THE SERMON ON THE MOUNT

Books in the PREACHING THE WORD Series:

JEREMIAH AND LAMENTATIONS:
From Sorrow to Hope
by Philip Graham Ryken

MARK, VOLUME ONE:
Jesus, Servant and Savior
by R. Kent Hughes

MARK, VOLUME TWO:
Jesus, Servant and Savior
by R. Kent Hughes

LUKE, VOLUME ONE:
That You May Know the Truth
by R. Kent Hughes

LUKE, VOLUME TWO:
That You May Know the Truth
by R. Kent Hughes

JOHN:
That You May Believe
by R. Kent Hughes

ACTS:
The Church Afire
by R. Kent Hughes

ROMANS:
Righteousness from Heaven
by R. Kent Hughes

EPHESIANS:
The Mystery of the Body of Christ
by R. Kent Hughes

COLOSSIANS:
The Supremacy of Christ
by R. Kent Hughes

1 & 2 TIMOTHY AND TITUS:
To Guard the Deposit
by R. Kent Hughes and Bryan Chapell

HEBREWS, VOLUME ONE:
An Anchor for the Soul
by R. Kent Hughes

HEBREWS, VOLUME TWO:
An Anchor for the Soul
by R. Kent Hughes

JAMES:
Faith That Works
by R. Kent Hughes

PREACHING THE WORD

THE SERMON ON THE MOUNT

The Message of the Kingdom

R. Kent Hughes

R. Kent Hughes, General Editor

CROSSWAY BOOKS • WHEATON, ILLINOIS
A DIVISION OF GOOD NEWS PUBLISHERS

The Sermon on the Mount

Published by Crossway Books
a division of Good News Publishers
1300 Crescent Street
Wheaton, Illinois 60187

Cover banner by Marge Gieser

Art Direction: Cindy Kiple

First printing 2001

Printed in the United States of America

Library of Congress Cataloging-in-Publication Data

Hughes, R. Kent.
The sermon on the mount : the message of the kingdom / R. Kent Hughes.
p. cm. — (Preaching the Word)
Includes bibliographical references and index.
ISBN 1-58134-063-X (alk. paper)
1. Sermon on the mount. I. Title. II. Series.
BT380.2.H83 2001
226.9'06—dc21 2001000453
CIP

15 14 13 12 11 10 09 08 07 06 05
15 14 13 12 11 10 9 8 7 6 5 4 3 2

To Lane Dennis
humble servant of Jesus Christ

*"Therefore everyone who hears these words
of mine and puts them into practice is like a wise man
who built his house on the rock."*
(Matthew 7:24)

Table of Contents

Acknowledgments

When people ask me which book influenced me most outside the Scriptures, my answer is Dr. Martyn Lloyd-Jones's *The Sermon on the Mount.* As a young pastor in the early seventies, I was stunned by the primary truth of the Beatitudes as opened by the Doctor. I wrote Lloyd-Jones at Westminster Chapel and some months later received back a card in his own crabbed hand. It is one of my treasures. No proper acknowledgment could be made apart from him. Likewise, I must mention the excellent work of my administrative assistant Mrs. Lillian Smith, who we both know is smarter than I am. Thanks for your careful attention to detail and support through this exhilarating study. Also, thanks to my long-time friend, Herbert Carlburg, whose attention to detail astounds us all. Of course, any defects in this work are solely mine. Thanks also to the congregation of College Church. There is a sense in which the congregation makes the preacher.

A Word to Those Who Preach the Word

There are times when I am preaching that I have especially sensed the pleasure of God. I usually become aware of it through the unnatural silence. The ever-present coughing ceases and the pews stop creaking, bringing an almost physical quiet to the sanctuary — through which my words sail like arrows. I experience a heightened eloquence, so that the cadence and volume of my voice intensify the truth I am preaching.

There is nothing quite like it — the Holy Spirit filling one's sails, the sense of his pleasure, and the awareness that something is happening among one's hearers. This experience is, of course, not unique, for thousands of preachers have similar experiences, even greater ones.

What has happened when this takes place? How do we account for this sense of his smile? The answer for me has come from the ancient rhetorical categories of *logos*, *ethos*, and *pathos*.

The first reason for his smile is the *logos* — in terms of preaching, God's Word. This means that as we stand before God's people to proclaim his Word, we have done our homework. We have exegeted the passage, mined the significance of its words in their context, and applied sound hermeneutical principles in interpreting the text so that we understand what its words meant to its hearers. And it means that we have labored long until we can express in a sentence what the theme of the text is — so that our outline springs from the text. Then our preparation will be such that as we preach, we will not be preaching our own thoughts about God's Word, but God's actual Word, his *logos*. This is fundamental to pleasing him in preaching.

The second element in knowing God's smile in preaching is *ethos* — what you are as a person. There is a danger endemic to preaching, which is having your hands and heart cauterized by holy things. Phillips Brooks illustrated it by the analogy of a train conductor who comes to believe that he has been to the places he announces because of his long and loud heralding of them. And that is why Brooks insisted that preaching must be "the bringing of truth through personality." Though we can never *perfectly* embody the truth we preach, we must be subject to it, long for it, and make it as much a part of our ethos as possible. As the Puritan William Ames said, "Next to the Scriptures, nothing makes a sermon more to pierce, than when it comes out of the inward affection of the heart without any affectation." When a preacher's ethos backs up his *logos*, there will be the pleasure of God.

Last, there is *pathos* — personal passion and conviction. David Hume, the Scottish philosopher and skeptic, was once challenged as he was seen going to hear George Whitefield preach: "I thought you do not believe in the gospel." Hume replied, "I don't, but *he does*." Just so! When a preacher believes what he preaches, there will be passion. And this belief and requisite passion will know the smile of God.

The pleasure of God is a matter of *logos* (the Word), *ethos* (what you are), and *pathos* (your passion). As you *preach the Word* may you experience his smile — the Holy Spirit in your sails!

R. Kent Hughes, General Editor
Wheaton, Illinois

1

The Riches of Poverty

MATTHEW 5:1-3

"Blessed are the poor in spirit, for theirs is the kingdom of heaven."
— MATTHEW 5:3

Jesus' Sermon on the Mount is so famous and powerful that we can hardly overstate its influence. St. Augustine, for example, described it as "a perfect standard of the Christian life." The great preacher-poet John Donne spoke of it in the most ornate terms:

> As nature hath given us certain elements, and all our bodies are composed of them; and art hath given us a certain alphabet of letters, and all words are composed of them; so, our blessed Saviour, in these three chapters of this Gospel, hath given us a sermon of texts, of which, all our sermons may be composed. All the articles of our religion, all the canons of our Church, all the injunctions of our princes, all the homilies of our fathers, all the body of divinity, is in these three chapters, in this one sermon in the Mount.

Dietrich Bonhoeffer based his classic, *The Cost of Discipleship*, upon its exposition. The influence of the Sermon on the Mount is truly past reckoning.

The Sermon on the Mount has even exerted a great influence on those outside the Christian faith. Its influence upon Gandhi's political approach is a matter of common knowledge. Those who hate Christianity and its ethics likewise have made it an object of contempt. It is seen as the source of the "slave morality" that Nietzsche so hated. When Nietzsche's teaching bore its terrible fruit during the ascendancy of National Socialism in Germany, the Sermon was vigorously attacked by men like Alfred Rosenberg, and a modified version was produced for those who wanted to remain within the Christian tradition and accommodate themselves to Hitler's philosophy. So like it or not, everyone in western civilization has been touched in some way by the Sermon on the Mount. No one can legitimately minimize its influence.

For the Christian believer, it is simply the greatest sermon ever preached. Why is this? To begin with, it came from the lips of Jesus. The original sermon was probably quite long, possibly even several hours, and what we have in Matthew 5 — 7 (which takes about ten minutes to read) is a distillation of his teaching. The Sermon on the Mount is the compacted, congealed theology of Christ and as such is perhaps the most profound section of the entire New Testament and the whole Bible. Every phrase can bear exhaustive exposition and yet never be completely plumbed. Along with this, it is the most penetrating section of God's Word. Because the theme is entering the kingdom of heaven, it shows us exactly where we stand in relation to the kingdom and eternal life (see 5:3; 7:21). As we expose ourselves to the X-rays of Christ's words, we see whether we truly are believers; and if believers, the degree of the authenticity of our lives. No other section of Scripture makes us face ourselves like the Sermon on the Mount. It is violent, but its violence can be our ongoing liberation! It is the antidote to the pretense and sham that plagues Christianity.

For me personally, the Sermon has been the most important factor in my spiritual life. Every time I return to it, especially the Beatitudes, I am brought up short as I face the bedrock reality of this amazing revelation. My dream and prayer is that somehow the spirituality of the Sermon on the Mount will penetrate our hearts, lifting us from the mediocrity that characterizes our society.

We will begin with the Beatitudes, which someone has, not inaccurately, called the "Beautiful Attitudes" of the kingdom, for they give us the character of those who are true children of God. Many suggested titles say essentially the same thing: "The Character of the Kingdom," "The Manifesto of the Kingdom," "The Norms of the Kingdom." The first four Beatitudes focus on our relationship to God, and the second four on our relationship to our fellowman. Each of the eight builds upon the other, so that there is an amazingly beautiful and compelling progression. At the same time there is a profound unity. The first Beatitude (verse 3) and the last Beatitude (verse 10) end with the same reward, "the kingdom of heaven," which according to Hebrew style means that the Beatitudes between them all deal with that very same theme.

As we begin our study, we must envision the snowballing of interest in Jesus' ministry leading up to this event. He has been traveling around Galilee teaching in the synagogues, and people are coming to him by the droves for healing. News has spread all the way to Syria, and every kind of case imaginable is coming to him. Great multitudes were following him clear out into the wilderness beyond the Jordan. Matthew 5:1, 2 tells us: "Now when he saw the crowds, he went up on a mountainside and sat down. His disciples came to him, and he began to teach them, saying . . ."

In the midst of his escalating ministry, Jesus chose a prominent rise or hill, sat down in the customary teaching posture of a rabbi, surrounded by many disciples (that is, those who were at that time interested in learning), and began to teach them.

Those of us who grew up in the fifties are quite familiar with the name Mickey Cohen because he was the most flamboyant criminal of the day. Perhaps some have even heard of Cohen's becoming a "Christian."

The story goes like this: At the height of his career, Cohen was persuaded to attend an evangelistic service at which he showed a surprising interest in Christianity. Hearing of this, and realizing what a great influence a converted Mickey Cohen could have for the Lord, some prominent Christian leaders began visiting him in an effort to convince him to accept Christ. Late one night, after repeatedly being encouraged to open the door of his life on the basis of Revelation 3:20 ("I stand at the door and knock. If anyone hears my voice and opens the door, I will go in and eat with him, and he with me"), Cohen prayed.

Hopes ran high among his believing acquaintances. But with the passing of time no one could detect any change in Cohen's life. Finally they confronted him with the reality that being a Christian meant he would have to give up his friends and his profession. Cohen demurred. His logic? There are "Christian football players, Christian cowboys, Christian politicians; why not a Christian gangster?"[1]

The absurdity of what happened to Mickey Cohen dramatically underscores what is happening to untold numbers today. Though many ostensibly have "accepted Christ," they continue life as they always have. There is no repentance. They remain self-sufficient, even puffed up. Indeed, they are nowhere near the kingdom because they have not experienced the poverty of spirit that the first Beatitude insists is the initial ground of the kingdom of heaven.

What evangelical Christianity needs is an exposure to the life-giving logic of the Beatitudes and the blessedness of their fearsome surgery.

BLESSEDNESS: THE APPROVAL OF GOD

Each of the eight Beatitudes opens with the word "blessed." So it is essential that we understand here in the beginning what this word means, because it bears on everything that will be said in the remainder of this book.

Contrary to popular opinion, *blessed* does not mean "happy," even though some translations have rendered it this way. Happiness is a subjective state, a feeling. But Jesus is not declaring how people feel; rather, he is making an objective statement about what God thinks of them.[2] *Blessed* is a positive judgment by God on the individual that means "to be approved" or "to find approval." *So when God blesses us, he approves us.*[3]

Of course, there is no doubt that such blessing will bring feelings of happiness and that blessed people are generally happy. But we must remember that the root idea of "blessed" is an awareness of approval by God. Blessedness is not simply a nice wish from God; it is a pronouncement of what we actually are — *approved*. Blessedness indicates the smile of God or, as Max Lucado has so beautifully put it, *The Applause of Heaven*.

As we begin this study of the Beatitudes, let us realize that if God's blessing/approval means more to us than anything else — even the approval of our friends, business acquaintances, and colleagues — then the Beatitudes are going to penetrate our hearts, speaking to us in the deepest of ways.

The question is, do we really want his approval more than anything else? Not, do we want to be happy (as proper as that desire is) but, do we truly want God's approval above all else?

If so, then we must heed every word of the first Beatitude, for it gives us the condition of blessing in just three words: "poor in spirit." "Blessed/approved are the poor in spirit."

It is so essential that we get off to a good start with the first Beatitude if we are to understand them all that I would like to encourage the following prayer.

Dear Lord,

I long for your smile upon my life. So please open my heart to the meaning of the Beatitudes.

I open myself to their light. Shine their rays into the deepest part of my life. Sear my soul. Heal me.

Build the character of the kingdom in me, so that you can call me blessed.

Amen.

UNDERSTANDING POVERTY OF SPIRIT

Let us understand what poverty of spirit is not. It is not the conviction that one is of no value whatsoever. It does not mean the absence of self-worth or, as one theologian put it, "ontological insignificance." It does not require that we believe ourselves to be zeros. Such an attitude is simply not scriptural, for Christ's death on our behalf teaches us that we are of great value (1 Corinthians 6:20; 7:23).

Neither does "poor in spirit" mean shyness. Many people who are naturally shy and introverted are extremely proud. Nor does "poor in spirit" mean lacking in vitality, spiritually anemic, or gutless.

Certainly, "poor in spirit" also does not refer to showy humility like that of Uriah Heep in Charles Dickens's *David Copperfield*, who kept reminding people that he was a "very humble person."

The great British preacher Martyn Lloyd-Jones tells of meeting such a man on one of his preaching missions. When Dr. Lloyd-Jones arrived at the train station, the man asked for the minister's suitcase and in fact almost ripped it from his hand saying, "I am a deacon in the church where you are preaching tomorrow. . . . You know, I am a mere nobody, a very unimportant man. Really. I do not count; I am not a great man in the church; I am just one of those men who carry the bag for the minister."

Lloyd-Jones observes, "He was anxious that I should know what a humble man he was, how 'poor in spirit.' Yet by his anxiety to make it known, he was denying the very thing he was trying to establish. Uriah Heep — the man who thus, as it were, glories in his poverty of spirit and thereby proves he is not humble."[4] We all have met this kind of person, who by his own self-conscious diffidence is begging for us to say that he is not really nothing but actually quite wonderful. When this attitude is present, there is an absence of poverty of spirit.

What, then, does "poor in spirit" mean? The history of the Greek word for "poor," *ptochos*, provides some insight. It comes from a verbal root that denotes "to cower and cringe like a beggar." In classical Greek *ptochos* came to mean "someone who crouches about, wretchedly begging." In the New Testament it bears something of this idea because it denotes a poverty so deep that the person must obtain his living by begging. He is fully dependent on the giving of others. He cannot survive without help from the outside. Thus an excellent translation is "beggarly poor."

Now, if we take this meaning and combine it with the following words ("in spirit") we have the idea, "Blessed are the *beggarly* poor in spirit." The sense is: "Blessed are those who are so desperately poor in their spiritual resources that they realize they must have help from outside sources."

"Poverty of Spirit, then, is the personal acknowledgment of spiritual bankruptcy."[5] It is the awareness and admission that we are utterly sinful and without the moral virtues adequate to commend us to God. John Wesley said of the poor in spirit, "He has a deep sense of the loathsome leprosy of sin which he brought with him from his mother's womb, which overspreads his whole soul, and totally corrupts every power and faculty thereof."[6]

It is the recognition of our personal moral unworthiness. The "poor in spirit" see themselves as spiritually needy. My favorite rendering of the verse is:

> Blessed are those who realize that they have nothing within themselves to commend them to God, for theirs is the kingdom of heaven.

The World Rejects Poverty of Spirit

Poverty of spirit is the antithesis of the proud selfishness and self-sufficiency of today's world. The world has its own ideas of blessedness. "Blessed is the man who is always right." "Blessed is the man who is strong." "Blessed is the man who rules." "Blessed is the man who is satisfied with himself." "Blessed is the man who is rich." "Blessed is the man who is popular."

Today's men and women think that the answer to life is found in self. Actress Shirley MacLaine is not alone in her journey into self. Many in the church travel with her. Karl Jung is their Virgil, and the subterranean god of self is their Inferno. Christian narcissism is promoted as biblical self-love. King Jesus becomes the imperial self. When this happens, Christianity suffers a massive shrinkage, as David Wells explains:

> Theology becomes therapy. . . . The biblical interest in righteousness is replaced by a search for happiness, holiness by wholeness, truth by feeling, ethics by feeling good about one's self. . . . The past recedes. The Church recedes. The world recedes. All that remains is self.[7]

Someday, if history is allowed to continue, a perceptive artist may sculpt a statue of twentieth-century man with his arms wrapped around himself in loving embrace, kissing his image in a mirror.

To this, Jesus answers, "Blessed [approved of God] are the poor in spirit, for theirs is the kingdom of heaven."

Poverty of Spirit Is Essential for Knowing God's Approval

We must understand and embrace a true poverty of spirit, for that is the only way we can ever know God's smile. David became the greatest king of Israel, and the key to his rise to greatness was his poverty of spirit. Listen to his words when it all began: "Who am I, and what is my family or my father's clan in Israel, that I should become the king's son-in-law?" (1 Samuel 18:18). Later in life, before his fall, he said, "Who am I, O Sovereign LORD, and what is my family, that you have brought me this far?" (2 Samuel 7:18).

Similarly, Gideon, whom we celebrate for his amazing deliverance of Israel with just 300 men, began with these words: "But LORD . . . how can I save Israel? My clan is the weakest in Manasseh, and I am the least in my family" (Judges 6:15).

Significantly, when Jesus began his public ministry he opened the scroll to Isaiah 61:1 and began with this opening line: "The Spirit of the Lord is on me, because he has anointed me to preach good news to the poor" (see Luke 4:18). In Isaiah's context the poor were the exiled people of Israel who had not compromised and who looked to God alone to save them and establish his kingdom. These are always the people to whom he comes. The incarnate Son of God was born of a woman who sang, "My soul glorifies the Lord and my spirit rejoices in God my Savior, for he has been mindful of the humble state of his servant" (Luke 1:46-47). When Christ was born, the angels announced it to humble shepherds, not to the Establishment (Luke 2:8-15).

And when Jesus was presented in the Temple, aged Simeon and Anna, representatives of the poor of Isaiah's prophecy, exalted God because of him (Luke 2:25-38). These are the people *to* whom Christ is born, and *in* whom he is born. Lay this to heart: "The LORD is close to the brokenhearted and saves those who are crushed in spirit" (Psalm 34:18). This is the way it will always be.

Poverty of Spirit Is Essential for Salvation

Poverty of spirit is an indispensable sign of grace. No one can truly know Christ without it. There are most likely scores of evangelicals in your own community, prominent "Christians," who do not know Christ. They are tares amidst wheat who perhaps do not even know it (Matthew 13:24-30). They have never come to a blessed emptiness, to the very end of themselves. They have never confessed, "There is nothing in me to commend me to God"; and thus they are lost.

The changeless truth is, no one can come to Christ without poverty of spirit. This is not to say that one must have a *perfect* sense of one's spiritual insufficiency to be saved. Very few, if any, come to this. Rather, it means that the spiritually proud and self-sufficient, those who actually think there is something within them that will make God accept them — these people are lost.

Positively stated, "Those who acknowledge themselves as spiritually bankrupt enter the kingdom of heaven." No one enters God's kingdom without such an acknowledgment, regardless of how many times he or she has walked the aisle, raised a hand, signed a decision card, prayed "the sinner's prayer," or given his or her testimony.

Salvation is by faith alone, *sola fide* (Ephesians 2:8-9; Romans 11:6);[8] but poverty of spirit is the posture of faith. God pours out his grace to the spiritually bankrupt, for only they are open to believe and receive his grace and salvation. He does this with no one else. No one can enter the kingdom without poverty of spirit.

Poverty of Spirit Is Essential for Spiritual Growth

We never outgrow the first Beatitude, even though it is the basis by which we ascend to the others. In fact, if we outgrow it, we have outgrown our Christianity — we are post-Christian.

That is what was happening in the Laodicean church. Christ rebuked that failing church with these stern words:

> *"You say, 'I am rich; I have acquired wealth and do not need a thing.' But you do not realize that you are wretched, pitiful, poor, blind and naked. I counsel you to buy from me gold refined in the fire, so you can become rich; and white clothes to wear, so you can cover your shameful nakedness; and salve to put on your eyes, so you can see." (Revelation 3:17-18)*

Just as no one can come to Christ without poverty of spirit, no one can continue to grow apart from an ongoing poverty of spirit.

Poverty of spirit is foundational because a continual sense of spiritual need is the basis for ongoing spiritual blessing. A perpetual awareness of our spiritual insufficiency opens us to continually receiving spiritual riches. Poverty of spirit is something we never outgrow. In fact, the more spiritually mature we become, the more profound will be our sense of poverty.

It is because of this that every believer should commit the Beatitudes to memory and make the first Beatitude, especially, his or her conscious refrain: "Blessed are the beggarly poor in spirit"; "blessed are the spiritually bankrupt, for theirs is the kingdom of heaven."

THE RICHES OF POVERTY

Now we turn to the statement of the reward: "for theirs is the kingdom of heaven." "Theirs" is emphatic. It means theirs in the sense of *theirs alone*, barring all others who approach God with a different spirit than that of beggarliness.[9] Again, none but those who are "poor in spirit" will enter the kingdom of heaven.

The reward of the kingdom is both now and future. It is present because all who have life are in the kingdom now. We are seated with Christ in the heavenly places *now* (Ephesians 2:6). We are subjects of Christ *now*. We are overcomers *now*. We are a kingdom of priests *now*. This means we are kings and queens, and that we reign in life and exercise vast authority and power. It means that our poverty of spirit, our weakness, is a reservoir of authority and power. Our weakness is the occasion for his power, our inadequacy for his adequacy, our poverty for his riches, our inarticulation for his articulation, our tentativeness for his confidence (see 2 Corinthians 12:9, 10; Colossians 2:9, 10).

As kings and queens, we are also free. Pride makes slaves out of all whom it possesses; not so with poverty of spirit. We are free to be full of God, free to be all that he would have us to be, free to be ourselves. We reign now and for all eternity. The kingdom is ours — ours alone!

CRUCIAL TEACHING

The supreme lesson of this Beatitude is that without poverty of spirit no one enters the kingdom of heaven. Its prominent position — as the opening sentence of the Sermon on the Mount — declares for all time that no one is saved who believes there is something within him that will make God prefer or accept him.

Self-righteousness, moral pride, vain presumption will damn the soul! Jesus made this crystal-clear with the account of the tax-gatherer and the Pharisee who went up to the Temple to pray:

"Two men went up to the temple to pray, one a Pharisee and the other a tax collector. The Pharisee stood up and prayed about himself: 'God, I thank you that I am not like other men — robbers, evildoers, adulterers — or even like this tax collector. I fast twice a week and give a tenth of all I get.' But the tax collector stood at a distance. He would not even look up to heaven, but beat his breast and said, 'God, have mercy on me, a sinner.' I tell you that this man, rather than the other, went home justified before God. For everyone who exalts himself will be humbled, and he who humbles himself will be exalted." (Luke 18:10-14)

We must realize that:

The first link between
my soul and Christ is
not my goodness
but my badness;
not my merit
but my misery;
not my standing
but my falling.

Fortunately, this truth can penetrate the most privileged of hearts, as it did to one of England's distinguished judges. The church he attended had three mission churches under its care. On the first Sunday of the new year all the members of the missions came to the big city church for a combined Communion service. In those mission churches, which were located in the slums of the city, were some outstanding cases of conversions — thieves, burglars, and so on — but all knelt side by side at the Communion rail.

On one such occasion the pastor saw a former thief kneeling beside the aforementioned jurist, a judge of the High Court of England. After his release the thief had been converted and became a Christian worker. Yet, as the judge and the former thief knelt together, neither seemed to be aware of the other.

After the service, the judge happened to walk out with the pastor and said, "Did you notice who was kneeling beside me at the Communion rail this morning?"

The pastor replied, "Yes, but I didn't think that you did."

The two walked along in silence for a few more moments, when the judge declared, "What a miracle of grace."

The pastor nodded in agreement. "Yes, what a marvelous miracle of grace."

Then the judge asked, "But to whom do you refer?"

The pastor responded, "Why, to the conversion of that convict."

"But I was not referring to him. I was thinking of myself," explained the judge.

Surprised, the pastor replied, "You were thinking of yourself? I don't understand."

"Yes," the judge went on. "It was natural for the burglar to respond to God's grace when he came out of jail. His life was nothing but a desperate history of crime, and when he saw the Savior he knew there was salvation and hope and joy for him. He understood how much he needed that help.

"But I . . . I was taught from earliest infancy to be a gentleman — that my word was my bond, that I was to say my prayers, go to church, receive Communion. I went up to Oxford, took my degrees, was called to the bar, and eventually ascended to judge. My friend, it was God's grace that drew me; it was God's grace that opened my heart to receive Christ. I'm a greater miracle of his grace."

Listen again to Jesus' words, "Blessed [approved of God] are the [beggarly] poor in spirit, for theirs is the kingdom of heaven [now and forevermore]."

The question I must ask is, have you experienced true poverty of spirit? Can you say,

Nothing in my hand I bring,
Simply to Thy cross I cling;
Naked, come to Thee for dress
Helpless, look to Thee for grace;
Foul, I to the fountain fly;
Wash me, Saviour, or I die.
— AUGUSTUS M. TOPLADY, 1740-1778

Is this your heart's cry? Or are you a church attender without Christ? Are you an unregenerate evangelical? Are you a Christless "Christian"? If so, hear God's Word and take it to heart: "Blessed are the poor in spirit, for theirs is the kingdom of heaven."

The other great lesson for all who are born again, regardless of their spiritual maturity, is that poverty of spirit is necessary for continuing spiritual blessing.

I personally can say that the most profitable spiritual experiences of my life have come out of times of profound spiritual poverty, times when God has brought me face to face with the fact of my need, times when I once again realized there was nothing within me to commend me to him. Sometimes he has done this through professional failure, sometimes through intellectual shortcomings, sometimes through social or family pressures.

Whatever the case, in him my bankruptcy has been the opening for his riches. And it can be yours as well. "Blessed are the poor in spirit, for theirs is the kingdom of heaven."

2

The Comfort of Mourning

"Blessed are those who mourn, for they will be comforted."
— MATTHEW 5:4

Charles Colson, in his brilliant book of essays *Who Speaks for God?*, tells of watching a segment of television's *60 Minutes* in which host Mike Wallace interviewed Auschwitz survivor Yehiel Dinur, a principal witness at the Nuremberg war-crime trials.

During the interview, a film clip from Adolf Eichmann's 1961 trial was viewed that showed Dinur entering the courtroom and coming face to face with Eichmann for the first time since being sent to Auschwitz almost twenty years earlier. Stopped cold, Dinur began to sob uncontrollably and then fainted while the presiding judge pounded his gavel for order.

"Was Dinur overcome by hatred? Fear? Horrid memories?" asks Colson, who then answers:

> No; it was none of these. Rather, as Dinur explained to Wallace, all at once he realized Eichmann was not the godlike army officer who had sent so many to their deaths. This Eichmann was an ordinary man. "I was afraid about myself," said Dinur. "I saw that I am capable to do this. I am . . . exactly like he."
>
> Wallace's subsequent summation of Dinur's terrible discovery — "Eichmann is in all of us" — is a horrifying statement; but it indeed captures the central truth about man's nature. For as a result of the Fall, sin is in each of us — not just the susceptibility to sin, but sin itself.[1]

Colson follows his penetrating observation with this question: Why is it that today sin is so seldom written or preached about? The answer is in Dinur's dramatic collapse, for to truly confront the sin within us is a devastating experience. If pastors preached on sin, says Colson, many people would flee their church pews never to return.[2]

The abiding fact is that man has always been in need of such an encounter. And to this end Jesus has given the second Beatitude, because it shows the necessity of truly facing one's sin.

So no one would miss the point, the Lord put this in the most striking language.

TRUTH UPSIDE-DOWN

When read apart from its context, the second Beatitude is startling: "Blessed are those who mourn, for they will be comforted." This is, of course, a paradox — and it is meant to grab us.

G. K. Chesterton once defined a paradox as "truth standing on its head calling for attention," and this is certainly true here. Jesus states one of the essential truths of life in such a way that it cries for all to come and take a good long look, a look that can bring life. "Blessed/approved are those who mourn."

The intimate connection of this second Beatitude with the first is beautiful and compelling. The first Beatitude, "Blessed are the poor in spirit," is primarily *intellectual* (those who understand that they are spiritual beggars are blessed); the second Beatitude, "Blessed are those who mourn," is its *emotional* counterpart. It naturally follows that when we see ourselves for what we are, our emotions will be stirred to mourning.

Again, as with the previous Beatitude, we cannot place enough stress on the importance of these spiritual truths as they relate to the gospel. The Beatitudes are *not* the gospel because they do not explicitly explain Christ's atoning death and resurrection and how one may receive him. But they are *preparatory* to the gospel.

The Beatitudes are preparatory in the sense that they slay us so that we may live. They hold us up against God's standards for the kingdom so that we can see our need and fly to him. They cut through the delusions of formula Christianity and expose the shallowness of evangelicals who can give all the "right" answers but do not know Christ.

THE BLESSED PARADOX

To begin with, what does the paradoxical pronouncement "Blessed are those who mourn" mean? Let us first note what it does not mean.

Jesus does not mean, "Blessed are grim, cheerless Christians." Some believers have apparently interpreted it this way. The Victorian preacher Charles Spurgeon once remarked that some preachers he had known appeared to have their neckties twisted around their souls.[3] Robert Louis

Stevenson must have known some preachers like that because he once wrote, ironically, in his diary, "I've been to church today and am not depressed." Christ certainly is not pronouncing a Beatitude on a forlorn disposition.

Neither does Jesus mean, "Blessed are those who are mourning over the difficulties of life." The Bible does not say that mourning by itself is a blessed state. Sorrow is not blessed any more than laughter is. In fact, some mourning is cursed. For example, Amnon mourned because his lust was not fulfilled by Tamar (2 Samuel 13:2). Also, Ahab mourned because he wanted but couldn't get Naboth's vineyard (1 Kings 21:4).

Mourning over Sin

A great day has come when we see our sinful state for what it is apart from God's grace and begin to mourn over its devastating dimensions in our souls, words, and deeds as described in Romans chapter 3.

• *Souls*: "There is no one righteous, not even one; there is no one who understands, no one who seeks God. All have turned away, they have together become worthless; there is no one who does good, not even one" (vv. 10-12).

• *Words*: "Their throats are open graves; their tongues practice deceit"; "the poison of vipers is on their lips"; "their mouths are full of cursing and bitterness" (vv. 13-14).

• *Deeds*: "Their feet are swift to shed blood; ruin and misery mark their ways, and the way of peace they do not know" (vv. 15-17).

Such are we all if left to ourselves. There is always room for decline if we refuse the grace of God.

But it is an even greater day when we are truly confronted with our individual sins, when we refuse to rationalize them, when we reject facile euphemisms, when we call sin "sin" in our lives. And it is the greatest of all days yet when in horror and desolation over our sin and sins we weep, so that the divine smile begins to break.

Mourning over the Sins of the World

Such personal mourning is naturally expansive because one who truly mourns over his own sins will also sorrow over the power and effects of sin in the world. David mourned for the sins of others in Psalm 119:136: "Streams of tears flow from my eyes, for your law is not obeyed." The great characteristic of Jeremiah, the Weeping Prophet, was that he wept for his people (Jeremiah 9:1; 13:17).

Of course, our sinless Lord Jesus was also deeply grieved by sin in the world. Through the mystery of the Incarnation his heart became a spiritual seismograph, registering the slightest tremors of the earth's pain and sorrow. No wonder some thought Jesus was Jeremiah returned from the grave (Matthew 16:14).

Now we begin to see the force of the brilliant paradox of the second Beatitude. The Lord Jesus has stood truth on its head, and it shouts for us to take notice and understand. "Blessed [approved] are those who mourn [over sin — that is their own sin and the sin that poisons the world], for they will be comforted." Christ shouts for our understanding. Blessed are we if we hear and put our understanding to work.

MOURNING IS NOT POPULAR

It is very important to see that mourning is definitely not in vogue today, despite its necessity for spiritual health. However, before elaborating on this point we must emphasize that humor and laughter are good and necessary for the believer. Solomon says that a merry heart acts as a "good medicine" (Proverbs 17:22), and we have found this to be true. Abraham Lincoln said, "If I did not laugh, I would die." The need for laughter in the church was underlined by missionary statesman Oswald Sanders with these questions:

> Should we not see that lines of laughter about the eyes are just as much marks of faith as are the lines of care and seriousness? Is laughter pagan? We have already allowed too much that is good to be lost to the church and cast many pearls before swine. A church is in a bad way when it banishes laughter from the sanctuary and leaves it to the cabaret, the nightclub, and the toastmasters.[4]

Laughter is essential, but the world despises sorrow so much that it has gone wild in its attempt to avoid it. Moderns have structured their lives to maximize entertainment and amusement in an attempt to make life one big party. They laugh when there is no reason to laugh. In fact, they laugh when they ought to cry.

Solomon was right that a merry heart acts like a "good medicine." But that does not mean you cannot overdose! Much of our culture has overdosed on amusement, as Neil Postman has so convincingly chronicled in his highly regarded *Amusing Ourselves to Death.*

The world thinks mourners (those who mourn the course of the world, who mourn sin) are mad. John Wesley observed that they consider it ". . . to be more moping and melancholy, if not downright lunacy and distraction."[5] Some have actually argued that Martin Luther was insane because of his deep mourning over his sin before his new birth. They judge his behavior as psychotic. Indeed, the world regards pain of heart with suspicion and restraint.

The church is much the same. Some actually hold that if we are good Christians, filled with the Spirit, we will experience no sorrow and will wear eternal beatific smiles like plastic Mona Lisas.

I personally know of preachers who though they maintain that they belong in the evangelical tradition never mention sin in their preaching because that makes people unhappy. The result is a Christianity that is pathetically shallow — if indeed it is Christianity at all!

True Christianity manifests itself in what we cry over and what we laugh about. So often we laugh at the things that we should weep over and weep over the things we should laugh at. In our heart of hearts, what do we weep about? What do we laugh about?

GOOD MOURNING!

In matters of spiritual life and health, mourning is not optional. Spiritual mourning is necessary for salvation. No one is truly a Christian who has not mourned over his or her sins. You cannot be forgiven if you are not sorry for your sins.

This was powerfully argued in the article "There Is One Thing Worse than Sin," which first appeared in the *Chicago Sun-Times*. In it, Dr. Thomas F. Roeser compared the equally reprehensible sins of Congressmen Daniel Crane and Gerald Studds. Both had been censured by the House of Representatives — Crane for having sexual relations with a seventeen-year-old female page and Studds for having relations with a seventeen-year-old male page. Roeser observed:

> Being censured is the only thing Crane and Studds have in common. The nation got a glimmer of their philosophical differences when Crane admitted tearfully to his district, then to the full House, that he "broke the laws of God and man," casting a vote for his own censure, facing the House as the Speaker announced the tally. Studds, in contrast, acknowledged he was gay in a dramatic speech to the House, then defended the relationship with the page as "mutual and voluntary." He noted that he had abided by the age of consent, and said the relationship didn't warrant the "attention or action" of the House. Studds voted "present" on the census and heard the verdict from the Speaker with his back to the House.

Roeser went on to contrast the different moral traditions both these men represent — properly excusing neither one for his sin.

> But there's one consolation for Crane. His . . . philosophy teaches that there is one thing worse than sin. That is denial of sin, which makes forgiveness impossible.[6]

The saddest thing in life is not a sorrowing heart, but a heart that is incapable of grief over sin, for it is without grace. Without poverty of spirit no one enters the kingdom of God. Likewise, without its emotional counterpart — grief over sin — no one receives the comfort of forgiveness and salvation.

GOOD GRIEF!

If you have never sorrowed over sin in your life (not just its consequences, but sin itself), then consider long and carefully whether you really are a Christian. Genuine believers, those who are truly born again, have mourned, and continue to mourn, over sin.

For Christians, mourning over sin is essential to spiritual health. The verb used here is the most intensive of the nine verbs employed in the New Testament for mourning, and it is continuous.[7] Godly believers, therefore, perpetually mourn, and thus perpetually repent of their sins.

It is significant that the first of Martin Luther's famous *95 Theses* states that the entire life is to be one of continuous repentance and contrition. It was this attitude in the Apostle Paul that caused him to affirm, well along into his Christian life, that he was the chief of sinners (1 Timothy 1:15).

What is the result of our mourning? In the first Beatitude we saw that an ongoing poverty of spirit leaves us open to ongoing blessings of the kingdom. Here, our ongoing mourning opens us to His unspeakable comfort and joy.

This naturally anticipates and introduces the paradoxical reward: ". . . for they will be comforted."

THE COMFORT OF MOURNING

Notice that the comfort is actually immediate. Don't misinterpret the future tense, which is used merely to sequence mourning and comfort. The actual sense of Christ's words is, "Blessed are the mourners, for they will be immediately comforted, and they will continue to be so."

Forgiveness

Notice, above all, that the basis of comfort is forgiveness. Believers are the only people in the world who are free from the guilt of their sins. The word "they" is emphatic. The sense is: "Blessed are those who mourn, for *they alone* will be comforted." We actually know we are mourners if we have the paradoxically comforting sense of God's forgiveness.

This forgiveness is also accompanied by changed lives, diminishing the sources of so much personal sorrow — arrogance, judgmentalism, selfishness, jealousy, to name a few. Therefore, comfort springs from within — from changed lives.

The Holy Spirit

The very Greek word used here for "they will be comforted" has the root from which we get *paraclete*, which is also used for the Holy Spirit, the One who comes alongside and comforts us. God's comfort is relational. It comes in the form of his divine companionship. He is our ally. He personally binds up our sorrows and consoles us.

How comprehensive our comfort is! It is immediate. It comes to us alone. It comes personally in the Person of the Holy Spirit. And it is based on the forgiveness of our sins. That is why we are called "blessed."

What a stupendous paradox! Jesus stands truth on its head to get our attention, and he says, "Would you be comforted? Then mourn. Would you be happy? Then weep."

Salvation

To those who are not yet believers, perhaps unsaved evangelicals, understand that this paradox is meant to lead you to salvation. If a spirit of mourning is welling up within you, then let your mourning elevate you to him.

Do as the prodigal son did. He recognized his condition and mourned over it and in the midst of his misery said:

> *"I will set out and go back to my father and say to him: Father, I have sinned against heaven and against you. I am no longer worthy to be called your son; make me like one of your hired men." So he got up and went to his father. But while he was still a long way off, his father saw him and was filled with compassion for him; he ran to his son, threw his arms around him and kissed him. (Luke 15:18-20)*

Do you acknowledge that there is nothing within you to commend you to God? Are you mourning? Do you ache with the guilt of your sin before God and man? If so, and if you are a Christian, return to the Lord and be restored to fellowship. If you are not a believer, come to him now and he will give you the kingdom. He will put his robe on your shoulders, his ring on your hand, his sandals on your feet, and will prepare a feast for you. You will be comforted!

That is what he has done for Charles Colson and multitudes of others. Colson says of his own experience:

> That night when I . . . sat alone at my car, my own sin — not just dirty politics, but the hatred and evil so deep within me — was thrust before my eyes, forcefully and painfully. For the first time in my life, I felt unclean, and worst of all, I could not escape. In those moments of clarity I found myself driven irresistibly into the arms of the living God.[8]

Charles Colson followed his mourning to God. And so can you. Be comforted now!

3

The Strength of Gentleness

"Blessed are the meek, for they will inherit the earth."
— MATTHEW 5:5

Two men faced each other on the pavement before the governor's palace. One was Jesus Christ, the meekest man who ever lived. The other was Pontius Pilate, a man of extraordinary pride.

Jesus appeared as the epitome of weakness, a poor Jew caught on the inexorable tides of Roman history, frail and impotent, a man destined to be obliterated from the earth. Pilate was the personification of Roman power. The tides of history were with him. As part of Rome, he was heir to the earth.

The two figures are opposite ends of a tragic paradox. Jesus Christ, the prisoner, was the free man. He was in absolute control. Jesus, the meek, would inherit not only the earth but the universe. On the other hand, Pilate, the governor, was the prisoner of his own pride. He could not even control his soul. He had no inheritance.

Jesus not only taught the paradox "Blessed are the meek, for they will inherit the earth" — he lived it.

Christ was master of the paradox. His teaching is salted with shining contrasts like:

Last is first.
Giving is receiving.
Dying is living.
Losing is finding.
Least is greatest.
Poor is rich.
Weakness is strength.
Serving is ruling.

For Christ, paradoxes were an especially effective way of getting people to see essential spiritual truth — in this instance, "Blessed are the meek, for they will inherit the earth."

The beauty of a paradox is that it grabs our attention because it falls on the ear with an elevating dissonance. In the case of Matthew 5:5, it seems far truer to say, "Blessed are the proud, the intimidating, for they will inherit the earth." But Jesus is teaching the survival not of the fittest but of the meekest! How in the world are the meek going to inherit anything? Life simply does not work that way. Jesus' Beatitude contravenes the laws of nature — and of society. Just look at those who occupy the executive suites — the strong, the self-sufficient, the overbearing, the capable, the aggressive, the ambitious. The world belongs to the "John Waynes." It belongs to those who proudly intone:

Out of the night that covers me,
Black as the Pit from pole to pole,
I thank whatever gods may be
For my unconquerable soul.[1]

The last thing the average man wants to be known for is meekness.

It seems that Jesus has made a great mistake, but of course we know that our Lord has not. Indeed this Beatitude provides an infallible law of life and a remarkable power for living and dying.

TENDER STEEL

So to begin, what does "Blessed are the meek" mean? Specifically, what does the word "meek" — or as many translations have it, "gentle" — mean?

Understand first that meekness is *not* weakness. It does not denote cowardice or spinelessness or timidity or the willingness to have peace at any cost. Neither does meekness suggest indecisiveness, wishy-washiness, or a lack of confidence. Meekness does not imply shyness or a withdrawn personality, as contrasted with that of an extrovert. Nor can meekness be reduced to mere niceness.

Bearing this in mind, we must note that the Greek word's development in classical literature and its other usages in the New Testament absolutely confirm the popular translations of *meek* and *gentle*.

In classical Greek the word was used to describe tame animals, soothing medicine, a mild word, and a gentle breeze.[2] "It is a word with a caress in it."[3] The New Testament bears the same sense. John Wycliffe translated the third Beatitude, "Blessed be mild men."[4] *Gentleness* and *meekness* are, indeed, caressing words.

Meekness/gentleness also implies self-control. Aristotle explained that it is the mean between excessive anger and excessive angerlessness. So the man who is meek is able to balance his anger. It is strength under control.[5] The meek person is strong! He is gentle, meek, and mild, but he is in control. He is as strong as steel.

TRUSTING STEEL

A reading of Psalm 37 shows that Jesus consciously alluded to verse 11, "But the meek will inherit the land," when he formulated the third Beatitude. This statement's location in the heart of this great Psalm is deeply revelatory of what meekness/gentleness rests upon. The Israelites to whom the Psalm was written, despite living in the land, did not truly possess it because of the working of evil men. What were they to do? In a word, *trust* ("trust," vv. 3, 5; "be still . . . wait," v. 7). Thus a deep trust in the sovereign power of God is the key to meekness.

Gentle Jesus himself forever displayed the dynamic of trust that is part and parcel of meekness. "When," as Peter records, "they hurled their insults at him, he did not retaliate; when he suffered, he made no threats. Instead, he entrusted himself to him who judges justly" (1 Peter 2:23).

JESUS' MEEKNESS

Jesus said of himself, "I am gentle and humble in heart" (Matthew 11:29). As the incarnation of meekness, he displayed it in two ways, both of which showed his power.

In respect to his own person, he practiced neither retaliation nor vindictiveness. When he was mocked and spat upon, he answered nothing, for he trusted his Father. As we have noted, when he was confronted by Pilate, he kept silent. When his friends betrayed him and fled, he uttered no reproach. When Peter denied him, Jesus restored him to fellowship and service. When Judas came and kissed him in Gethsemane, Jesus called him "friend." And Jesus meant it. He was never insincere. Even in the throes of death, he pleaded, "Father, forgive them, for they do not know what they are doing" (Luke 23:34). In all of this Jesus, meek and mild, was in control. He radiated power.

Yet, when it came to matters of faith and the welfare of others, Jesus was a lion. He rebuked the Pharisees' hardness of heart when he healed the man's withered hand on the Sabbath (Matthew 12:9-45). He was angered when his disciples tried to prevent little children from coming to him (Mark 10:13-16). Jesus made a whip and drove the moneychangers from the temple (John 2:14-17). He called Peter "Satan" after the outspoken fisherman tried to deter him from His heavenly mission (Matthew 16:21-23). All of this came from Jesus, the incarnation of gentleness.

Bringing this all together, we have an amazing picture. The one who is meek has a gentle spirit because he trusts God. Indeed, there is a caress about his presence. At the same time the meek person possesses immense strength and self-control, which he exhibits in extending love rather than retaliation against those who do him evil. He stands up fearlessly in defense of others or of the truth as the occasion arises.

JESUS' SMILE

Our Lord's words "Blessed are the meek" make it clear that a gentle and meek spirit has the divine approval. Therefore the presence or lack of such is indicative of one's spiritual status.

Of course, no one perfectly manifests meekness in his or her life. No one's life is a perpetual caress. No one is so strong that his or her only response is love. No one totally escapes pride and self. Nevertheless, Jesus' warnings are clear.

• *Harshness*: If you are mean in your treatment of others, if there is an absence of gentleness in your treatment of others, take heed.

• *Grasping*: If you make sure you always get yours first, if *numero uno* is the subtle driving force in your life, if you care little about how your actions affect others, beware.

• *Vengeful*: If you are known as someone never to cross, if you always get your "pound of flesh," be on your guard.

• *Uncontrolled*: If rage fills your soul so that life is a series of explosions occasioned by the "fools" in your life, watch out.

Again, this is not to suggest that you are not a Christian if you fall into these sins, but rather to point out that if they are part of your persona, if you are a self-satisfied "Christian" who thinks that the lack of gentleness and meekness is "just you" and people will have to get used to it, if you are not repentant, you are probably not a Christian.

Jesus' words are not demanding perfection. The point is, however, that if a gentle/meek spirit is not at least imperfectly present in your life, if it is not incipient and growing, you may very well not have the smile of Christ, which is everything.

THE SUBLIME PARADOX

The reward for meekness is truly amazing: "They will inherit the earth."

As was mentioned, the inspiration for this magnificent paradox is Psalm 37, which encourages God's people not to fret because of evil, but rather to trust because "the meek will inherit the land" (v. 11; cf. vv. 9, 22, 29, 34). In the New Testament, God's people are not a physical nation — they are gathered from all nations and tongues. And the land/earth they inherit is not a physical plot of ground — it is heaven itself. The time is coming when, as fellow heirs with Christ (Romans 8:17), we will reign with him in his earthly kingdom. We will inherit the earth. We will even judge the world (1 Corinthians 6:2). The paradox will be literally fulfilled, far beyond our wildest dreams.

But there is also a present inheritance that abundantly enriches our earthly existence. There is a sense in which those who set their minds on riches never possess anything. This was given classic expression by one of the world's wealthiest men when asked how much is enough money. "Just a little bit more," he answered. He owned everything, yet possessed nothing!

It is the meek who own the earth now, for when their life is free from the tyranny of "just a little more," when a gentle spirit caresses their approach to their rights, then they possess all. As Izaak Walton explained:

> I could there sit quietly, and looking on the waters see fishes leaping at flies of several shapes and colors. Looking on the hills, I could behold them spotted with woods and groves. Looking down the meadows, I could see a boy gathering lilies and lady-smocks, and there a girl cropping columbines and cowslips, all to make garlands suitable to this present month of May. As I thus sat, joying in mine own happy condition, I did thankfully remember what my Saviour said, that the meek possess the earth.[6]

The meek are the only ones who inherit the earth. The "they" in "they shall inherit" is emphatic: "*They alone*, *only they*, shall inherit the earth." They are rich right now; and fifty billion trillion years into eternity they will be lavishing in the unfolding of "the incomparable riches of his grace" (Ephesians 2:7).

BECOMING MEEK

There are three concurrent paths to Christlike meekness.

First, we must realize that a gentle, caressing spirit is a gift of the Holy Spirit (Galatians 5:23). Therefore, it comes only through grace. We must cast ourselves on God, asking in humble prayer that he give us life, make us his children, and instill in us a spirit of meekness. At the same time, we can ask confidently because we know that if we ask anything according to his will he will do it (cf. John 14:13; 1 John 5:14). Such asking ought to be continual because every soul needs to grow in grace regardless of one's level of spiritual maturity.

Second, we must yoke ourselves to Jesus, for he was the incarnation of meekness. Our Lord said of himself, "Take my yoke upon you and learn from me, for I am gentle and humble in heart, and you will find rest for your souls. For my yoke is easy and my burden is light" (Matthew 11:29, 30). Jesus promises us that if we yoke ourselves to him, we will learn gentleness and humility.

In Biblical times a young ox was yoked to an older, experienced ox so that the older might train him to perform properly. By bearing the same yoke, the untrained ox learned the proper pace and how to heed the direction of the master. We learn by being yoked to Christ, as we surrender our lives to him for direction.

Third, we must give close attention to the progression of thought in the Beatitudes, for it provides us with a three-step ladder to meekness. The initial step begins in the first Beatitude (Matthew 5:3) with poverty of spirit, which comes from a true knowledge of ourselves. We realize that there is nothing within us that would commend us to God. We fall short. We need God.

In the next Beatitude (v. 4) we progress to mourning. We most naturally lament our state of spiritual poverty. This mourning is an enviable state because in it we are blessed and comforted.

We should note that poverty of spirit and mourning are negative. However, when true poverty of spirit and spiritual mourning are present, they make way for the positive virtue of meekness. In a sense, meekness is superior to the two preceding states because it grows out of them. The process is all so natural, so beautiful, and yet also quite supernatural!

We must stop here and say to ourselves, "I see how the progression works, and I see that it comes by grace, but how can I know when I am truly meek?" That is a good question. Martyn Lloyd-Jones gave his congregation in Westminster Chapel the answer, and I can say it no better. "The man who is truly meek is the man who is amazed that God and man can think of him as well as they do and treat him as well as they do."[7] The test as to whether we are truly meek is not whether we can say we *are* poor sinners, but rather what we *do* when someone else calls us vile sinners. Try it!

THE NEED FOR GENTLE CHRISTIANS

We need to rise above superficial Christianity. None of us must imagine that because we have good manners and display the proper social conventions we are fulfilling the meekness called for in this third Beatitude.

Evangelical passwords and civilities are not enough. God will not be impressed, nor will the world. May the paradoxes of the Sermon on the Mount penetrate our beings and drive us to an ongoing poverty of spirit, ongoing mourning, and ongoing meekness.

We cannot afford *not* to have this happen! Those closest to us need to see positive spiritual reality in our lives, especially the paradox of Christian meekness. They need to see its strength as we are willing to put our lives on the line for others and to stand tall for truth when necessary. They need to see gentleness and a non-retaliatory spirit within us. And when they do, they will see Jesus. That is who the world really needs to see!

4

The Fullness of Hunger

"Blessed are those who hunger and thirst for righteousness, for they will be filled."

— MATTHEW 5:6

Nutritionists have dramatized the importance of diet by telling us that we are what we eat. The thinking is, if we eat too many doughnuts and cream puffs, we'll become walking pastries. And the argument is pretty sound, as far as it goes.

In the realm of the mind and the spirit, "you are what you eat" is more penetrating. If you feed on violence, excitement, erotica, and materialism, you will eventually personify them. You will become what you eat.

I think we can accurately say that Elvis Presley never understood this. His life was a pitiful pursuit of materialism and sensuality. In Elvis's hey-day he earned between $5 million and $6 million a year. It is estimated that he grossed $100 million in his first two years of stardom.

He had three jets, two Cadillacs, a Rolls-Royce, a Lincoln Continental, Buick and Chrysler station wagons, a Jeep, a dune buggy, a converted bus, and three motorcycles.

His favorite car was his 1960 Cadillac limousine. The top was covered with pearl-white Naugahyde. The body was sprayed with forty coats of a specially prepared paint that included crushed diamonds and fish scales. Nearly all the metal trim was plated with eighteen-karat gold.

Inside the car there were two gold-flake telephones, a gold vanity case containing a gold electric razor and gold hair clippers, an electric shoe buffer, a gold-plated television, a record player, an amplifier, air conditioning, and a refrigerator that was capable of making ice in two minutes. He had everything.

Elvis's sensuality is legendary. Those friends and relatives most familiar with his state in the last months of his life tragically reveal that Elvis had very much become the victim of his appetites. He was what he had eaten — in the profoundest sense.

Elvis Presley's tragic life dramatizes the significance of the Lord's teaching in this fourth Beatitude, because in it Jesus sets forth the appetite and menu that bring spiritual well-being: "Blessed are those who hunger and thirst for righteousness, for they will be filled."

In this splendidly paradoxical sentence Jesus tells us what we ought to eat and how we must eat if we are to have spiritual health and ultimate satisfaction. Spiritual health comes from hunger.

A HEALTHY HUNGER

Because Christ declares that hunger for righteousness is essential to spiritual health and satisfaction, we must carefully consider what it means. Some have supposed that it is the *objective righteousness* described in Romans that God reckons to the believer's account, sometimes called imputed righteousness — "righteousness from God" (Romans 1:17; 3:21, 22; cf. Philippians 3:9). However, while the gift of such righteousness is foundational to every believer's salvation, that is not what is meant here.

Others have confined the meaning to *social righteousness*, the righteous treatment of the poor and oppressed. This is certainly part of the meaning because in the preceding context (4:12-17) Matthew quotes Isaiah 9:1, 2, which goes on to describe the social justice that will result from the coming of Messiah's reign. However, the root meaning here is determined by the seven occurrences of "righteousness" in the Sermon on the Mount that indicate it means a *subjective righteousness*, an inner righteousness that works itself out in one's living in conformity to God's will — righteous living. Thus, those who "hunger and thirst for righteousness" long to live righteously, and for righteousness to prevail in the world. It is a passionate desire, which begins with one's own life, that all things should be lived in line with God's will.

This desire to live in compliance with God's will is expansive. It includes an increasing sense of a need for God - a desire to be like him. To hunger and thirst for this righteousness means longing after the practical righteousness that the Beatitudes represent both personally and in the world. The one who hungers and thirsts wants the character of the kingdom. He pants after the fruit of the Spirit. He wants God's will and all it entails.

A DESPERATE HUNGERING

The fourth Beatitude is a call to pursue conformity to God's will stated in the most extreme of terms. The intensity of the expression is difficult for us to feel because if we are thirsty today, all we need to do is turn on the tap for cold, refreshing water; or if we are hungry, we just open the refrigerator.

However, to the ancient Palestinian the expression was terribly alive because he was never far from the possibility of dehydration or starvation.

It is not a comfortable picture. Jesus is far from recommending a genteel desire for spiritual nourishment, but rather a starvation for righteousness, a desperate hungering to be conformed to God's will.

The Beatitude is further intensified by the fact that this hungering is continual. "Blessed are those who are hungering and thirsting for righteousness." King David, at his best, was like this. He walked with God as few mortals have. He penned some of our favorite Psalms about his lofty spiritual experiences. And at the same time he wrote of his continual thirst and hunger: "O God, you are my God, earnestly I seek you; my soul thirsts for you, my body longs for you, in a dry and weary land where there is no water" (Psalm 63:1). "And I — in righteousness I will see your face; when I awake, I will be satisfied with seeing your likeness" (Psalm 17:15).

This is the way it is for a healthy believer. He or she never has enough of God and righteousness. He or she is always hungry.

SUCH HUNGERING EITHER REPULSES OR DRAWS US

The language of this Beatitude does not make sense to the modern ear. Indeed, it is too strong for some Christians. It rules out sleek, self-satisfied, halfhearted religion. In fact, hungering and thirsting for righteousness is the only approach the Beatitude accepts.

For some, Jesus' pronouncement may uncover buried, almost forgotten glimmers of past life when you first came to Christ and perpetually hungered and thirsted for righteousness. You couldn't get enough of Jesus or his Word. You were joyously desperate for the things of God. You also cared about the world and its spiritual famine. You welcomed opportunities for self-sacrifice and were willing to go for it all. But time blunted your desires, "the realities of life" took over, and that delectable hunger ceased. Now you are content with a life of lesser, limited devotion.

Yet you have not quite forgotten the joy and warmth of earlier times, and Jesus' words here still stir you. If so, you should heed his call, because you can be restored to what you were meant to be.

You must never be spiritually satisfied. You must pray that each decade of your life will find you more thirsty for a life pleasing to God.

"Blessed are those who desperately hunger and thirst for righteousness," says our Lord.

HUNGERING PEOPLE KNOW CHRIST

Jesus pronounces the spiritually famished to be "blessed" or approved. The reason is this: Those who truly hunger and thirst know Christ. And that is why this is such a penetrating warning to evangelicals. Concern for righteous living is on the decline in the evangelical church. Many watch more murders and adulteries on television in one week than their grandparents read about in a lifetime — and with no twinge of conscience. Their casual viewing is a tacit approval of evil. The pollsters tell us that the ethical gap is narrowing between the church and the world. And many evangelicals are no more concerned about the unrighteous plight of the world than their non-Christian neighbors. Some professing evangelicals would regard a desperate longing for righteousness as odd, even fanatical.

If you have no longing for righteousness, you had better initiate a careful analysis of your soul. Christ's words are such a gracious test, because each of us knows in his heart of hearts whether he really does long for righteous living.

However, if you do hunger and thirst for righteousness, if the Lord has given you a holy discontent with your life, you have his smile!

A HUNGERER'S REWARD

This Beatitude is, of course, another attention-grabbing paradox. It suggests that those who continually hunger are satisfied. Yet, how can one be hungry and satisfied at the same time? Or how can one be satisfied and experience hunger? Satisfied but never satisfied? Full yet empty? Content but discontent?

Paradoxical Satisfaction

How does it work? Like this. Someone left a plate of brownies in my church office. I resisted temptation (for a minute or two!) and then poured myself a cup of coffee and retreated to my study, brownie in hand. When I bit in, I tasted the best of brownies, for it was layered with caramel. I was "in heaven" with my brownie and cup of coffee. And I was completely satisfied — for about half an hour. Then I began to hunger and thirst for more! And I ate again with the same effect. It was a sublime cycle.

There you have the idea. The paradox describes a spiritual cycle. The more one conforms to God's will, the more fulfilled and content one becomes. But that in turn spawns a greater discontent. Our hunger increases and intensifies in the very act of being satisfied.

Paul lived in the blessing of this paradox. He wrote to Timothy, "I know whom I have believed" (2 Timothy 1:12). Yet to the Philippians he expressed a profound longing for Christ — "to know Christ and the power of his resurrection and the fellowship of sharing in his sufferings, becoming like him in his death" (Philippians 3:10). Paul knew Christ intimately, but the intimacy and satisfaction made him long for more. Bernard of Clairvaux sang of this cycle. Read his great words slowly:

We taste Thee, O Thou living Bread,
And long to feast upon Thee still;
We drink of Thee, the Fountainhead,
And thirst our souls from Thee to fill.

Complete Satisfaction

The world only offers us empty cups. That is why our text emphasizes that "they alone [those who hunger and thirst] will be filled." No one can know anything of this satisfaction but a believer.

The Scriptures joyfully attest to the satisfaction that Christ brings:

> *"But whoever drinks the water I give him will never thirst. Indeed, the water I give him will become in him a spring of water welling up to eternal life." (John 4:14)*

> *"I am the bread of life. He who comes to me will never go hungry, and he who believes in me will never be thirsty." (John 6:35)*

> *. . . for he satisfies the thirsty and fills the hungry with good things. (Psalm 107:9)*

Eternal Satisfaction

The image of a divine feast is used more than once by Jesus to illustrate the satisfactions of the kingdom. On one occasion Jesus told his disciples, "And I confer on you a kingdom, just as my Father conferred one on me, so that you may eat and drink at my table in my kingdom" (Luke 22:29-30). Now that will be eternal satisfaction!

We need to believe the words of Isaiah: "Come, all you who are thirsty, come to the waters; and you who have no money, come, buy and eat! Come, buy wine and milk without money and without cost. Why spend money on what is not bread, and your labor on what does not satisfy? Listen, listen to me, and eat what is good, and your soul will delight in the richest of fare" (Isaiah 55:1, 2).

We need to practice Jesus' words: "But seek first his kingdom and his righteousness, and all these things will be given to you as well" (Matthew 6:33).

GOD'S CALL: A PROFOUND HUNGER

Consider the force of this fourth Beatitude as we have opened it: "Blessed are those who hunger and thirst [like the starving do for food and the thirsty do for water] for righteousness [righteous living], for they will be filled [satisfied completely]."

"You are what you eat" is not as simple as it may first appear. It is profoundly esoteric. The tragedy of our time is that the world is hungering and thirsting after sex and wealth, violence and excitement. The church's tragedy is that many in her are seeking the same thing — and their diets are making them as empty and pathetic as the world.

We must remember that Jesus has provided us with the menu and appetite. The main course is righteousness — conformity to his will. The method is desperation. We are to hunger for righteousness-and so pursue it with all that is in us. The result is profound satisfaction, now and forever.

HOW IS YOUR APPETITE?

The answer lies in the spiritual logic of the Beatitudes.

- We must begin with the first Beatitude, true poverty of spirit, realizing that there is nothing within us that commends us to God. We must affirm our spiritual bankruptcy.
- Next, we must graduate to the second Beatitude, truly mourning our sins as well as the sin around us.
- Then we must ascend to the third Beatitude, by allowing our spiritual bankruptcy and mourning to instill in us a truly meek and gentle spirit.
- Finally, as we live the logic of the Beatitudes, we will be able to desperately hunger and thirst for righteousness.

There are few things more important than our spiritual appetite. We are what we eat.

Evangelicals, we need to hear Jesus' words afresh: "If you knew the gift of God and who it is that asks you for a drink, you would have asked him and he would have given you living water" (John 4:10).

5

The Dividend of Mercy

"Blessed are the merciful,
for they will be shown mercy."
— MATTHEW 5:7

Years ago a small-town merchant had identical twin boys who were inseparable. They were so close that they even dressed alike. It was said that their extraordinary closeness was the reason they never married. When their father died, they took over the family business. Their relationship was considered "a model of creative collaboration."

Because he was busy, one of the brothers neglected to ring up a sale and absentmindedly left a dollar bill on top of the cash register while he went to the front of the store to wait on another customer. Remembering the dollar, he returned to deposit it only to find the bill was gone. He asked his brother if he had seen it, but the brother said he had not.

An hour later he asked his brother again, but this time with an obvious note of suspicion. His brother became angry and defensive. Every time they tried to discuss the matter, the conflict grew worse, culminating in vicious charges and countercharges. The incredible outcome was the dissolution of their partnership, the installation of a partition down the middle of the store, and two competing businesses. This continued for twenty years — an open, divisive sore in the community.

One day a car with an out-of-state license pulled up in front of the stores. A well-dressed man entered one brother's shop and asked how long the store had been there. Learning it had been twenty years, he said, "Then you are the one with whom I must settle an old score."

> Some twenty years ago I was out of work, drifting from place to place, and I happened to get off a boxcar in your town. I had absolutely no money

> and had not eaten for three days. As I was walking down the alley behind your store, I looked in and saw a dollar bill on the top of the cash register. Everyone else was in the front of the store. I had been raised in a Christian home and I had never before in all my life stolen anything, but that morning I was so hungry I gave in to the temptation, slipped through the door, and took that dollar bill. That act has weighed on my conscience ever since, and I finally decided that I would never be at peace until I came back and faced up to that old sin and made amends. Would you let me now replace that money and pay you whatever is appropriate for damages?[1]

When the stranger finished his confession, he was amazed to see the old store owner shaking his head in deep sorrow and beginning to weep. Finally the old man gained control and, taking the gentleman by the arm, asked him to go to the store next door and tell its owner the same story. The stranger complied. Only this time two old men who looked almost identical wept side by side.[2]

From our distance we cannot say whether the two brothers professed to be believers, or were even churchgoers. Given the time and the culture, they probably owned some religious inclinations. Indeed, they could have been enthusiastic churchmen — even evangelicals. But whatever their spiritual profession, their merciless, unforgiving spirits revealed hearts that had never understood the mercy of God. For if they had, they themselves would have been merciful.

The fifth Beatitude — "Blessed are the merciful, for they will be shown mercy" — is the perfect corrective for all those who are caught in bitterness.

If you have problems similar to the two unhappy brothers, this chapter could lead you to liberation.

THE MERCIFUL

The basic idea of the Greek word translated *merciful* is "to give help to the wretched, to relieve the miserable." Here the essential thought is that mercy gives attention to those in misery. From this we make the important distinction between mercy and grace. *Grace* is shown to the undeserving; *mercy* is compassion to the miserable. Thus the synonym for *mercy* is *compassion*. Mercy, however, is not simply *feeling* compassion. Mercy exists when something is done to alleviate distress. This is uniform in the Old Testament (cf. Hosea and Amos 5). Jesus made this perfectly clear when, after he told the Parable of the Good Samaritan, he asked his questioner:

> *"Which of these three do you think was a neighbor to the man who fell into the hands of robbers?" The expert in the law replied, "The one who had mercy on him." Jesus told him, "Go and do likewise." (Luke 10:36-37)*

Mercy Is Compassion in Action

We must never imagine that we are merciful because we *feel* compassionate toward someone in distress. Mercy means *active* goodwill. This was well understood by the nineteenth-century preacher who happened across a friend whose horse had just been accidentally killed. While a crowd of onlookers expressed empty words of sympathy, the preacher stepped forward and said to the loudest sympathizer, "I am sorry five pounds. How much are you sorry?" And then he passed the hat. True mercy demands action.

Mercy Is Forgiving

New Testament scholar Robert Guelich has shown that especially in this Beatitude *merciful* describes one who forgives and pardons another who is in the wrong.[3] An inspiring display of this forgiving aspect of mercy in Scripture is that of Joseph to his brothers. The only reason they had not murdered him as a boy was that as they were ready to perform the act, they saw an approaching caravan and decided to sell him into slavery instead. Years later, when Joseph had his guilty brothers literally "at his mercy," he showed them exactly that. There was *compassion* as he wept for their misery, and then *action* as he met their needs. There was *forgiveness* as he restored them all to his grace, saying, "You intended to harm me, but God intended it for good" (Genesis 50:20).

The merciful person remembers his own sin and God's mercy to him, he understands the weaknesses of others, and he forgives. W. E. Sangster, the much-loved pastor of the renowned Westminster Central Hall, London, was graced with this quality in his own life. "It was Christmas time in my home," as he tells it:

> One of my guests had come a couple of days early and saw me sending off the last of my Christmas cards. He was startled to see a certain name and address. "Surely, you are not sending a greeting card to him," he said. "Why not?" I asked. "But you remember," he began, "eighteen months ago . . ." I remembered, then, the thing the man had publicly said about me, but I remembered also resolving at the time with God's help . . . to forget. And God had "made" me forget! I posted the card.[4]

I once had an associate who was like this. On one memorable occasion the name of someone came up who had grievously slandered him, and I said something derogatory about that person. But to my embarrassment (and instruction!), my friend began to quietly defend his slanderer: "Life has been hard for him . . . we have no idea of the pressures he has been under . . . he has done a lot of good things too." My colleague had compassion on the miserable soul who had given him so much trouble and, from what I could tell, had forgiven him! How beautiful that was! Our text tells us what God thinks of this: "Blessed are the merciful." Jesus says, "Such are the ones whom I approve."

THEY SHALL RECEIVE MERCY

The reason the merciful are blessed is that "they will be shown mercy." The word "they" in the phrase is emphatic: "Blessed are the merciful, for they [they alone] will be shown mercy." Other Scriptures teach the same idea. James says, "Judgment without mercy will be shown to anyone who has not been merciful" (James 2:13). Jesus himself says, "For if you forgive men when they sin against you, your heavenly Father will also forgive you. But if you do not forgive men their sins, your Father will not forgive your sins" (Matthew 6:14, 15).

Predictably, some have completely missed the point here, supposing that this Beatitude teaches that one can merit God's mercy by performing acts of mercy. Such an idea is at complete variance with the rest of Scripture, which teaches salvation by grace alone (Ephesians 2:8, 9). Moreover, if receiving God's forgiveness could only be merited by becoming forgiving, none of us would ever be truly forgiven, for none would ever absolutely meet this standard.

What this Beatitude means is that those who are truly God's children, and as such are objects of his mercy, will themselves be merciful and will receive mercy in the end. Showing mercy is evidence that we have received mercy.

This interpretation suggests two very penetrating tests. The first is this: If we have no mercy toward those who are physically and economically in distress, we are not Christians. Notice I did not say we become Christians by showing mercy toward the unfortunate, but that we are not believers if we are unwilling to show mercy to them. This is precisely the point of the Parable of the Good Samaritan. Jesus told the story to demonstrate that the religious establishment of his day did not fulfill the Great *Shema* — loving God with all one's might and one's neighbor as oneself (Luke 10:25-28). The fact that the priest and the Levite turned away from the needy man proved they did not love their neighbor as themselves; they thus failed to fulfill the Law and were lost. But the Samaritan's act of mercy showed that he loved his neighbor as himself, and that he was living within the gracious parameters of the Law. He was a lover of God and man.

If we remain impassive or callous to human need and refuse to do anything about it, we need to take a good long look at ourselves and see if we really are believers. John says it best: "If anyone has material possessions and sees his brother in need but has no pity on him, how can the love of God be in him?" (1 John 3:17). This is a test evangelicals haven't liked. Today, I suspect, there are some who would reject this test outright. If so, they are in great peril of soul. True belief is never to be divorced from attitude and action.

The second test involves the corresponding aspect of mercy — forgiveness. The test is this: If we refuse to exercise mercy by extending forgiveness, we are not Christians. Of course, it is frightening to maintain that we cannot be truly forgiven unless we have forgiving spirits. But it is true, because when God's grace comes into our hearts it makes us merciful. Forgiveness demonstrates whether we have been forgiven. So the telling line is this: If we refuse to be merciful, there is only one reason — we have never understood the grace of Christ. We are outside grace and are unforgiven.

Jesus taught this in the Parable of the Unmerciful Slave (Matthew 18:21-35). The slave owed his master an immense sum — in today's currency about twenty million dollars. The debt was impossible to repay, so he pleaded with his master who, with astonishing compassion, forgave him the entire debt. Incredibly, however, the wicked slave went out, found one of his fellow slaves who owed him 2,000 dollars, and threw him in prison. When the other slaves reported this injustice to their master, he summoned the wicked slave:

> *"'You wicked servant,' he said, 'I canceled all that debt of yours because you begged me to. Shouldn't you have had mercy on your fellow servant just as I had on you?' In anger his master turned him over to the jailers to be tortured, until he should pay back all he owed. This is how my heavenly Father will treat each of you unless you forgive your brother from your heart." (Matthew 18:32-35)*

These are hard, violent, surgical words. But they are mercifully so. The Lord here warns the religious person who attends church, can recite the appropriate answers, leads an outwardly moral life, but holds a death grip on his grudges. Jesus warns the one who will not forgive his relatives or his former business associates regardless of their pleas. He warns the one who nourishes hatreds, cherishes animosities, and otherwise lives in settled malice.

Such a person had better take stock of his life.

Some words of qualification are in order. The warning is not for those who find that bitterness and hatred recur even though they have forgiven the offender. The fact that you have forgiven and continue to forgive is a sign of grace, despite the ambivalences and imperfections of your forgiveness. The warning is for those who have no desire to forgive. Their souls are in danger.

There may also be some who find forgiveness difficult because they have been recently offended and are still in such emotional shock that they *cannot* properly respond. The warning is not for these.

The overall lesson is, if we are Christians, we can forgive and will forgive, however imperfectly it may be. We cannot live like the miserable brothers who divided over a dollar bill.

ON FORGIVING

The late Corrie ten Boom recalled in her book *The Hiding Place* a postwar meeting with a guard from the Ravensbruck concentration camp, where her sister had died and she herself had been subjected to horrible indignities.

> It was at a church service in Munich that I saw him, the former S.S. man who had stood guard at the shower room door in the processing center at Ravensbruck. He was the first of our actual jailers that I had seen since that time. And suddenly it was all there — the roomful of mocking men, the heaps of clothing, Betsie's pain-blanched face.
>
> He came up to me as the church was emptying, beaming and bowing. "How grateful I am for your message, Fraulein," he said. "To think that, as you say, He has washed my sins away!"
>
> His hand was thrust out to shake mine. And I, who had preached so often to the people in Bloemendaal the need to forgive, kept my hand at my side.
>
> Even as the angry, vengeful thoughts boiled through me, I saw the sin of them. Jesus Christ had died for this man; was I going to ask for more? Lord Jesus, I prayed, forgive me and help me to forgive him.
>
> I tried to smile, I struggled to raise my hand. I could not. I felt nothing, not the slightest spark of warmth or charity. And so again I breathed a silent prayer. Jesus, I cannot forgive him. Give me Your forgiveness.
>
> As I took his hand the most incredible thing happened. From my shoulder along my arm and through my hand a current seemed to pass from me to him, while into my heart sprang a love for this stranger that almost overwhelmed me.[5]

Forgiveness is possible for the most grievous of wounds. When I was a young man, I was acquainted with a Christian who took in a troubled teenager and tried to help him. The boy brutally murdered this man's daughter. Amazingly, my friend visited him in prison, forgave him, and eventually led him to Christ.

If you are a Christian, regardless of the wrong done to you, you can forgive. By God's grace, you can forgive the domestic wrong. By God's grace, you can forgive the professional wrong. For your soul's sake, you must.

When we began our study of the Beatitudes, we observed that they were given to us so we could ascertain two things: first, the authenticity of our faith, and second, the health of our spiritual lives. In the searchlight of this Beatitude, "Blessed are the merciful, for they will be shown mercy," is your salvation authentic? Are you merciful? Are you forgiving? Or do you hold grudges as your treasured possessions?

If you have come to understand that you are without grace and mercy, then no more fitting word could be commended to you here than this parable:

> *"Two men went up to the temple to pray, one a Pharisee and the other a tax collector. The Pharisee stood up and prayed about himself: 'God, I thank you that I am not like other men — robbers, evildoers, adulterers — or even like this tax collector. I fast twice a week and give a tenth of all I get.' But the tax collector stood at a distance. He would not even look up to heaven, but beat his breast and said, 'God, have mercy on me, a sinner.' I tell you that this man, rather than the other, went home justified before God. For everyone who exalts himself will be humbled, and he who humbles himself will be exalted." (Luke 18:10-14)*

Now do as the sinner did. Confess your sin. Affirm your faith in Christ as your only hope of salvation. Rest in his mercy. Thank him for saving you.

If you need to develop the compassion and forgiveness of a merciful spirit, here are some suggestions:

• *Confession*: Admit your need to God. Pray to this effect: "Father, I know your mercy. I have been merciful at times. But, God, I need more compassion, and I need to forgive. I know this is your will for me. Help me."

• *Scripture*: Read the Scriptures that have to do with mercy and compassion. Begin with Hosea 6:6, and then read Jesus' application of it in Matthew 9:9-13 and 23:23. Also examine Micah 6:8 and Amos 5:21-24. And especially meditate on Luke 10:30-37. Regarding forgiveness, read Matthew 6:14, 15 and 18:21-35.

• *Mercy*: Then get out and do mercy. Volitionally forgive those who have wronged you. Purposely become involved with those who are hurting.

Enjoy God's smile! "Blessed are the merciful, for they will be shown mercy."

6

The Reward of Purity

"Blessed are the pure in heart, for they will see God."
— MATTHEW 5:8

In 1982 the *Los Angeles Times* carried the story of Anna Mae Pennica, a sixty-two-year-old woman who had been blind from birth.[1] At age forty-seven she married a man she met in a Braille class; and for the first fifteen years of their marriage he did the seeing for both of them until he completely lost his vision to retinitis pigmentosa. Mrs. Pennica had never seen the green of spring or the blue of a winter sky. Yet because she had grown up in a loving, supportive family, she never felt resentful about her handicap and always exuded a remarkably cheerful spirit.

Then in October 1981 Dr. Thomas Pettit of the Jules Stein Eye Institute of the University of California at Los Angeles performed surgery to remove the rare congenital cataracts from the lens of her left eye — and Mrs. Pennica saw for the first time ever! The newspaper account does not record her initial response, but it does tell us that she found that everything was "so much bigger and brighter" than she ever imagined. While she immediately recognized her husband and others she had known well, other acquaintances were taller or shorter, heavier or skinnier than she had pictured them.

Since that day Mrs. Pennica has hardly been able to wait to wake up in the morning, splash her eyes with water, put on her glasses, and enjoy the changing morning light. Her vision is almost 20/30 — good enough to pass a driver's test.

Think how wonderful it must have been for Anna Mae Pennica when she looked for the first time at the faces she had only felt, or when she saw the kaleidoscope of a Pacific sunset or a tree waving its branches or a bird in flight. The gift of physical sight is wonderful. And the miracle of seeing for the first time can hardly be described.

A GREATER SEEING

Yet there is a seeing that surpasses even this — and that is seeing God. Since nothing is higher than God, seeing God is logically the greatest joy one can experience. Thus, when we pass from this world and see the face of Christ, the joy of that first split second will transcend all the accumulated joys of life. It will be the highest good, the *summum bonum*, the greatest joy, beside which the wonderful story of Mrs. Pennica's "miracle" fades in comparison.

This is what the sixth Beatitude is about — seeing God. "Blessed are the pure in heart, for they will see God." Jesus' words tell us how to get 20/20 spiritual vision. If we want to see God, this is *the* great text.

THE BEATITUDE: "BLESSED ARE THE PURE IN HEART"

As we begin, we must determine what "pure" means. Its Old Testament usage tells us that it refers to internal cleansing. Very likely Jesus' reference to "pure in heart" comes from the famous rhetorical answer to the questions of Psalm 24:3, 4: "Who may ascend the hill of the LORD? Who may stand in his holy place? He who has clean hands and a pure heart." Significantly, the Old Testament prophets looked forward to the time when God would give the people clean hearts. Ezekiel records God's words:

> *"I will sprinkle clean water on you, and you will be clean; I will cleanse you from all your impurities and from all your idols. I will give you a new heart and put a new spirit in you; I will remove from you your heart of stone and give you a heart of flesh." (36:25, 26)*

Jeremiah similarly envisaged a new covenant in which God would put his "law in their minds and write it on their hearts" (31:33).

In Jesus' day the need was urgent because of the Pharisees' externalizing. Hence Jesus' warning:

> *"Woe to you, teachers of the law and Pharisees, you hypocrites! You clean the outside of the cup and dish, but inside they are full of greed and self-indulgence. Blind Pharisee! First clean the inside of the cup and dish, and then the outside also will be clean. Woe to you, teachers of the law and Pharisees, you hypocrites! You are like whitewashed tombs, which look beautiful on the outside but on the inside are full of dead men's bones and everything unclean. In the same way, on the outside you appear to people as righteous but on the inside you are full of hypocrisy and wickedness." (Matthew 23:25-28)*

The Pharisees could well be characterized as saying, "Blessed are the outwardly clean, for they shall see God." So we see the necessity for the sixth Beatitude's call for a radical inner purity: "Blessed are the pure in heart, for they will see God."

In addition to this primary meaning, "pure" also calls for a purity of devotion. William Barclay tells us that the Greek word was used to describe clear water, sometimes metals without alloy, sometimes grain that had been winnowed, and sometimes feelings that are unmixed.[2] As it is used in our text, it carries the idea of being free from every taint of evil.

We must keep this squarely in mind because it is normally supposed that "pure" as in "pure in heart" primarily refers to being pure in mind regarding matters of sensuality. It certainly includes these matters. But the idea cannot be so limited, for it goes far deeper. Here in the sixth Beatitude it means a heart that does not bring mixed motives and divided loyalties to its relationship with God. It is a heart of singleness in devotion to God — pure, unmixed devotion. James refers to this idea when he says, "Purify your hearts, you double-minded" (James 4:8). That is, "Get rid of your mixed motives, your duplicity, your double-mindedness; be simple and pure in your devotion. (Cf. the commendations for an "undivided heart" in Psalm 86:11, Jeremiah 32:39, Ezekiel 11:19, 1 Corinthians 7:35.)

Negatively, we can imagine this idea from everyday life if we reflect on those people who, having been introduced to us, keep talking and smiling, while at the same time looking behind and around us at other people and things. They really are not interested in us; they only see us as objects or a means to an end. In the God-man relationship such behavior is scandalous. Positively stated then, "pure" is represented by the words *focus*, *absorption*, *concentration*, *sincerity*, and *singleness*.

"Blessed are the pure" is a searching statement, because focusing on God with a singleness of heart is one of the biggest challenges to twentieth-century Christians. Very few in this frenetic age are capable of the spiritual attention this Beatitude calls for.

Depth of Devotion

The depth of what is called for here is seen in the qualifying words "in heart." We are to be singly focused "in heart" on God. In the Bible, *heart* means more than just the mind; it also includes the emotions and the will. It is the totality of our ability to think, feel, and decide. So "pure in heart" means that not only our minds but our feelings and actions are to be concentrated singly on God. If our focus is merely intellectual, we are not pure in heart. As Martyn Lloyd-Jones paraphrases it, "Blessed are those who are pure, not only on the surface but in the center of their being and at the source of every activity."[3] This is a daunting requirement — a radical cleanness of heart, totally focused on God.

The depth of this heart requirement is further underlined by the realization that it is from the heart that all our human problems come. Jeremiah said, "The heart is deceitful above all things and beyond cure" (Jeremiah 17:9). Jesus said, "For out of the heart come evil thoughts, murder, adultery, sexual immorality, theft, false testimony, slander" (Matthew 15:19). Again he said, "Nothing outside a man can make him 'unclean' by going into him. Rather, it is what comes out of a man that makes him 'unclean.' . . . For from within, out of men's hearts, come evil thoughts" (Mark 7:15, 21). The Scriptures are conclusive. But our hearts tell us the same. All we have to do is look into our own hearts of darkness, observing the mixed motives, the distractions, the divided loyalties, to know this is perfectly true. The dictum of Ivan Turgenev, the nineteenth-century Russian novelist, speaks for us all:

I do not know what the heart
of a bad man is like.
But I do know what the heart
of a good man is like.
And
it is terrible.

An Impossible Depth

The looming question is, therefore, how can we ever accomplish this? This Beatitude is beyond our reach. Jesus is asking for perfection. And at the end of the first section of the Sermon on the Mount, this is precisely what he says: "Be perfect, therefore, as your heavenly Father is perfect" (Matthew 5:48). This drives us to despair, for none of us *perfectly* models any of the Beatitudes. None of us perfectly exhibits a poverty of spirit. None of us perfectly mourns our sins. None of us is perfectly humble and gentle. None of us perfectly thirsts. No one is perfectly pure in heart.

Then what are we to do? There is only one answer. We must cast ourselves on the grace of God and thus receive his radical renewal. We must ask him to implant and nourish the character of the kingdom in our lives. If we do this, these qualities will take root and grow within us, though we will never attain absolute perfection in this life.

If the character of the kingdom is not present, then we must question whether we are truly believers. Here, with the sixth Beatitude — "Blessed [approved] are the pure in heart" — we must ask ourselves, "Is my heart clean, and do I know anything of single-hearted devotion to God?" The answers to these searching questions may indicate the authenticity of our faith or, if we are believers, the state of our spiritual health.

God demands a humanly impossible character, and then gives us that character by his grace. And with that he bestows a humanly impossible vision.

THE BOON: "FOR THEY WILL SEE GOD"

The Beatitude's sublime benefit is a vision of God himself. Here, as in the preceding Beatitudes, the word "they" is emphatic: "for they [they alone] will see God." And as with the other Beatitudes, the future is in immediate reference to what goes before. They will see God as they become pure in heart. And the seeing is continuous.

What this means is that it is possible to actually see God in this life — now. I think this is what blind and deaf Helen Keller meant when someone bluntly said to her, "Isn't it terrible to be blind?" To which she responded, "Better to be blind and see with your heart, than to have two good eyes and see nothing." Perhaps if it were possible for her to have heard of Mrs. Pennica's miraculous operation, she would have said, "That is wonderful. But there is yet a better seeing."

Seeing God Now

Christians see God now. Of course, they do not see him in his total being, because that would be too much for them. However, they do see him in many ways. That has been my experience. Before I became a Christian I won a Bible-reading contest, but the words meant nothing to me. Just a short time later when I met Christ, the Word of God came alive. I couldn't get enough. I even read at night with my flashlight! The Bible was living, and I saw God in its pages.

Believers also see and celebrate God in creation. Psalm 29 records that David watched a thunderstorm and saw God. Of thunder he says, "The voice of the LORD is over the waters; the God of glory thunders, the LORD thunders over the mighty waters. The voice of the LORD is powerful; the voice of the LORD is majestic" (vv. 3, 4). When David saw the lightning his response was, "The voice of the LORD strikes with flashes of lightning" (v. 7). This kind of seeing is the special possession of the believer. We see the footprints and the hand of God in nature.

Those of faith also see him in the events of life — even difficulties. Job exclaimed after his varied experiences of life, "My ears had heard of you but now my eyes have seen you" (Job 42:5).

Seeing More of God

The sixth Beatitude tells us that the purer our hearts become, the more we will see of God in this life. The more our hearts are focused on God, absorbed with him, concentrated on his being, freed from distractions, sincere — *single*, the more we will see him. As our hearts become purer, the more the Word lives and the more creation speaks. Even the adverse circumstances of life seem to sharpen our vision of God.

Seeing God in this life is the *summum bonum — the* highest good, because those who see him become more and more like him. "And we, who with unveiled faces all reflect the Lord's glory, are being transformed into his likeness with ever-increasing glory, which comes from the Lord, who is the Spirit" (2 Corinthians 3:18).

Ultimate Seeing

But there is even more to seeing God, for the "pure in heart" will one day see him face to face. As we have said, in that split second of recognition believers will experience more joy than the sum total of accumulated joys of a long life. They will behold the dazzling blaze of his being that has been, and will always be, the abiding fascination of angels. Scripture and reason demand that we understand that it will be the greatest event of our eternal existence — the *visio Dei*, the vision of God. We need to believe it! We need the faith and vision of Job who said, "I know that my Redeemer lives, and that in the end he will stand upon the earth. And after my skin has been destroyed, yet in my flesh I will see God; I myself will see him with my own eyes — I, and not another. How my heart yearns within me!" (Job 19:25-27). Fainting hearts should be our reaction at the prospect of the vision of God.

Now think of the complete Beatitude: "Blessed [approved of God] are the pure in heart [those with a clean, unmixed heart for God] for they will [continuously] see God [in life and in eternity]." Have we experienced, do we know, a purity of heart, an unmixed devotion to God? This is not to suggest that this is our perfect experience at every moment. But rather, do we *ever* experience it? Moreover, is this singleness our desire? If not, listen closely, for the answer exists.

ON RECEIVING SIGHT

The irony of Mrs. Pennica's "miracle," according to Dr. Pettit, was that "surgical techniques available as far back as the 1940s could have corrected her problem." Mrs. Pennica lived forty of her sixty-two sightless years needlessly blind!

Now hear this, and hear it well: The "technique" for curing spiritual blindness has existed for two millennia. The procedure is radical and 100% effective, because God is the physician. You must be born again. To be pure in heart, you must be given a new heart.

When Jesus informed Nicodemus of this necessity, Nicodemus quite naturally questioned how it could be. Jesus answered, "Flesh gives birth to flesh, but the Spirit gives birth to spirit" (John 3:6), saying in effect, "That which is animal is animal, that which is vegetable is vegetable, and that which is of the Spirit is spirit. Nicodemus, it is radical indeed." Jesus explained how spiritual birth happens in these words: "You should not be surprised at my saying, 'You must be born again.' The wind blows wherever it pleases. You hear its sound, but you cannot tell where it comes from or where it is going. So it is with everyone born of the Spirit" (John 3:7, 8). That is to say, "Nicodemus, it is the work of the Holy Spirit. You do not see his work, just as you do not see the wind, but only its effects." To us he says, "Trust God's Word, believe that Jesus' death on the cross paid the penalty for your sins, and thereby receive a new, pure heart in place of your heart of darkness." It is a miracle. It is all of God. It is free. It is yours as you believe.

Do you believe?

ON IMPROVING VISION

For those of us who are Christians, this text is also an opportunity to develop and enhance the purity and focus of our hearts.

First, *be absolutely honest with God about your heart's condition.* Is your heart inwardly clean? And more, is it pure in its focus on God? Ask the Holy Spirit to show you the exact state of your heart.

Second, *acknowledge that only God can make your heart pure.* This is not to suggest passivity. Paul tells us, "Therefore, my dear friends, as you have always obeyed — not only in my presence, but now much more in my absence — continue to work out your salvation with fear and trembling, for it is God who works in you to will and to act according to his good purpose" (Philippians 2:12, 13). James says, "Come near to God and he will come near to you. Wash your hands, you sinners, and purify your hearts, you double-minded" (James 4:8). The Biblical balance is: I must do everything I can and still realize that it is not enough; only God can make my heart pure (cf. Romans 11:6 and Ephesians 2:7a).

Third, *fill yourself with God's Word.* In the Upper Room Jesus told his disciples, "You are already clean because of the word I have spoken to you" (John 15:3). Immersion and interaction with God's Word will purify.

Fourth, *think about what you will be in eternity.* Make that hope a prominent aspect of your meditation. The Apostle John is very exact in explaining what such a hope will do to us:

> *Dear friends, now we are children of God, and what we will be has not yet been made known. But we know that when he appears, we shall be*

like him, for we shall see him as he is. Everyone who has this hope in him purifies himself, just as he is pure. (1 John 3:2, 3)

You and I are going to be transformed at the *visio Dei* into the likeness of Christ. This is the most stupendous thing we could ever be told! This is our purifying hope.

Hear Paul's charge to look for that day:

For the grace of God that brings salvation has appeared to all men. It teaches us to say "No" to ungodliness and worldly passions, and to live self-controlled, upright and godly lives in this present age, while we wait for the blessed hope — the glorious appearing of our great God and Savior, Jesus Christ, who gave himself for us to redeem us from all wickedness and to purify for himself a people that are his very own, eager to do what is good. (Titus 2:11-14)

7

The Paternity of Peace

"Blessed are the peacemakers,
for they will be called sons of God."
— MATTHEW 5:9

The celebrated historians Will and Ariel Durant, in their book *The Lessons of History*, begin the chapter on "History and War" with these words: "War is one of the constants of history, and has not diminished with civilization and democracy. In the last 3,421 years of recorded history only 268 have seen no war."[1] That is a chilling statement. And it would, no doubt, be even more so if the facts of *unrecorded* history could be known.

War is the constant reality of life. Today anyone old enough to understand what is being said on television knows that multiple wars are being fought at this very moment. The proposed solutions are many. Some are tongue-in-cheek, like the despairing scenario that the Durants put in the mouth of a fictitious general:

> States will unite in basic cooperation only when they are in common attacked from without. Perhaps . . . we may make contact with ambitious species on other planets or stars; soon thereafter there will be interplanetary war. Then, and only then, will we of this earth be one.[2]

Seriously, some do argue the necessity that one of the superpowers gain ascendancy over the rest (through battle no doubt!) and then war will be outlawed — a *Pax Romana* revived. Others hold that the inhabitants of the world simply must come to the conclusion that war is unprofitable and refuse to fight. Do you remember the old bumper sticker, "What if they had a war and nobody came?" Another suggestion, akin to this but more elevated, is that nations must challenge the evil precedents of history and live by the Golden Rule, as legend says a Buddhist king once did.

This last idea touches on the solution, but it does not go far enough. The answer to war is not simply a matter of bootstrap ethics; it is profoundly theological. What is needed is a radical change in the human race if there is to be peace. No one can live the Golden Rule by mere human will. No one can master even one of the Beatitudes in his own strength. Peace is impossible for humans qua humans.

Thus the grand relevance of the seventh Beatitude: "Blessed are the peacemakers, for they will be called sons of God." This divine pronouncement, understood, taken to heart, and applied by the Holy Spirit, can not only bring inner peace to our troubled hearts but also make us instruments of peace — peacemakers. It has the potential to give us peace within and to make us mediators of peace in the lives of those around us and in society at large.

"BLESSED ARE THE PEACEMAKERS"

Fundamental to understanding what Christ is saying is the precise meaning of the exquisite word "peacemakers." Taking the first half of the word, *peace*, we understand it to mean much the same as the Hebrew word *shalom*, which bears the idea of wholeness and overall well-being. When a Jew said, "Shalom," he was wishing another more than the absence of trouble, but all that made for a complete, whole life. God's peace is not narrowly defined. It is much more than the absence of strife; it encompasses all of the person — it is positive.

The second half of the word, *makers*, demands that we understand that the person is not passive but is a source of peace. As it is used here, it is a dynamic word bursting with energy. Both parts of the word "peacemakers," taken together, describe one who actively pursues peace in its fullness. He pursues more than the absence of conflict; he pursues wholeness and well-being.

Bearing this in mind, we can then understand what a peacemaker is not. A peacemaker is not, as is commonly supposed, the kind of person who is easygoing and *laissez-faire*, who does not care what anyone else does as long as it does not directly affect him. Neither is the peacemaker always tolerant — "you do your thing and I'll do mine." Nor is the peacemaker an appeaser — the kind who wants "peace at any price." Appeasement does not make for peace. It just puts off the conflict. The history of Europe during the 1930s is the classic example of this.

The true peacemaker, contrary to what most people think, is not afraid of making waves.

WHAT A PEACEMAKER IS

What then is a peacemaker like? To begin with, he is characterized by *honesty*. If there is a problem, he admits it. The prophet Ezekiel warned against those who act as if all is well when it is not, who say "'Peace,' when there is no peace" (13:10). Such, according to Ezekiel, are merely plastering over cracked walls. The plaster obscures the cracks, but when the rain comes, the true state of the walls is revealed and the walls crumble (vv. 10, 11). Jeremiah, employing similar phrasing, put it memorably: "They dress the wound of my people as though it were not serious. 'Peace, peace,' they say, when there is no peace" (Jeremiah 6:14). The peacemaker does not do this. He is painfully honest about the true status of relationships in the world, in the society in which he moves, and in his own personal dealings. He admits failed relationships. He admits that he is at odds with others if it is so. He honestly acknowledges tension if others have something against him. He does not pretend. He refuses to say, "Peace, peace!" when there is no peace.

How this speaks to real life! We tend to putty over the cracks. This is particularly a male tendency. Even in our most intimate relationships, men tend to act as if everything is OK when it is not. Men often avoid reality because they want peace. But their avoidance heals the wound only slightly and prepares the way for greater trouble.

Next, a peacemaker is willing to *risk pain*. Any time we attempt to bring peace personally or societally, we necessarily risk misunderstanding and failure. If we have been wrong, there is the pain of apologizing. On the other hand, we may have to shoulder the equally difficult pain of rebuking another. In any case, the peacemaker has to be willing to "risk it." The temptation is to let things slide. It is so easy to rationalize that trying to bring true peace will "only make things worse."

These two qualities of the peacemaker — honesty about the true status of peace and a willingness to risk pain in pursuing peace — beautifully anticipate the next quality, which is a paradox: *the peacemaker is a fighter*. He makes trouble to make peace. He wages peace.

God's Word enjoins such peacemaking, telling us to "make every effort to keep the unity of the Spirit through the bond of peace" (Ephesians 4:3) and to "make every effort to do what leads to peace and to mutual edification" (Romans 14:19). "If it is possible, as far as it depends on you, live at peace with everyone" (Romans 12:18). St. Francis of Assisi understood this call to the active pursuit of peace:

Lord, make me an instrument of Thy peace.
Where there is hate, may I bring love;
Where offense, may I bring pardon;
May I bring union in place of discord.

That the peacemaker is a fighter in no way justifies a verbal "license to kill." He should never be thoughtless or pugnacious. Rather his personality must be permeated with the *shalom* of God. He is gentle. James wrote, "But the wisdom that comes from heaven is first of all pure; then peace-loving, considerate, submissive, full of mercy and good fruit, impartial and sincere. Peacemakers who sow in peace raise a harvest of righteousness" (3:17-18). The peacemaker is positive. He is tolerant in the best sense of the word. He realizes we are all of fallen stock and so does not demand perfection of others. He is humble. His ego is in hand. And he is loving.

How beautiful true peacemakers are. Filled with peace themselves, they are honest about the state of the relationships around them, whether personal or in the church or in the world. They are honest about what is in their own hearts and sensitive to where others are. They refuse to be satisfied with cheap peace, to say "peace, peace" when there is none. They are willing to risk pain and misunderstanding to make things right. Peacemakers will even *fight* for peace.

THE ULTIMATE PEACEMAKER

Our Lord himself is, of course, the supreme peacemaker. He is the glorious "Prince of Peace" prophesied by Isaiah, the messianic fulfillment of the new covenant of peace (cf. Isaiah 9:6; 52:7-10; Ezekiel 37:24-28). At his birth the angels celebrated this fulfillment, singing, "Glory to God in the highest, and on earth peace to men on whom his favor rests" (Luke 2:14).

What we must see is that there was nothing cheap about his peacemaking. The Apostle Paul wrote, "For God was pleased to have all his fullness dwell in him, and through him to reconcile to himself all things, whether things on earth or things in heaven, by *making peace* through his blood, shed on the cross" (Colossians 1:19, 20, italics added). Jesus saw the gravity of our problem, and he refused to sweep it under the rug. Only a drastic solution would suffice, and so he "[made] peace" (the same root words as in Matthew 5:9 for "peacemakers") "*through His blood.*" Christ is our supreme example of sacrificial aggression in bringing peace.

He also became the source of peace among all men.

> *But now in Christ Jesus you who once were far away have been brought near through the blood of Christ. For he himself is* our peace, *who has made the two one and has destroyed the barrier, the dividing wall of hostility, by abolishing in his flesh the law with its commandments and regulations. His purpose was to create in himself one new man out of the two, thus making peace, and in this one body to reconcile both of them to God through the cross, by which he put to death their hostility. He came and*

preached peace to you who were far away and peace to those who were near. (Ephesians 2:13-17, italics added)

By becoming "our peace," he thus dispenses his *shalom* in our hearts. "Peace I leave with you," said Jesus, "my peace I give you" (John 14:27). This, in turn, enables us to promote in each other everything that makes for well-being. The cost of this enabling power is beyond computation. It was attained for us "with the precious blood of Christ, a lamb without blemish or defect" (1 Peter 1:19).

Jesus not only made possible peace with God and peace among men — he gave us the example of how a peacemaker goes about his work.

Do nothing out of selfish ambition or vain conceit, but in humility consider others better than yourselves. Each of you should look not only to your own interests, but also to the interests of others. Your attitude should be the same as that of Christ Jesus: who, being in very nature God, did not consider equality with God something to be grasped, but made himself nothing, taking the very nature of a servant, being made in human likeness. And being found in appearance as a man, he humbled himself and became obedient to death — even death on a cross! (Philippians 2:3-8)

In obtaining our peace, our Lord didn't grasp his glory and dignity, but instead he humbled himself. The example stands for us who are called to peacemaking. This is expensive! It costs to make peace. Peacemakers are willing to lower themselves, to even lose their dignity in order to bring *shalom* to life. This is the way peacemakers always have been.

A RADICAL CALL

We cannot overemphasize the radical nature of the call to be peacemakers. Peacemaking, as commended by Jesus, is not a natural human quality. It is above human nature. It is impossible. As such, it is a wonder that this Beatitude has been a favorite text of those who know little about Christianity. Secular pacifists love to quote Matthew 5:9 along with Isaiah 2:4 ("They will beat their swords into plowshares and their spears into pruning hooks. Nation will not take up sword against nation, nor will they train for war anymore"). They argue that the Beatitudes (especially the seventh) are "the real gospel"; if only men would practice them, the world would be renewed. Of course, they are correct, as far as they go. For if the Beautiful Attitudes really were practiced, war would be no more. However, peacemaking cannot take place without a radical change in the human heart and the enabling of the Holy Spirit.

The radicalness of Christ's call to peacemaking demands a renovation of human personality. One must first have a profound experience of the *shalom* of God. No one can become a peacemaker until he has found peace himself. The tragedy is that people do not go to the heart of the matter. Without grace, we are natural enemies of God and of one another. Our hearts must be changed. We cannot give what we do not possess.

This inner change, coupled with dependence on the Spirit, is what makes a peacemaker. The Holy Spirit molds the character of peacemakers' lives so that their ethos becomes increasingly gentle, humble, and loving. He elevates their integrity so that they can honestly evaluate the development of peace in their personal lives and society. He steels them *not* to say there is peace when there is no peace. The Spirit leads them to risk pain and misunderstanding in the pursuit of peace. He also leads them in developing the divinely aggressive spirit that wages peace.

CALLED SONS OF GOD

Now let us consider the sublime benefit: "They will be called sons of God." They have divine paternity, an inheritance from above. The meaning here is breathtaking. Again, as in the six previous Beatitudes, the pronoun is emphatic. The Greek word order is, "for they sons of God shall be called." The idea is that they, and no others, shall be called God's sons. Moreover, the passive voice indicates that it is God, not man, who assigns the title "sons."

The sublimity of this promise comes from the fact that the title "sons of God" refers to character (cf. Luke 6:35). The peacemaker partakes of the character of God. He is like God in the way he lives. No wonder God says, "Blessed are the peacemakers." The proper question to ask next is, what title does God assign to *us*?

ARE WE PEACEMAKERS?

If we are not peacemakers but troublemakers, there is high probability that we are not true children of God, regardless of how prominently we wear our evangelicalism. Peacemakers are sometimes troublemakers for the sake of peace, but not troublemakers who spread rumors and gossip about others. If you are constantly fomenting discontent, if you find joy in the report of trouble and scandal, if you are omnicritical, always fault-finding, if you are unwilling to be involved in peacemaking, if you are mean — if these negative qualities characterize your life, you are probably not a true Christian (cf. 1 Corinthians 6:9-11; Galatians 5:19-21 on the fate of those involved in slander, hatred, discord, dissension, and factions).

Again, this is not a matter of whether you fall into these things or are struggling to control them, but rather whether these elements are a part of your character. If this is what you are like, then you need to take a day off from your regular schedule and spend it with the Scriptures open before you, seeking the face of God. His Word promises you peace.

> *For God was pleased to have all his fullness dwell in him, and through him to reconcile to himself all things, whether things on earth or things in heaven, by making peace through his blood, shed on the cross. (Colossians 1:19, 20)*

> *Therefore, since we have been justified through faith, we have peace with God through our Lord Jesus Christ. . . . For if, when we were God's enemies, we were reconciled to him through the death of his Son, how much more, having been reconciled, shall we be saved through his life! (Romans 5:1, 10)*

Now for some advice regarding the "hows" of being a peacemaker. As we first saw, a peacemaker must experience the peace of God himself. The futility of Christians attempting to make peace when their inner lives are walking civil wars is evidenced by the logic that we can impart only that which we possess. If we are believers but have receded from the fullness of Christ's *shalom*, we must come to him honestly and ask for a fresh implanting of his peace.

Then we must remember that this seventh Beatitude is the last Beatitude that describes the *character* of the Christian, and that all the other Beatitudes build up to it. Peacemakers are developed as they ascend the ladder (the spiritual logic) of the Beatitudes.

Beatitude One:	These have experienced poverty of spirit (the recognition that there is nothing within them to commend them to God). In fact, it remains their ongoing awareness and as such is the ground for ongoing spiritual blessing.
Beatitude Two:	These have come face to face with their own sin, and they mourn over it.
Beatitude Three:	Due to the authenticity of their poverty of spirit and mourning, these experience gentle ness and humility in dealing with others.
Beatitude Four:	Because these have experienced poverty of spirit and mourning and meekness, they hunger and thirst for all righteousness.

Beatitude Five:	The reality of their own need has made these merciful to others.
Beatitude Six:	These have been cleansed by the blood of Christ, and their pure lives are focused on him, and thus they are blessed with an ongoing vision of God.
Beatitude Seven:	And now these, having been so infused by Christ's peace and the character of the kingdom, are peacemakers.

Peacemakers are those through whom the entire Beatitudes course again and again — sometimes in order, sometimes out of order, sometimes singly, sometimes all together. They have the character of the King — they are peacemakers.

8

The Joy of Persecution

MATTHEW 5:10-12

"Blessed are those who are persecuted because of righteousness, for theirs is the kingdom of heaven."

— MATTHEW 5:10

From William Blake's *Auguries of Innocence* come these wise, moving lines:

Joy and woe are woven fine,
A clothing for the soul divine,
Under every grief and pine
Runs a joy with silken twine.[1]

Blake understood that joy and woe are part of the fabric of life that God weaves and lovingly fits as perfect clothing for his children. This is mysterious and paradoxical. But there is great comfort in the fact that God is the weaver.

As we take up the final Beatitude we find a divinely composed paradox that has similar mystery, for it involves the relationship of persecution and joy. To read this Beatitude for the first time is shocking. Imagine hearing these lines for the first time ever.

"Blessed are those who are persecuted because of righteousness, for theirs is the kingdom of heaven. Blessed are you when people insult you, persecute you and falsely say all kinds of evil against you because of me. Rejoice and be glad, because great is your reward in heaven, for in the same way they persecuted the prophets who were before you." (Matthew 5:10-12)

One of the Puritan commentators believed that the reason Christ repeated himself was because the statement was so incredible! And he was probably right.

Until now all the Beatitudes have been given in the third person — "Blessed are those," and that is the way this Beatitude begins. But the repetition in verse 11 changes to the direct address of the second person — "Blessed are *you* when people insult *you*, persecute *you* . . ." (emphasis added). The repetition of the Beatitude, its personalization, and its position at the end of the list tell us that it is of supreme importance for the church. Significantly, when stretched on the loom of adversity the church has repeatedly woven persecution and joy into garments of divine praise.

JOY IN PRISON

Supernatural joy amidst trial has been the experience of the church. When Peter and the other apostles were flogged before the Sanhedrin soon after Pentecost, "the apostles left the Sanhedrin, rejoicing because they had been counted worthy of suffering disgrace for the Name" (Acts 5:41).

Samuel Rutherford, the saintly Scottish pastor, wrote from his prison sty, "I never knew by my nine years of preaching so much of Christ's love, as He taught me in Aberdeen by six months imprisonment." "Christ's cross," he also said, "is such a burden as sails are to a ship or wings to a bird."[2]

And in our own time a Romanian pastor describes how he was imprisoned and tortured mercilessly and yet experienced joy. Locked in solitary confinement, he had been summoned by his captors, who cut chunks of flesh from his body, and was then returned to his cell, where he was starved. Yet in the midst of this sadism, there were times when the joy of Christ so overcame him that he would pull himself up and shuffle about the cell in holy dance. So remarkable was his joy that on his release from prison and his return to his home, he chose to fast the first day in memorial to the joy he had known in prison.

Hearing stories like these, we naturally ask how it is possible. In partial answer, notice that they did not *enjoy* persecution. To suggest that one should enjoy persecution is to suggest a perversion. We also must understand that persecution of itself is neither blessed nor joyous. However, there is a kind of persecution that has God's blessing and results in joy.

THE PERSECUTION THAT BRINGS JOY

The Beatitude does not say, "Blessed are the persecuted, period!" Unfortunately, this is the way it is sometimes interpreted. And those who read it like this delude themselves into thinking that any time they experience conflict they are bearing the reproach of Christ.

Joseph Bayly's satire *The Gospel Blimp* humorously portrays this fallacy. Some believers in a small town, eager to share their faith, hit on the idea of a gospel blimp. The blimp was piloted back and forth across town, dragging Scripture banners and dropping tracts, called "gospel bombs," into backyards. At first the town's people put up with the intrusion, but their tolerance changed to hostility when the blimp's owners installed a loudspeaker and began assaulting the people with gospel broadcasts. The locals had had enough, and the local newspaper ran an editorial:

> For some weeks now our metropolis has been treated to the spectacle of a blimp with an advertising sign attached at the rear. This sign does not plug cigarettes or a bottled beverage, but the religious beliefs of a particular group in our midst. The people of our city are notably broad-minded, and they have good-naturedly submitted to this attempt to proselyte. But last night a new refinement (some would say debasement) was introduced. We refer, of course, to the airborne sound truck, the invader of our privacy, that raucous destroyer of communal peace.[3]

That night the gospel blimp was sabotaged, and of course the Christians saw it as "persecution."

Sadly, Christians are very often persecuted not for their Christianity, but for lack of it. Sometimes they are rejected simply because they have unpleasing personalities. They are rude, insensitive, thoughtless — or piously obnoxious. Some are rejected because they are discerned as proud and judgmental. Others are disliked because they are lazy and irresponsible. Incompetence mixed with piety is sure to bring rejection.

Christ's words must be read in their entirety. "Blessed are those who are persecuted because of righteousness." In context, this is the righteousness (righteous living) taught in the preceding Beatitudes. The world cannot tolerate such a life. Why?

First, poverty of spirit runs counter to the pride of the unbelieving heart. Those whom the world admires are the self-sufficient who need nothing else, not the poor in spirit.

Second, the mourning, repentant heart that sorrows over its own sin and the sins of society is not appreciated by the world.

Third, the gentle and meek person, the one who has the strength not to take up a personal offense, is regarded as weak by those who do not know Christ. Conventional wisdom has it that "meekness is weakness."

Fourth, hungering and thirsting for the spiritual — for Christ — is foreign and repugnant to a world that lusts after only what it can touch and taste.

Fifth, the truly merciful person who not only feels compassion and forgiveness but who gives it is out of step with the grudge-bearing callousness of our age. This person is an awkward, embarrassing rebuke to the uncaring.

Sixth, the pure, single-minded heart focused on God provides a convicting contrast to impure, self-focused culture.

Seventh, the peacemaker is discomforting because he will not settle for a cheap or counterfeit peace and has an embarrassing inclination to wage peace.

The foundational reason such a person will be persecuted is that he or she is like Christ. This is Jesus' point when he completes verse 11 with "because of me" instead of "because of righteousness," used in verse 10. Everyone who lives like Jesus will be persecuted. Listen to Jesus' testimony in John 15:18-20:

> *"If the world hates you, keep in mind that it hated me first. If you belonged to the world, it would love you as its own. As it is, you do not belong to the world, but I have chosen you out of the world. That is why the world hates you. Remember the words I spoke to you: 'No servant is greater than his master.' If they persecuted me, they will persecute you also. If they obeyed my teaching, they will obey yours also."*

Jesus tells us that since the wind was in his face, it will be in ours too.

Hear Paul's advice to Timothy: "In fact, everyone who wants to live a godly life in Christ Jesus will be persecuted" (2 Timothy 3:12). Paul also warned the Thessalonians, "You know quite well that we were destined for them [trials]. In fact, when we were with you, we kept telling you that we would be persecuted. And it turned out that way, as you well know" (1 Thessalonians 3:3, 4). Likewise, he told the Christians in Antioch, "We must go through many hardships to enter the kingdom of God" (Acts 14:22).

Few people who have lived in our time have understood and expressed this better than Dietrich Bonhoeffer:

> Suffering, then, is the badge of true discipleship. The disciple is not above his master. . . . That is why Luther reckoned suffering among the marks of the true church, and one of the memoranda drawn up in preparation for the Augsburg Confession similarly defines the church as the community of those "who are persecuted and martyred for the Gospel's sake." . . . Discipleship means allegiance to the suffering Christ, and it is therefore not at all surprising that Christians should be called upon to suffer. In fact, it is a joy and a token of His grace.[4]

During a stressful time in Charles Spurgeon's life when he was depressed by criticism, his wife took a sheet of paper, printed the eight Beatitudes on it in large, old English style script, and tacked it to the ceiling over his bed. She wanted the reality to saturate his mind morning and evening: Everyone who lives righteously will be persecuted. There are no exceptions!

HOW DO WE MEASURE UP?

The logic is revealing: since the first seven Beatitudes describe the character of the true believer, we must conclude that ostracism, persecution, and rejection are just as much signs of the believer as being poor in spirit or merciful. We should not be surprised when persecution comes but rather, surprised when it does not. Therefore, if the person who claims to follow Christ never experiences any persecution at all, it may be reasonably asked if he really is a Christian.

If we evangelicals have never experienced rejection for the sake of the kingdom, are we citizens of the kingdom? If we have not been out of step with the surrounding culture and suffered its disapproval because we practice the ethics of God's children, are we truly God's children?

Of course, we should be careful not to condemn ourselves if at the moment we are not undergoing persecution. No one is persecuted all the time. Also, we must be careful not to imagine persecution in overly dramatic terms. Most of it is mundane, and some is even quite "civilized."

THE NATURE OF PERSECUTION

The word rendered "persecuted" in Matthew 5:10 bears the root idea of "pursue" or "chase." A good translation is "harass" — "Blessed are the harassed." The reiteration of the Beatitude in verse 11 amplifies this idea: "Blessed are you when men cast insults at you, and persecute you, and say all kinds of evil against you falsely." This casting of insults means literally "to cast in one's teeth," so that the sense here is of throwing insults in one's face. Persecution can go to physical extremes as the church's bloody history records; but most often it is verbal harassment, sometimes audible, sometimes whispered, sometimes direct, sometimes innuendo. Verbal abuse and social ostracism may call for as much heroism as braving the arena.

Other examples of what believers endure include the conscientious worker who has given twenty years of faithful service but has been repeatedly passed over because the brass are uncomfortable with his uncompromising ethics; or the friendly student who is systematically excluded from conversation because he does not rubber-stamp all that is said; or the housewife who is considered dull by her neighbors because she does not delight in their gossip. Such indifference and condescension can sometimes be harder to take than physical violence.

THE REAL TRAGEDY OF PERSECUTION

These are hard things. But the tragedy today is not that they happen to believers, but that very often, they do not. One reason for this is that many

Christians are cut off from the world. They go to a church that is 100 percent Christian, attend Bible studies that are 100 percent Christian, attend Christian schools, exercise with believers, garden with churchgoers, and golf with believers — and thus are sealed from persecution. Others keep their Christianity secret so as not to make waves with non-Christian associates. The tragedy is that hidden Christianity is probably not Christianity at all.

But by far the greatest reason there is so little persecution is that the church has become like the world. If you want to get along, the formula is simple. Approve of the world's morals and ethics — at least outwardly. Live like the world lives. Laugh at its humor. Immerse yourself in its entertainment. Smile benignly when God is mocked. Act as if all religions converge on the same road. Don't mention hell. Draw no moral judgments. Take no stand on the moral/political issues. Above all, do not share your faith. Follow this formula and it will be smooth sailing.

But the fact is, the church must be persecuted or it is no church at all. People need to be told that if they follow Christ, there will be a price to pay. It will affect how they get along at school. It will affect their profile at the club. It will affect how they make their living.

The early church had no doubt about where a believer's duty lay. One hundred years after Jesus preached the Sermon on the Mount, a man approached the great church father Tertullian with a problem — his business interests and Christianity conflicted. He ended by asking, "What can I do? I must live!" Tertullian replied, "Must you?" When it came to a choice between loyalty to Christ and living, Tertullian held that the real Christian chooses Christ.

It is a glorious thing when the church and the individual are persecuted for righteousness' sake, because that means they are like Christ.

THE JOY OF PERSECUTION

Persecution is glorious because it is the persecuted who know elite joy. In Matthew 5:12 Christ, the ultimate persecuted man, said, "Rejoice and be glad, because great is your reward in heaven, for in the same way they persecuted the prophets who were before you." The persecuted ought to rejoice in the fact that they keep "classy" company with the likes of Jeremiah and Elijah.

But the ultimate source of the believer's rejoicing is the ultimate reward, for Jesus says, "great is your reward in heaven." When John D. Rockefeller died, the public became understandably curious about the size of the famous man's fortune. One reporter, determined to find out, secured an appointment with one of Rockefeller's highest aides. He asked the aide how much Rockefeller left behind. The man answered simply, "He left it all."

Not so for those who have been persecuted for the sake of righteousness!

The reward is "great," *polus*, which means "immeasurably great." God will not permit what has been done for his glory to go unrewarded. Hear Paul's assurances: "For our light and momentary troubles are achieving for us an eternal glory that far outweighs them all" (2 Corinthians 4:17). "I have fought the good fight, I have finished the race, I have kept the faith. Now there is in store for me the crown of righteousness, which the Lord, the righteous Judge, will award to me on that day — and not only to me, but also to all who have longed for his appearing" (2 Timothy 4:7, 8).

What then will it be like for such saints the first thirty seconds in heaven? The first half hour? The first day? The first 10,000 years?

Certainly Christians' persecutions for the sake of righteousness are "as sails to a ship or wings to a bird" in the voyage through life — and on to heaven.

9

"The Salt of the Earth"

MATTHEW 5:13

The Beatitudes of Jesus are sometimes called the "Beautiful Attitudes" because they describe the inner character of those who are members of the kingdom of God. Realizing that the Beatitudes are essentially interior, one might be tempted to think they can be lived in isolation — away from the world that is so contradictory to the things of God. But actually it is impossible to live these eight norms of the kingdom in private. They are powerfully social and outward when put to work. That is why Christ crowns them with two brilliant and searching metaphors (salt and light) that tell us how those who live the Beatitudes must relate to the world. These beautiful crowning metaphors are amazingly penetrating. We will consider the first, salt, in this chapter.

> *"You are the salt of the earth. But if the salt loses its saltiness, how can it be made salty again? It is no longer good for anything, except to be thrown out and trampled by men." (v. 13)*

Since Jesus Christ spoke these words early in his ministry, when he only had a few poor, uneducated followers, his words no doubt appeared to some as presumptuous and even absurd. "You, you alone, are the salt of the earth — not just of Palestine, but of the whole earth." The Lord was saying that his disciples would perform a vast universal task that would affect all mankind. He was expressing a strange confidence in his followers. In essence he was saying, "I have great faith in you. I believe that you will function as salt for *all* the world. I believe in you." Stranger still, we know that they and their followers accomplished just that, despite their shortcomings and inconsistencies.

As we examine this portion of Christ's Sermon on the Mount, we will see an unforgettable description of the church's mission in a fallen world.

THE SALTED CHURCH

To begin with, the church is to be a salty church. What did Jesus mean when he said, "You are the salt of the earth"? Fundamental to understanding his meaning is the fact that in the ancient world the number-one function of salt was its use as a preservative. There were no ice-making machines in those days. Refrigeration was beyond man's wildest dreams. The only way to preserve meat then was to salt it down or soak it in a saline solution. In fact, this was common practice right into the twentieth century in remote areas. It was particularly the experience of pioneer missionaries. As one describes it:

> This was absolutely imperative. Under the high temperatures and hot weather of the region, decay and decomposition of meat was astonishingly rapid. We had no winter weather or cool, frosty nights to chill the flesh.
>
> Besides this, swarms of ubiquitous flies soon hovered over the butchered carcasses. The only way to prevent them from ruining the meat . . . was to soak the slabs of meat in a strong solution of salt.[1]

This preserving use of salt was what made it possible for David Livingstone's body to be shipped back to England for burial in Westminster Abbey. Having died in deepest Africa, Livingstone's servant buried the great missionary's heart in African soil, then salted down his body and shipped it home for an honored burial. The understanding that salt is a preservative is fundamental to understanding Jesus' words.

In view of this, the underlying implication of his saying, "You are the salt of the earth" is that the world tends toward decomposition and is actually rotting away. Jesus was under no illusion about the world apart from himself. When the world is left to itself, it festers and putrefies, for the germs of evil are everywhere present and active. This is the consistent teaching of Scriptural teaching and Biblical history. The world began as a perfect creation, but when sin came, decay set in, and as a result the world became rotten, so that God eventually removed nearly the entire population of the world by the Flood. Given another chance, man fell into immediate debauchery, leading after a time to Sodom and Gomorrah. We live in a world that constantly tends toward decay. Some of the Christless structures of the world may look okay, but inside they are rotting away, and it is just a matter of time before they fall. In today's disintegrating world only the most extreme Pollyanna would contradict this.

This suggests to us the function of the church: The church, as salt, functions as a retardant to decay and a preservative in a disintegrating world. Jesus was saying in effect, "Humanity without me is a dead body that is rotting and falling apart. And you, my followers, are the salt that must be rubbed into the flesh to halt the decomposition." The church must be rubbed into the world — into its rotting flesh and wounds so that it might be preserved. This matter of being a preservative has a positive and a negative side. On the negative side, the presence of a salty Christian will retard decay simply because his or her life is a reproach to the sin of those they are around. We all know there are certain people in whose presence a filthy story is naturally told, and there are others before whom no one would think of telling such a story. The salty Christian is not self-righteous or condemning, but his or her life makes ungodly conversation seem shabby and inappropriate.

I believe such Christians exert an incalculable influence on society! Their mere presence reduces crime, restrains ethical corruption, promotes honesty, quickens the conscience, and elevates the general moral atmosphere. The presence of such people in the military, in business, in education, in a fraternity or sorority will amazingly elevate the level of living. And their absence will allow unbelievable depths of depravity. Believers, salty believers, are the world's preservative. The question we must ask ourselves is, what happens when we get to know people without Christ? Does it make a difference in their lives? Are we salt?

There is also a positive aspect. Not only are our lives meant to reprove evil, but they are also meant to elicit the best from those around us. To live a life that is so salted that others are drawn to God and want to live lives like ours is indeed beautiful! Sad to say, not everyone who claims to be a Christian has this effect. Henrik Ibsen, in one of his plays, put this complaint on the lips of the Roman Emperor Julian:

> Have you looked at these Christians closely? Holloweyed, pale-cheeked, flat-breasted all; they brood their lives away, unspurred by ambition: the sun shines for them, but they do not see it: the earth offers them its fullness, but they desire it not; all their desire is to renounce and to suffer that they may come to die.[2]

Algernon Charles Swinburne gave his estimation of Christianity when he wrote, in his poem "Hymn to Prosperine":

> *Thou hast conquered,*
> *O pale Galilean.*

Oliver Wendell Holmes put it this way: "I might have entered the ministry if certain clergymen I knew had not acted and looked so much like undertakers." Some Christians behave as if they were baptized in lemon juice!

That is not the way true salted Christians are! Rather, that is the way life is without Christ — insipid and dull. That is why our culture attempts to numb itself with its pleasure mania and with drugs. People are literally dying of boredom. Our entertainment industry does its best to make life look otherwise. Fictional good is made out to be boring and flat, while fictional evil is exciting and intriguing. But it is the other way around. As Malcolm Muggeridge wrote:

> Nothing is so beautiful, nothing so continually fresh and surprising, so full of sweet and perpetual ecstasy as good; no desert is so dreary, monotonous and boring as evil.[3]

In Biblical times, as today, salt was not only a preservative, but also a spice, a condiment. Christianity is what brings spice and zest to life. The bland is made savory, and the unpalatable becomes a delight! Believers must be salty not only because they are righteous, but because life is alive. They ought to write the best books, be the most courteous, work the hardest, be the best musicians and artists and craftsmen and students.

All of which anticipates another result of being salty — salt creates thirst. Jesus made people thirsty for God. Whenever anyone encountered Jesus, whether a Pharisee like Nicodemus or an outcast like Mary Magdalene, that person became thirsty for God. Are we salty enough to make people thirsty for Jesus?

Also consider this: Even a little salt makes itself known. When we sit down for dinner, all it takes is one little bite to know whether the food has been salted or not. Just a pinch of salt goes a long way! William Wilberforce, the man who almost single-handedly brought about the Slavery Emancipation Bill in England, was living proof of this. Dwarfed by disease, he did not appear to be a person who would accomplish anything. However, Boswell wrote of him, after listening to one of his speeches, "I saw a shrimp mount the table; but as I listened, he grew and grew until the shrimp became a whale."[4] Tiny, elfish, misshapen, he was salt to British society, not only bringing preservation but enticement to Christ by his beautiful life. A little salt will make its presence felt.

How wonderful Jesus' metaphor is! And how beautiful is the life of a salty believer — bringing preservation to a decaying world as a living reproof to sin, an enticement to Christ, one who brings spice and flavor to life, one who makes others thirsty for Christ and life in Heaven.

If we are salt, how are we to maximize our effectiveness? We must be spread out upon the decaying world. Salt can sit for years in the saltshaker, but it will never do any good until it is poured forth. In Jesus' time its effect was maximized when it was poured upon and rubbed into the meat. We must allow God to rub us into the world, without our becoming like the world. We may fear that we will disappear, and disappear we may. But that is the point: Salt dispenses its power as it dissolves into the world's flesh. That is when its effect is greatest. As pungent people, empowered by the presence of Christ's Spirit within us, we are to penetrate society. We are to become involved in life — in the community, in our schools, in politics, in our neighborhoods, in the world at large. Does this text affirm us or mock us? Are *we* salt?

THE DESALTED CHURCH

Is there such a thing as a desalted church? Our Lord indicates this is a possibility: ". . . if the salt loses it saltiness." Some translations render this "tasteless." In actual fact, salt is an extremely stable compound and does not become tasteless. The consensus of most scholars is that Jesus is referring to its adulteration or dilution, which can happen in several ways that we will not go into. The point is, it is dangerously easy for Christians to lose their salty, preserving influence in the world. While many believers are pungent and salty, there are others who are virtually indistinguishable from the surrounding culture. I do not think any of us can look at professing Christianity at large or at American Christianity or at our local Christianity or at our own hearts without admitting that the possibility of saltless, insipid, bland Christianity is very real.

The reality is, to use a different analogy, if we are not heating the world, the world is freezing us. We export our influence on those around us, but if there are more imports than exports, if there are not greater influences going out from us than are coming in, we will become like the world. If we are not salting the world, the world is making us rot. The great tragedy is that often the world does us more harm than we do it good.

We need to ask ourselves if there is any difference between our approach to materialism, for example, than that of the world. Are there any distinctions between our approach to pleasure than that of unbelievers? Do we approach happiness differently? Is there a difference in our application of ethics? Does our compassion know the limitations of the world, or is it stronger? The answers to these questions will reveal whether the salt is penetrating the meat or if the salt is being adulterated. We must answer these questions with a conscience informed by the Word of God.

THE RE-SALTED CHURCH

Can a church be re-salted? The Lord brought this question up when he asked, "How can it be made salty again?" As we have said, salt cannot lose its saltiness, and therefore it cannot again be made salty. I believe Jesus is talking about salt that is so adulterated it has lost its preservative powers. In the context of his times Christ is saying that if salt has lost its savor, there is no *natural* hope for it. Is there any hope for us if we have become desalted? The answer is no — not in ourselves anyway. However, Jesus extends the metaphor into the supernatural, and here we must say that the answer is yes! Jesus is not saying that if a Christian loses his pungency, he cannot get it back, even by going to the source from which it came. Nothing but our own sin can keep us from being resalted.

I once met a man who, in his sixties, was re-salted. He told me about how his life had become bland and insipid, and then he was confronted again with the necessity of a vital life for Jesus Christ and committed his life to him. For the next ten years of his life he was incredibly salty in the world. The effect of his life is literally known by thousands. So one can be re-salted!

But there is an urgency in what Jesus had to say, and the urgency is seen in the concluding sentence of verse 13 as he warned about the destiny of saltless salt: "It is no longer good for anything, except to be thrown out and trampled by men." Nothing good can be done with saltless salt. All it is good for is to be tossed onto the road where perhaps it will fill in a few cracks as it is further adulterated. There, since it has lost its pungent saltiness, it sterilizes the soil and retards plant growth, bringing to the roadway a blighted barrenness. This substance, so beneficial in its pungent, pure form, now brings only desolation. The Christian life that has lost its saltiness is good for nothing at all! There is only one thing to do with it — throw it away and walk on it. We see testimony of this in church history. We search in vain for the once-great churches of Asia Minor with their flourishing parishes. The churches of Corinth and Ephesus are all but nonexistent. We look in vain for the church of North Africa where the great Augustine ministered. Salt that lost its saltiness was cast out and was trodden underfoot by the men of this world. This does not mean a loss of salvation but of vibrancy and fruitful testimony.

Seeing this, we must dispense with any illusion that the churches of western Christianity are eternal. The reality is that much organized Christianity is already falling because it has lost its pungency. The best evangelical traditions are not immune from inconsistency, preaching that is barely Biblical, and a status-quo mentality. I am sometimes asked, "Are evangelicals born again?" And the answer is, "Not necessarily." True Christianity lives the Beatitudes, however imperfectly. True Christianity is pungent and salty.

Yet with all of this, Christ's expression of this metaphor is essentially positive. Jesus said, "You [emphatic: you alone] are the salt of the earth." Jesus says, "I believe in you. I have called you." Jesus believes that we can have a healing, preserving influence on our own society and world. He believes that we can bring flavor to life — that we can make the world thirsty for him.

We are salt, and he wants us to cultivate our saltiness by constantly communing with him and being constantly filled with the Spirit. Then he wants us to get out of the saltshaker and into the world — rubbed into the rotting wounds of the world. And he wants us to remember that though we are not much, a little salt goes a long way!

10

"The Light of the World"

Matthew 5:14-16

The story of how Jesus identified himself as "the light of the world" is remarkably beautiful and instructive. It happened on the day following the spectacular nighttime ceremony known as the Illumination of the Temple, which took place in the temple treasury before four massive golden candelabra that were topped with huge torches. It is said that the candelabra were as tall as the highest walls of the temple, and that at the top of these candelabra were mounted great bowls that held sixty-five liters of oil. There was a ladder for each candelabrum, and when evening came, healthy young priests would carry oil up to the great bowls and light the protruding wicks. Eyewitnesses said that the huge flames that leapt from these torches illuminated not only the temple but all of Jerusalem. After the torches were roaring high above the people, the *Mishna* tells us:

> Men of piety and good works used to dance before them with burning torches in their hands singing songs and praises and countless Levites played on harps, lyres, cymbals, and trumpets and instruments of music.[1]

The exotic rite celebrated the great pillar of fire (the glorious cloud of God's presence) that led the people of Israel during their sojourn in the wilderness and spread its fiery billows over the tabernacle.

It was in the temple treasury the following morning, with the charred torches still in place, that Jesus lifted his voice above the crowd and proclaimed, "I am the light of the world. Whoever follows me will never walk in darkness, but will have the light of life" (John 8:12). There could scarcely be a more emphatic way to announce one of the supreme truths of his existence. Christ was saying in effect, "The pillar of fire that came between you and the Egyptians, the cloud that guided you by day in the wilderness and illumined the night and enveloped the tabernacle, the glorious cloud that filled Solomon's temple — that was me!" Jesus is the light of the world! He is everything suggested by the storied cloud of glory. Moreover, he is everything suggested by the glowing metaphor of light — and much more.

This great fact that he is the light of the world is foundational to our thinking and must control it as we examine the unforgettable words of Matthew 5:14-16, where our Lord applies the metaphor to *us*.

THE SPIRITUAL FACTS ABOUT LIGHT IN THE WORLD

The foundational fact that Jesus is the light of the world is glorious, but it suggests the equally foundational but inglorious fact that the world is in darkness. The physical earth is shrouded with dark clouds, suspended in dark space. The darkness of the world is a spiritual darkness that dominates the entire world system, and it is terrible. But the real horror is that the inhabitants of the earth love it! John tells us, "This is the verdict: Light has come into the world, but men loved darkness instead of light because their deeds were evil" (John 3:19). Darkness by itself is one thing, but intentional darkness is far worse. To be subject to the darkness of the night before the dawn is one thing, but it is quite another thing to deliberately live in caves and refuse to come to the light. Why this preference for darkness? John tells us that the world loves darkness because its deeds are evil. Unconsciously, and sometimes consciously, the world reasons very much as Lady Macbeth did as she planned a murder:

> *Come, thick night,*
> *And pall thee in the dunnest smoke of hell,*
> *That my keep knife see not the wound it makes,*
> *Nor Heaven peep through the blanket of the dark.*

That is a grim, unhappy picture, but it is Biblical and therefore true. The world is in darkness.

But it is the reality of the world's darkness that makes Jesus' pronouncement so thrilling. "You [emphatic: you alone] are the light of the world [and no one else!]." If we are truly believers, we are the light of the world! To say such a thing about ourselves without divine precedent and sanction would be the height of arrogance. But Jesus said it, and it is easily one of the most amazing statements to ever fall from Christ's lips — especially realizing what we are like when left to ourselves. It is a fact — we are light.

How can this be? Dr. Barnhouse, the master of illustration, used to explain it this way. He said that when Christ was in the world, he was like the shining sun that is here in the day and gone at night. When the sun sets, the moon comes up. The moon, the church, shines, but not with its own light. It shines with *reflected* light. When Jesus was in the world he said, "I am the light of the world." But as he contemplated leaving this world, he said, "You are the light of the world." At times the church has been at full moon, dazzling the world with an almost daytime light. These have been times of great enlightenment, times such as those of Paul and Luther and Wesley. And at other times the church has been only a thumbnail moon, with very little light shining upon the earth. Whether the church is a full moon or a new thumbnail moon, waxing or waning, it reflects the light of the sun.[2]

Our light is a reflected or derived light. It does not originate from us. That is a great illustration, as far as it goes. However, I believe the Scriptures teach that the light is more than reflected, that we in fact become light ourselves. Ephesians 5:8 says, "for you were once darkness, but now you are light in the Lord. Live as children of light." Somehow our incorporation in Christ allows us to some extent to be light, however imperfect. Our light is still derived from him — not a ray of it comes from ourselves — but it is more than reflected. We "participate in the divine nature," as Peter says (2 Peter 1:4). This is a mystery.

But the beautiful thing is, it works! The church has had some great shining lights. When the English martyrs Hugh Latimer and Nicholas Ridley were being taken to the stake to be burned, Latimer turned to Ridley and said, "Be of good cheer, Brother Ridley, we have lighted such a candle in England as by the grace of God shall never be put out." Latimer and Ridley continue to shine as great lights in the world. There are also lesser lights, for the mystery works for all believers, even children. When my now grown daughter Holly was in the first grade, she weekly approached her teacher, Mrs. Smith, and timidly said, "Mrs. Smith, will you come to church?" Mrs. Smith would promise to do so. And when Mrs. Smith did not show up, Holly would approach her on Monday morning and say, "Mrs. Smith, you didn't come to church." Who could resist those big, sad, brown eyes? Finally Mrs. Smith came, and she came again, and she came to know Jesus. Today she is a remarkable, radiant sunbeam herself. This is a mystery, and it is beautiful. Somehow believers shine with the light of Christ, and it goes forth with life-changing effect. The facts are: Jesus is the light; the world is in darkness; somehow believers are light. If we are believers, we will shine somehow, some way.

The question is, how can we shine even more? A man returning from a journey brought his wife a matchbox that would glow in the dark. After he gave it to her, she turned out the light, but it could not be seen. Both thought they had been cheated. Then the wife noticed some French words on the box and asked a friend to translate them. The inscription said: "If you want me to shine in the night, keep me in the light." So it is with us! We must expose ourselves to Jesus, delight in his Word, and spend time in prayer soaking up his rays. As Paul says:

> *And we, who with unveiled faces all reflect the Lord's glory, are being transformed into his likeness with ever-increasing glory, which comes from the Lord, who is the Spirit. (2 Corinthians 3:18)*

If you want to shine in the night, keep your eye on the Light.

THE SPIRITUAL FUNCTION OF LIGHT IN THE WORLD

Our Lord dramatizes the function of light by giving two examples — a city perched on a hill and a light set in a home. First, believers are to function like a city set on a hill. Jesus says, "A city on a hill cannot be hidden" (v. 14b). There is no way to obscure a city on the crest of a hill. Having traveled a little in Ecuador, I can testify that the light of the city of Quito, situated at 10,000 feet, illumines the sky for seventy-five miles around. It cannot be hidden. Yet when you are in the great city itself, the light from the tiny villages higher above in the Andes is easily seen. Cities on hills cannot be hidden. Believers are like this. They are visible. There is no such thing as an invisible believer. As Dr. Lloyd-Jones said, "If we find in ourselves a tendency to put the light under a bushel, we must begin to examine ourselves and make sure that it really is 'light.'"[3]

That is good, gracious advice! Do we hide our light? And if so, are we really light? Christians are visible, and this visibility makes them like the beckoning lights of a city on a hill. Inside there is light and what goes with it — warmth and safety.

In addition to being like a hilltop city, Christians are like an ancient household lamp. Jesus goes on to say, "Neither do people light a lamp and put it under a bowl. Instead they put it on its stand, and it gives light to everyone in the house" (v. 15).

The point is unmistakable: The principal function of a household lamp, and of a believer, is to provide illumination to all around. This simple metaphor tells us so much. Light reveals things as they really are. All of us have at some time walked into an unfamiliar room and have felt our way to the lamp and turned the light on, discovering a room far different from what we imagined. Light also promotes life. In metropolitan Chicago where I live and minister, summer patio plants flourish in the basement all winter if we provide them with enough light — even if it is artificial. Even broken bones mend faster if we can soak up some sunlight. Light is persistent. It constantly assaults the surface of the earth and will penetrate the slightest crack. The darkest place is not safe from it if the tiniest opening appears. Light also awakens us.

Jesus, our Captain and Model, did all of these things and more by bringing spiritual light into the world. He did not make the darkness darker — he simply made it felt. His life was such that men and women were made to feel what they could not feel before — their sin, imperfection, and impurity. Christ made possible a clearer distinction between good and evil. He eliminated the option of thinking ourselves good by comparison with others. *He* was and is the standard! At the same time his perfectly beautiful life drew men and women to him. We are lamps, and the Householder places us strategically. "Neither do people light a lamp and put it under a bowl. Instead they put it on its stand." The light is placed strategically so it can shine to best advantage. And God does the placing. We are simply to shine where we are placed. In fact, it is in the darker and less promising places that light has the greatest effect. Consider Dr. Boris Kornfeldt who shared his faith with the diseased and sickly Alexander Solzhenitsyn in the Russian Gulag. God calls us to shine where we are. "Brighten the corner where you are."

How beautiful this all is! God has made us *visible* like a city on a hill. God has enabled us to *illumine* life like a lamp in a dark room. God has *placed* us where he wants us to shine to best advantage. Our presence is meant to reveal life, sin, and goodness as they are — to provide a light that draws others to it like a summer lamp. How beautiful it is when this happens. Some time ago a young man spent a week with my family. He had lived across the street from us a number of years earlier. He had been just a boy then but was a strapping 6'4" when he came to stay with us, visiting one of my sons. During that time he committed his life to Christ because of the light he had seen over the years. How wonderful it is when we see this occur.

THE SPIRITUAL RESPONSIBILITY THAT THESE FACTS AND FUNCTIONS BRING

The facts and functions of light in our lives and world bring us a great responsibility. Our Lord is very explicit about this: "In the same way, let your light shine before men, that they may see your good deeds and praise your Father in heaven" (v. 16). This is a command, not a suggestion. Jesus says, "If you are light, then shine!" This is not an option. Let us keep the emotion of this imperative before us as we consider what he says. The mode of shining, he tells us, is "good deeds." The word he uses is *kalos*, which carries the idea of attractiveness or beauty, rather than the more common *agathos*, which means good in quality. Jesus wants our light to shine through beautiful, attractive works! Of course, he is not recommending self-conscious, staged works. Yet he does suggest that we should let them be beautiful. Our

Lord would thus tell us that works of compassion and caring are top-priority. John Stott says it well:

> Indeed, the primary meaning of "works" must be practical, visible deeds of compassion. It is when people see these, Jesus said, that they will glorify God, for they embody the good news of his love which we proclaim. Without them our gospel loses its credibility and our God his honour.[4]

And why should we be given to beautiful, shining works? ". . . that they may see your good deeds and praise your Father in heaven." All glory to God! *Soli Deo Gloria*. As David said, "Not to us, O LORD, not to us but to your name be the glory" (Psalm 115:1). May that be our prayer as well.

Jesus' pronouncement "You [you alone] are the light of the world" is amazing and thrilling. It suggests that we become like him in relation to this world. We would not have dared to say it, but he did — to our everlasting amazement.

As light, becoming like him, we are sure to prevail. Ultimately he will completely vanquish the forces of darkness.

> *As by the sun in splendour*
> *The flags of night are furled,*
> *So darkness will surrender*
> *To Christ who lights the world.*[5]

The day is coming when darkness will be gone.

Moreover, in eternity we will be part of the shining light ourselves. Jesus said at the end of the Mystery Parables that "The righteous will shine like the sun in the kingdom of their Father" (Matthew 13:43). That is us — you and me! How can that be? I am not sure. C. S. Lewis once noted that the heavens only reflect or suggest the glory of God. But we *share* the glory of the Father with Christ. And we will be more glorious than the heavens. Lewis says:

> Nature is mortal. We shall outlive her. When all the suns and nebulae have passed away, each one of you will still be alive. Nature is only the image, the symbol. . . . We are summoned to pass in through nature beyond her to the splendor which she fitfully reflects.[6]

I believe that with all my heart. I do not understand it, but I believe that for us as Christians there is a glory awaiting us that involves, in some way, an even greater shining forth. I do not know if we will be 100 watts or 200,

300, or 1,000! We might be like fireflies or we might be like supernovas. But somehow we are going to enter into the fame and approval of God, and we will be glorious beings, far beyond all imagination.

But at the same time we are light right now. Jesus says, "You [you alone] are the light of the world." Let us covenant with all our being to shine as brightly as possible in this dark world. Let us covenant to expose ourselves to the face of Jesus in prayer. Let us covenant to be visible for him. Let us covenant to shine wherever he places us. Let us covenant to do beautiful works. Let us covenant to remind ourselves that we always will be light — and to live in that reality.

11

Jesus on Righteousness

Matthew 5:17-20

The structure of the Sermon on the Mount is remarkably beautiful. It begins in Matthew 5:1-12 with the Beatitudes, which give us a penetrating description of the inner character or righteousness of those who are members of the kingdom of heaven. Next, in verses 13-16 the Lord gives two brilliant metaphors — salt and light — indelibly impressing upon us the effects of such inner righteousness upon humanity. Then in verses 17-20 Jesus gives a summary description of the radical righteousness of the kingdom, also introducing six great examples of how this righteousness is in continuity with the Old Testament Law. Each example is introduced with a variation of Christ's formula, "You have heard that it was said . . . but I tell you" (see vv. 21, 27, 31, 33, 38, 43).

I think it is significant that these three sections of the sermon are increasingly personal. In the Beatitudes Christ speaks in the third person: "Blessed are the . . ." But in the final Beatitude and in the metaphors he switches to the second person: "Blessed are you . . . you are the salt . . . you are the light." Then in the applications that follow, he switches to the first person: "But I tell you. . . ." No scribe or rabbi had ever spoken like this. They typically spoke in the second or third person. "Rabbi Abin said in the name of Rabbi Elai in Rabbi Jochanan's name . . ." Jesus' radical style of address concerning radical righteousness was, "I tell you." This was radically personal and authoritative.

In verses 17-20 we will see Jesus' highly personal statement of the radical righteousness of the Sermon on the Mount as it relates to the Old Testament Law. Verses 17, 18 tell us of the radical righteousness of Christ and the Law, verses 19, 20 of the radical righteousness of Christians and the Law. We will consider the radicalness of our call — a call to strive for radical righteousness in a dark and decaying world.

CHRIST AND THE LAW (vv. 17, 18)

After presenting the radical Beatitudes and the two metaphors, Jesus evidently sensed that some of his listeners thought he was advocating an overthrow of the Old Testament Law. So he gave his unforgettable disclaimer, which set down for all time his relationship to the Law.

> *"Do not think that I have come to abolish the Law or the Prophets; I have not come to abolish them but to fulfill them. I tell you the truth, until heaven and earth disappear, not the smallest letter, not the least stroke of a pen, will by any means disappear from the Law until everything is accomplished." (vv. 17, 18)*

It seems clear enough from Jesus' opening words that he came to fulfill the Law, not to annul it. However, some have actually taught that Christ came to destroy the Law. For example, the second-century heretic Marcion rewrote the New Testament by eliminating its Old Testament references and simply removed this passage. And some of his disciples even went further by exchanging the verbs in the sentence so it would read, "I have come not to fulfill the Law and the Prophets, but to abolish them!"[1] Two centuries later Dr. Faustus, a leader of the Manichees who also repudiated the Old Testament and its God, attacked Augustine. Augustine's *Reply to Faustus* became the classic answer to such thinking.[2] In a nutshell, the answer was this: Jesus was not abolishing the Law when he countered the Pharisees saying, "You have heard it said . . . but I tell you." Rather, he was correcting the perversions that the scribes and Pharisees had made of the Law.

This understanding remained standard among the church fathers and through the Dark Ages. The Reformation leaders said exactly the same thing. Luther repeatedly returned to his statement that the true interpretation of the Law had been obscured by the rabbis. Calvin argued the same, saying of Christ's corrections, "He only restored it [the Law] to its integrity by maintaining and purifying it when obscured by the falsehood, and defiled by the leaven of the Pharisees."[3] Today Carl Henry agrees, saying, "What He [Christ] criticizes is not the law itself but contemporary formulations of the law."[4] Moreover, the fact that Christ brought an end to the ceremonial laws, such as the sacrifices and dietary restrictions, does not amount to abolishing the Law but rather fulfills it.

In reality, Christ established the Law and the Prophets. How did he do this? First and foremost, he fulfilled their messianic predictions. Both the Prophets and the Law pointed to Jesus. Here the terms "the Law" and "the Prophets" are taken together to signify the entire Old Testament. Jesus himself said, "For all the Prophets and the Law prophesied until John" (Matthew 11:13). Thus the entire Old Testament had a prophetic function that was fulfilled in Christ. Some of it was clearly predictive — for example, the predictions of Jesus' place of birth (Micah 5:2) and the crucifixion (Psalm 22, esp. v. 16). Other parts were not so clear, such as his call from Egypt (see Matthew 2:15 and Hosea 11:1). But whether obvious or hidden, Jesus fulfilled all the messianic predictions of the Old Testament. This was his principal fulfillment.

However, he also fulfilled the Old Testament in other ways. He fulfilled the Law by dying on the cross and satisfying the demands of the Law against those who would believe on him. The entire sacrificial system in Old Testament times pointed to him. In his experiments Ivan Pavlov would ring a bell whenever he fed his dogs. Eventually the dogs would salivate whenever they heard the bell. They knew the bell meant food for them.[5] The sacrifices of the Old Testament prepared the people by instilling in them the conditioned reflex that sacrifice meant death. And the Old Testament sacrifices prepared them for the Lord Jesus' death when he came to die for our sins. Jesus fulfilled what the sacrificial system had pointed to.

A third area of fulfillment of the Old Testament Law and Prophets is that Jesus perfectly kept all its commands. He was "born under law" (Galatians 4:4) "to fulfill all righteousness" (Matthew 3:15). He kept the Law perfectly, never falling short in even one point.

A fourth way of fulfillment is that Jesus fulfills the Law in believers by means of the Holy Spirit. That is the argument of Romans 8:2-4:

> *Through Christ Jesus the law of the Spirit of life set me free from the law of sin and death. For what the law was powerless to do in that it was weakened by the sinful nature, God did by sending his own Son in the likeness of sinful man to be a sin offering. And so he condemned sin in sinful man, in order that the righteous requirements of the law might be fully met in us, who do not live according to the sinful nature but according to the Spirit.*

We are able to fulfill the righteousness of the Law by the power of the Holy Spirit. This is what Ezekiel prophesied:

> *I will give them an undivided heart and put a new spirit in them; I will remove from them their heart of stone and give them a heart of flesh. Then they will follow my decrees and be careful to keep my laws. (11:19, 20)*

A fifth way that Jesus fulfilled the Old Testament Scriptures is that he brought the great doctrines of the Old Testament to fruition by his teaching and person. Bishop Ryle put it this way:

> The Old Testament is the Gospel in the bud; the New Testament is the Gospel in full flavor. The Old Testament is the Gospel in the blade; the New Testament is the Gospel in full ear.[6]

The only possible conclusion is that Jesus fulfilled the Law and the Prophets in a multifaceted, dynamic way and in no way destroyed the Law but rather completely superseded and fulfilled it. His claim is the most stupendous ever made. We stand in awe at the matchlessness of Christ! He is the Author of the Law, and he is its Fulfiller. Nothing compares with the superb and mysterious authority with which he puts forth the truth.

Notice too the perpetuity of the Law:

> *"I tell you the truth, until heaven and earth disappear, not the smallest letter, not the least stroke of a pen, will by any means disappear from the Law until everything is accomplished." (v. 18)*

Jesus' language is compelling. "The smallest letter" is the Hebrew yod, which looks something like an apostrophe. There are approximately 66,420 yods in the Old Testament.[7] "The least stroke" is the Hebrew serif, a tiny extension on some letters that distinguishes them from similar letters. Not one of the 66,000-plus yods or innumerable little serifs will pass from the Law (which here includes the Law and the Prophets) until "everything is accomplished." Our Lord is here teaching the inspiration and immutability of the Old Testament. He is not only saying that the Old Testament contains the truth or that it becomes the truth, but that "the Scripture cannot be broken" (John 10:35). Holy Scripture and its teaching will not change. Time and time again when our Lord quotes the Old Testament, he used the perfect tense, *gegraptai* — "It is written" — which means "it was written, it is written, and it always will be written." The Scriptures are more enduring than the universe. Jesus said, "Heaven and earth will pass away, but my words will never pass away" (Matthew 24:35).

So the radically righteous Christ saw the Old Testament Prophets and Law as God's perfect, enduring Word and, furthermore, saw his life as the fulfillment of the Law and the Prophets. We must see the profound continuity between Christ's righteousness and the righteousness called for by the Old Testament. The radical righteousness Christ lived and taught, including here in the Sermon on the Mount, is not out of line with the Old Testament. Christ's righteousness is radical not because it is new but because he lived it! The Old Testament is still tremendously important, even though we are under grace. The Law instructs us in the righteous demands of God. Through it we see how high his holiness and his standards are, and we see how far short we fall and thus desperately need God's grace. Luther said:

> The Law must be laid upon those that are to be justified, that they may be shut up in the prison thereof, until the righteousness of faith comes — that, when they are cast down and humbled by the Law, they should fly to Christ. The Law humbles them, not to their destruction, but to their salvation. For God woundeth that He may heal again. He killeth that he may quicken again.[8]

That was Luther's experience. He saw himself falling short of the righteousness of God. The Law drove him to the depths of despair and to his urgent need of grace. But when he believed in Christ and received his mercy, he became one of the most powerful lives in all of history.

There is a beautiful parallel between Martin Luther and John Wesley, who also was slain by the Law. He saw the requirements of God and tried to meet them, but he failed. But coming to the end of himself, he too believed and lived a powerful Christian life. We need to be people of both Testaments! Relying on the New Testament alone makes us one-legged believers. We need to spend time in the Old Testament and in the New. That is one of the practical implications of Christ's attitude toward the Law and the Prophets.

THE CHRISTIAN AND THE LAW (vv. 19, 20)

Verses 19, 20 give us specific advice as to how we should relate to the Old Testament.

> *"Anyone who breaks one of the least of these commandments and teaches others to do the same will be called least in the kingdom of heaven, but whoever practices and teaches these commands will be called great in the kingdom of heaven." (v. 19)*

Notice the word "great." We twentieth-century Americans like that word, though we are not careful about its use. Edwin Newman in his book *Strictly Speaking* humorously records the overuse of the word by Chicago's Mayor Richard J. Daley, Sr. when he addressed the 1960 Republican Convention.

> Daley therefore referred to the great city, that being Chicago; the great year, that being 1960, the only year available to him at the time; the great convention city, again Chicago; our great country; the great convention, that being the one that nominated Abraham Lincoln a hundred years earlier; a great country, the United States; these great centers, the local urban communities; the great central cities of our nation, which include Chicago; our great beach, the beach of Lake Michigan; and a great people, this being the American people.

Finally Newman observes, "This great speech by Chicago's great mayor lasted two minutes and drew great applause."[9]

Our use of the word *great* is not too great or meaningful. But when God says certain people will be called "great" — *megas* — big in the kingdom — he means it! In fact, we can only guess what this means, and our guesses will almost certainly fall short!

How does one become "great" in heaven? By keeping God's commandments and teaching them to others. Believers who by the power of the indwelling Spirit (Romans 8:1-14) fulfill the Law will be the big ones in heaven! On the other hand, the one who "breaks one of the least of these commandments and so teaches others to do the same will be called least in the kingdom of heaven." Such a person will still be there, but that is all.

The keeping of the precepts of God as recorded in the Old Testament will make a difference in our eternal reward. Following Christ is not simply following subjective inner impulses. It involves knowing what *he* desires. We need to be in touch with the teaching of all of God's Word as to the nature of righteousness. We need the Holy Spirit. Jesus' words have set us up for a supremely radical call. True belief necessitates radical personal righteousness.

> *"For I tell you that unless your righteousness surpasses that of the Pharisees and the teachers of the law, you will certainly not enter the kingdom of heaven." (v. 20)*

To the average man on the street, the Jews of Jesus' day, this was absolutely shocking! The scribes and Pharisees made obedience to God's Law the master passion of their lives. They calculated that the Law contained 248 commandments and 365 prohibitions, and they tried to keep them *all.* How could anyone surpass that? And how could such righteousness be made a condition to entering the kingdom? Jesus seemed to be saying, "Don't think I have come to make things easier by reducing the demands of the Law. Far from it! In fact, if your righteousness does not exceed that of the scribes and Pharisees, you'll never make it!"

What a dilemma! What is the solution? Part of the answer is that the Pharisees' righteousness was not so (to use Daley's word) great. It was merely external. It focused on the ceremonial. Its man-made rules actually were unconscious attempts to reduce the demands of the Law and make it manageable. Those rules insulated them from the Law's piercing heart demands. These men were also self-satisfied. A Pharisee could stand on a corner, look at a publican, and say, "I thank God I am not like that man." Jesus was demanding a deeper obedience. The Pharisees saw obedience quantitatively (obedience to myriad little laws), but Jesus saw it qualitatively. The righteousness that Christ demands is supremely radical. It is immeasurably higher than the rabbis' concept of righteousness. Jesus closes this whole section by saying, "Be perfect, therefore, as your heavenly Father is perfect" (v. 48).

Christ's intransigence, his hard unbending words, were actually full of grace. When he said, "For I tell you that unless your righteousness surpasses that of the Pharisees and the teachers of the law, you will certainly not enter the kingdom of heaven," he was speaking as kindly as he ever spoke, for he was explaining in the most dramatic terms the impossibility of salvation apart from his grace. This takes us right back to ground zero of the first Beatitude: "Blessed are the poor in spirit, for theirs is the kingdom of God" (5:3). "Blessed are those who are spiritually bankrupt, for theirs is the kingdom of heaven." "Blessed are those who realize they cannot make it on their own, for theirs is the kingdom of heaven."

Do you understand and acknowledge that there is no way but that of grace? If so, then also see that Jesus' words in verse 17 are our hope: "Do not think that I have come to abolish the Law or the Prophets; I have not come to abolish them but to fulfill them." This is our hope because Christ did what we could never do — he fulfilled the Law. His righteousness exceeded that of the scribes and Pharisees. And because he fulfilled the Law, he can give us a righteousness that exceeds that of the scribes and Pharisees. He fulfilled the Law by leading a perfectly righteous life. He fulfilled its demands against us by dying for us.

12

A Righteous Person's Relationships

MATTHEW 5:21-26

For the last 500 years there has been an ongoing debate over how Christ's teaching relates to that in the Old Testament. The Reformers believed that there is a perfect continuity, that Jesus' teaching did no more than explain what was already in the Law. In keeping with this view, they argued that Jesus' seeming corrections of the Old Testament, introduced by the phrase "You have heard that it was said . . . but I tell you," are actually corrections of the interpretations of the scribes and Pharisees, not of the Old Testament. His new teaching was simply an amplification of the deeper meaning of the old teaching.

The other branch of the Reformation, represented by the Anabaptists, believed that Jesus' new teaching was in radical discontinuity with the Old Testament. They believed that Jesus' teaching abrogated certain aspects of the Old Testament. To some it even seemed that Jesus' teaching was at odds with the Law given through Moses. For them, Christ's teaching was radically new.

There is a third position that I believe to be the correct one — namely, that Jesus' teaching is radically new and supersedes the old, but is also in continuity with it. The best way to think of it is that he completed the Law and the Prophets. His own words in verse 17, "I have not come to abolish . . . but to fulfill," carries the idea of completion. In fact, the word "fulfill" is sometimes translated "complete," as it well could be here.[1] For example, Jesus brought an end to the ceremonial laws of sacrifice and dietary laws, but that was not so much an abrogation of them as a fulfillment, for he validated and superseded them in his own person.

Here in the Sermon on the Mount, Jesus does the same thing with the Old Testament teachings. In superseding them, he did not bring discontinuity between the Old Testament precepts and his teaching but rather established continuity as he fulfilled them. Jesus brought radically new teaching that superseded the Old Testament Law and Prophets but did not contradict them. Christ's teaching harmonizes with the Old Testament and adds to it. It completes it!

In Matthew 5:21-26, Jesus holds up the first of six examples that show one's need for a righteousness that surpasses that of the scribes and Pharisees if one is to enter the kingdom of heaven (cf. v. 20). The first example is the Old Testament teaching on murder, which he explains by first giving us the traditional position and then his radically new teaching. Some might think, *What does an exposition on murder have to do with me?* Everything! In fact, this text is one of the foundational passages on human relationships in the Bible. Jesus begins with the prohibition against the ultimate fracture of human relationships that takes place through murder, then supplies his own teaching, which goes far beyond the mere preserving of life itself to the preserving of human relationships. In this section of his Sermon on the Mount, Jesus describes how a righteous person conducts his or her relationships.

The longer I live, the more I value my relationships. When I was younger, I had little idea of how important they are. I took them for granted. I did not fully understand that human relationships greatly affect our heavenly relationship.

THE TRADITIONAL TEACHING OF THE LAW REGARDING MURDER (v. 21)

> *"You have heard that it was said to the people long ago, 'Do not murder, and anyone who murders will be subject to judgment.'" (v. 21)*

This is an exact duplicate of the sixth commandment (Exodus 20:13) as taken from the Septuagint (LXX). The additional comment, "anyone who murders will be subject to judgment," is accurate and true. This was not only the Pharisees' interpretation. It was the interpretation of the Law itself. So this teaching and interpretation was true. The only criticism might be that it was too narrow. And that is where the radically new, superseding teaching of Christ comes in.

THE SUPERSEDING TEACHING OF CHRIST REGARDING MURDER (v. 22)

> *"But I tell you that anyone who is angry with his brother will be subject to judgment. Again, anyone who says to his brother, 'Raca,' is answerable*

to the Sanhedrin. But anyone who says, 'You fool!' will be in danger of the fire of hell." (v. 22)

This is an unusually strong statement. It forthrightly claims that those guilty of contemptuous anger are guilty enough to go to Hell. Jesus says in effect, "The Old Testament Law condemns murder, but I say that contemptuous anger will get you a fiery Hell just as surely." Jesus means what he says, and we need to let it sink in with all its absoluteness.

However, we must not think that he forbids all anger with other people. Jesus himself was angry when he cleared the temple (John 2:13-22). He was angry with those who assailed him for healing on the Sabbath (Mark 3:5 uses the word "anger"). And in Matthew 23:17 he called the Pharisees "blind fools." So we conclude that there is a place for anger. Jesus was angry at sin and injustice, but he never became angry at personal insult or affront. Peter says that when Jesus was dying, "when they hurled their insults at him, he did not retaliate; when he suffered, he made no threats. Instead, he entrusted himself to him who judges justly" (1 Peter 2:23). But we see that there is a place for righteous anger. Such anger brings pleasure to God.

But in the Sermon on the Mount Jesus is speaking of unrighteous anger, and his words leave no doubt about what he means. We are quick to get angry at personal affront but slow to become angry with sin and injustice, and we need to take our Lord's words to heart. To call someone the Aramaic word "*Raca*" is literally to call him "empty-headed." Commentators suggest a number of more contemporary substitutes like numbskull, nitwit, blockhead, bonehead, jerk, or brainless idiot. I can relate to all of them. And I have been called every one of them — sometimes even affectionately! *Raca* used in deadly earnest demotes another person to the level of a nothing, a nobody. It is an utterly contemptuous word.

The term "fool" is a translation of the Greek word *moros*, from which we derive *moron*. But its meaning did not involve judgment of one's IQ but rather one's moral condition. It was applied to those who denied God's existence and as a result fell to further evil. The psalmist's phrase, "The fool says in his heart, 'There is no God'" (Psalm 14:1) bears this idea.

A. B. Bruce perfectly summarizes the two words: "*Raca* expresses contempt for a man's head = you stupid! *More* expresses contempt for his heart and character = you scoundrel!"[2] These two words were not terms of endearment but of malignant contempt. Jesus here condemns angry contempt and all its cousins — animosity, malice, hostility, malevolence, wrath. He is not suggesting a ladder of offenses that result in progressively sterner judgments, as if "anger" gets a minor judgment, "*raca*" a stiffer penalty, and "fool" Hell. He is simply multiplying examples to make His point. And the point is, all such animosity can land one in Hell.

Jesus is saying that we must not think we are safe just because we have not shed blood. We are guilty enough to receive punishment if we have harbored anger and contempt. He says in essence, "You may think you are removed from murder morally. But you are wrong. Have you ever wished someone were dead? Then your heart has known murder!" In view of this, we cannot escape the truth that we are *all* murderers. We have all murdered others in mind and heart. We have treasured thoughts about others that are as foul as murder.

Here again we see that the radical righteousness Jesus demands is not merely a refraining from outward sin — it is interior. And again we are made to see that our only hope is Christ who fulfilled all righteousness and offers it to us as a free gift. Jesus' radical demand is meant to drive us to him for grace. Have you done so? Murderers are welcome.

What this means practically is that as believers we must purge ourselves of any delusion of spiritual superiority. It is all too true that a long association with Christ and his Word and his church can foster the feeling that one is a spiritual Brahman — looking down on the rest of empty-headed, foolish humanity. Such smugness makes the words *fool*, *nitwit*, and *idiot* as natural as breathing. Believers must purge themselves of any thought of superiority. If there is anyone who ought to know who they are and what is within them, it is believers. Furthermore, we must never devaluate others. No one is worthless. Some time ago my wife and I were watching TV. In the middle of a program she stepped out for a moment, and when she returned, she asked what had transpired. I responded, "A worthless dope peddler was leading the two young boys astray." My wife's response brought me up short. "No one is worthless!" she said. And she is absolutely right. My sentiment was wrong theologically, emotionally, and socially. God loves everyone, even the debased sinner!

We must be careful in our use of words like nitwit, fool, blockhead, idiot. We need to be positive about others — not condoning their sin, but remembering that God loves them. It was said of Alexander Whyte, the great preacher of Edinburgh, "Watch out for Whyte! All his geese become swans." Whyte had a way of seeing the best in people and bringing it out. This is the way of the righteous in his or her relationships. How much better than going through life seeing all the swans as geese!

Has Christ's radical righteousness truly penetrated our relationships with others? Or are we full of hostility that causes us to verbally or silently murmur "fool" or "worthless" as we go through life? If so, we need to repent, calling upon the Holy Spirit's renewing power. The righteous, those who have received the radical righteousness of Christ, must guard their hearts and mouths.

LIVING OUT CHRIST'S TEACHING (vv. 23-26)

Christ was so concerned that believers not harbor evil thoughts toward one another that he gave two illustrations of the positive steps they should take.

Example #1: Regarding Worship (vv. 23, 24)

> *"Therefore, if you are offering your gift at the altar and there remember that your brother has something against you, leave your gift there in front of the altar. First go and be reconciled to your brother; then come and offer your gift."*

Christ gives us a remarkable picture here. The worshiper has entered the great Temple of Herod with his sacrifice and has passed through the concentric courts (the Court of the Gentiles, the Court of Women, the Court of Men). Beyond him lies the Court of the Priests, into which only priests could pass. The worshiper is standing at the threshold of the court. His hands are on the sacrifice, and suddenly he remembers that he has wronged his brother. So he turns and retreats through the great courts. He must first make things right with his brother. Jesus' point is clear: It is far more important to be reconciled to your brother than to fulfill the external duties of worship. Worship is merely a pretense if we have offended others in such a way that they are holding grudges against us.

It is so natural to try to make up for our integrity with ceremony. Dr. Lloyd-Jones said:

> I think I can say again that we all know something about this tendency not to face directly the conviction which the Holy Spirit produces in our heart, but to say to ourselves: "Well, now; I am doing this and that; I am making great sacrifices at this point; I am being helpful in that matter; I am busily engaged in that piece of Christian work." The whole time we are not facing the jealousy we may feel against another Christian worker, or something in our personal, private life. We are balancing one thing with another, thinking this good will make up for that evil.[3]

Ceremony, regular attendance at worship, and giving will never produce a clear conscience. If we are at odds with others because of our actions and are unwilling to do anything about it, attendance at a worship service is an exercise in hypocritical futility. We need to first attempt to make things right. Similarly, sometimes the reason our prayers are hollow is because we have offended another brother or sister and are not willing to do anything about it.

Psalm 66:18 touches on this: "If I had cherished sin in my heart, the Lord would not have listened." Peter's advice to husbands in 1 Peter 3:7 is built on this principle: "Husbands, in the same way be considerate as you live with your wives, and treat them with respect as the weaker partner and as heirs with you of the gracious gift of life, so that nothing will hinder your prayers." The principle is transferable, of course. If a man or woman is living with his or her spouse in a way that lacks understanding and is difficult and unfeeling, the heavens can become like brass. Perhaps you are sensing a dryness in your life. You pray, you try to be as religious and good as possible, but somehow it just does not seem to be working. The reason might be that you have not faced up to your sin in a fundamental relationship.

We are called to sensitivity in our relationships with others. This does not mean morbid sensitivity to imagined offenses, but rather dealing with real offenses that the Holy Spirit brings to mind. There is an urgency to Jesus' words that he underlines with a second illustration taken from the legal realm.

Example #2: A Legal Situation (vv. 25, 26)

> *"Settle matters quickly with your adversary who is taking you to court. Do it while you are still with him on the way, or he may hand you over to the judge, and the judge may hand you over to the officer, and you may be thrown into prison. I tell you the truth, you will not get out until you have paid the last penny."*

Jesus' advice is to do what you can to make amends, and do it quickly. If you do not, an inevitable process (like the legal process) will catch up with you, and you will have to pay the maximum penalty. Personal conflicts can often be resolved if dealt with quickly. However, if one puts off dealing with them, you and everyone else will have to pay. We dare not ignore Jesus' advice.

What a remarkable message the Lord gave! If we have Christ's righteousness, we will not only refrain from the shedding of blood but will develop hearts that are liberated from the things that are the cause of murder — namely, contemptuous anger. We will be sensitive about our attitude toward others. Though we are by no means perfect, we are by God's grace learning that contempt and hostility — and their telltale language — are not to be part of our lives. Furthermore, we are learning that God places the highest priority on our relationships with our brothers and sisters in Christ. That is so important that he even recommends that we temporarily leave worship in order to take time to meet with the offended.

If we are guilty of offending another, may we covenant with God to deal with it soon. Some of us have been spiritually dry because we have been offensive to others. May we covenant now to confess our sins to those whom we have offended. Then the heavens will open again. The moment we truly decide to deal with the problem, God's re-creating forces go to work within us. Let us live as truly righteous people, so that others will see the radical righteousness of Christ and be drawn to him.

13

Radical Purity

MATTHEW 5:27-30

An acquaintance of mine had occasion to travel to another city where he met some old friends for dinner. It was good to see his friends, but what they shared with him was not so pleasant — their pastor had just resigned in disgrace because of adultery. The entire congregation was in deep mourning. They urged my friend to meet with their pastor, which he did. The meeting revealed a humiliated, broken man. Up to that time the pastor's outward life had been impeccable. No one would have dreamed this would happen to him, least of all himself, but it did. As he recounted his tale of woe, he kept saying, "I never thought this would happen to me." That was, and is, a tragic story, but sadder still is the fact that his story is not unique. It has happened to hundreds of other pastors in recent years. I have personally known men with high reputations in the Christian world — college presidents, vice presidents, professors, and pastors — who have fallen into immorality. Sometimes I have felt very much like Chuck Swindoll when he said, "If I hear of one more pastor who has fallen, I think I'm going to get sick." We cannot and must not deny the fact that sensuality has not only invaded the church of Jesus Christ but has penetrated high places in it.

As we all know, part of the problem stems from the fact that our society is blatantly sensualistic. Powerful voices in sociology and secular family counseling are promoting new normative definitions of what is acceptable. According to them, there are no constants in moral questions and personal relationships. All values are on trial. Relationships should last only as long as they are mutually fulfilling, we are told. Access to regular sexual satisfaction should be viewed as a basic human right. There is no true humanness devoid of sexuality. And so it goes. The situation is made more acute by the fact that the bulk of our national media apparently endorses this thinking. Much of our advertising is based on sexual stimulation. If you wear a certain brand of cologne or drive a particular luxury car, you will suddenly attract a bevy of beautiful supermodels. Popular songs romanticize infidelity. The advent of home video has extended a river of filth into the homes of millions. In 1953 Kinsey's famous report revealed that by age twenty-one, 23 percent of the female population had lost their virginity. In 1971 the figure was more than 46 percent.[1] In 1970 there were 1,046,000 unmarried adults sharing living quarters with a person of the opposite sex. In 1977 the figure was more than 1,900,000. And the figures have not gotten better since then, but increasingly worse.

The problem is immense. It's all around us, even in the church. How does one live in purity in an age of sensuality? Is that even possible? And if so, how? Our Lord speaks to this in the Sermon on the Mount as he gives the second illustration of the radical, superseding righteousness that he brings. The first illustration had been taken from the sixth commandment, which prohibits murder. This second illustration is built on the seventh commandment, which prohibits adultery. His theme is the radical purity of radical righteousness, and it is essential for us to hear and heed his words if we are to live purely in a sensual society.

THE TRADITIONAL STANDARD OF SEXUAL PURITY

In verse 27 Jesus reiterates the traditional standard of sexual purity: "You have heard that it was said, 'Do not commit adultery.'"

In the original, this is a letter-for-letter rendering of the Greek version (Septuagint) of the seventh commandment. It is a perfectly good, sublime statement of God's Law. The only criticism that one might venture is that it is only external, for it only mentions the outward act of adultery. It must be admitted, however, that the tenth commandment does allude to the internal aspect: "You shall not covet your neighbor's house. You shall not covet your neighbor's wife" (Exodus 20:17). However, for all practical purposes, Moses and the scribes did not emphasize the inward aspect of adultery as much as they did the outward manifestation.

For many, this became a conveniently narrow definition of sexual sin. It was all so clear. You were either an adulterer or you were not. And if you were a "caught" adulterer, you were dead. That really made it simple. How convenient! And how deadly! It is very natural for those of us who are nonadulterers to feel smug and conceited. "I haven't committed *that* sin! Jesus is speaking to the rest of you sinners, not to me! Listen up, you reprobates!" But Jesus knows our hearts, and he is not buying it. Instead, he communicates a radically new standard of sexual purity. It is in continuity with the Old Testament, but it supersedes and completes it.

THE RADICALLY NEW STANDARD OF SEXUAL PURITY

"But I tell you that anyone who looks at a woman lustfully has already committed adultery with her in his heart." (v. 28)

In understanding what Jesus means, first let us see what he does not mean. Jesus does not mean it is wrong to look at a woman admiringly, but it is wrong to do so lustfully. He does not forbid the natural, normal attraction that is part of our humanity. What he forbids is deep-seated lust that consumes the inner person. A. B. Bruce writes, "The look is not casual but persistent, the desire not involuntary or momentary, but cherished."[2] It is not the first glance that is sin, but the second that swells with lust and feeds upon the subject. Jesus' language is perfectly calculated. He uses a judicial form of statement that gives his pronouncement a final authoritative ring. The use of the aorist tense conveys that the person has *already* committed adultery with the woman. It is an accomplished, irreversible fact. This occurs in his heart, in the essence of his being. As Robert Guelich says, "Jesus categorically declares that the lustful desire to have another's wife incriminates one's very person."[3] Mental infidelity leaves one completely guilty.

Few male and female believers have not crossed the line from attraction to lust at some time. We are all adulterers by this standard. The great eighteenth-century commentator Albert Bengel knew this well and wrote, "Thus God looks upon the heart, in which, alas! what is not committed?"[4] The realization of this ought to deliver us from all judgmentalism and pious condescension toward those who have fallen to adultery. And it should instill within us a poverty of spirit and a humility that realizes we are spiritually bankrupt and makes us amazed that God loves us as he does.

There is another incontrovertible truth in Jesus' statement as well: Sensual sins are preceded by sensual fantasies. That was precisely the case with King David on a warm spring night in Palestine when he could not sleep and strode onto the rooftop garden for some cool evening air and a look at his city. As he gazed around, his eye caught the form of an unusually beautiful woman bathing. As to how beautiful she was, the Hebrew is explicit: "The woman was beautiful in appearance, very." She was young, in the flower of life, and the evening shadows made her even more enticing. David's look became a leer, and mental adultery ensued. And then he would not be denied, even when his servant meekly reminded him that she was the wife of Uriah the Hittite (2 Samuel 11:1-4). The fantasy preceded the act, and that is how it has always been. No sensual sin was ever committed that was not first imagined. Scripture says this, and our experience confirms it. Our imagination (one of the faculties that distinguish us from animals) is one of God's wondrous gifts. Through it we dream great dreams. Without it there would be no great works of art or great achievements of science. But as with any of God's gifts, it must be used responsibly. When abused, the imagination spawns great evil.

How marvelous our Lord's words are! In one single sentence he elevated our entire concept of sexual purity beyond the mere physical to a matter of the soul and heart. And in doing so, he has shown us our hearts and has uncovered the source of our trouble. His words cut. They are surgical. They expose to us our sin, and they show us his radical righteousness. The question now is, how can we live a life of purity in this age of sensuality?

THE RADICAL DEMANDS OF THE NEW STANDARD OF SEXUAL PURITY

> *"If your right eye causes you to sin, gouge it out and throw it away. It is better for you to lose one part of your body than for your whole body to be thrown into hell. And if your right hand causes you to sin, cut it off and throw it away. It is better for you to lose one part of your body than for your whole body to go into hell." (vv. 29-30)*

This is tough teaching! Oswald Chambers said, "This line of discipline is the sternest one that ever struck mankind."[5] It was also one of Jesus' favorite sayings because he used variations of it at various times (cf. 18:8, 9). Some have taken him literally. The most famous case is that of Origen of Alexandria who had himself physically emasculated in an attempt to overcome his sensual desires. It is significant that not long afterward, the Council of Nicea outlawed the practice. Apart from the fact that such mutilation is contrary to Scripture, poor Origen still had his eyes, and if he had removed them, he would still have had his mind's eye.

Jesus is speaking of what we call "spiritual mortification." John Stott explains it beautifully:

> What does this involve in practice? Let me elaborate and so interpret Jesus' teaching: "If your eye causes you to sin because temptation comes to you through your eyes (objects you see), then pluck out your eyes. That is, don't look! Behave as if you had actually plucked out your eyes and flung them away, and were now blind and so could not see the objects which previously caused you to sin. Again, if your hand or foot causes you to sin, because temptation comes to you through your hands (things you do) or your feet (places you visit), then cut them off. That is: don't do it! Don't go! Behave as if you had actually cut off your hands and feet, and had flung them away, and were now crippled and so could not do the things or visit the places which previously caused you to sin." That is the meaning of "mortification."[6]

Jesus is telling us that *anything* that stands between us and him must be ruthlessly, even savagely, torn out or cut off and thrown away. Drastic measures are always appropriate in order to protect one's spiritual health! Halfway measures will never do the job! How this strikes against our desire to seek the middle road, to never be too extreme either way. But it is Christ's advice, and some of us need to take some extreme measures today!

Of course, this great principle of mortification has universal application to all areas of life, but here Jesus specifically applies it to sensuality. So we will do the same. If the application seems negative, so be it, for the ultimate result is positive. Jesus tells us there must be a mortification of the eyes, that we must control our eyes. This advice may be more needful for men than women because they are more apt to be visually stimulated, but it does apply to both. In simplest terms, this forbids a second look. At the risk of sounding super-pious and goody-goody, I have tried to make this one of the canons of my own life. A godly man (one who is trying to be so) must not take a second look. When talking with the opposite sex, one should always maintain eye contact. Wandering eyes are sensual eyes and ultimately adulterous eyes. Job's reflections in chapter 31 of his book contain lifesaving wisdom:

> *I made a covenant with my eyes not to look lustfully at a girl . . . if my heart has been led by my eyes . . . If my heart has been enticed by a woman . . . (vv. 1, 7, 9)*

A wise man or woman will make a covenant with his or her eyes as to what they will look upon. Certainly this involves television and movies. There is probably no area in which Christians fail more than in what they allow to enter their minds through the media. There are times when we need to walk away from the screen. There are times to turn the dial. We are easily desensitized, and those impure things at which we laugh do not seem so bad the next time, and the last laugh will be on us. Certainly this also applies to books, magazines, and newspapers. We need to make a covenant with our eyes. We need to take extreme measures if necessary. Am I suggesting a new legalism with a list of yeses and nos? In no way! Jesus says, "If *your* right eye causes you to sin . . ." Not anyone else's eye, but *your* eye. We are all different. We stumble over different things. One thing may arouse one and leave another unmoved. One must cut something out, but another may be under no such obligation.

This all demands absolute honesty before Christ. I have heard of young men who attend smutty films and say they do not affect them at all. That is dishonest. Also, Jesus says there are places we must not go, and there are things we must not handle. There are even times we must use our limbs to flee. David should have looked the other way and walked back inside. I rather doubt that Joseph would have been able to resist Mrs. Potiphar if he had stayed around her for very long. Many Scriptures unite in a chorus to commend Joseph's example. For example, "Flee from sexual immorality" (1 Corinthians 6:18) and "Flee the evil desires of youth, and pursue righteousness" (2 Timothy 2:22). Jesus' advice is not totally negative. He does not merely call for a life of negation. Mortification is not only ultimately positive — it is positive in practice because it involves cultivating good thoughts and actions. Paul tells us, "Finally, brethren, whatever is true, whatever is noble, whatever is right, whatever is pure, whatever is lovely, whatever is admirable — if anything is excellent or praiseworthy — think about such things" (Philippians 4:8). A life filled with uplifting thoughts and overflowing with service will be less likely to be subject to the sins Jesus warns against.

But more than that, we must recognize the absolute necessity of the ministry of the Holy Spirit. We cannot mortify our flesh alone. Willpower will not do it! Paul is careful to tell us, "but if by the Spirit you put to death the misdeeds of the body, you will live" (Romans 8:13). Likewise, "continue to work out your salvation with fear and trembling, for it is God who works in you" (Philippians 2:12, 13). We can do this only by the power of Jesus.

We live in an age of extreme sensuality. Many say (and I think they are right) that never in the history of the western world, since the time of Greek and Roman paganism, has the state of marriage and sexual morality been so low. And even more tragic, immorality has invaded the church at every level, from teenage to mid-life, so that no age group is untouched. Moreover, the havoc this has wrought goes far beyond the relational horrors of divorce, illegitimacy, and abortion to the very perversion of faith. I know of one former church leader and theologian who after continuous adultery and finally dissolution of his marriage began to discard the essentials of his Christian faith. Why? When one's willful conduct contradicts one's theology, either the conduct or the theology must change. We must understand that much of the heresy we observe today has roots that are moral rather than intellectual. Therefore we must realize that what people do with their eyes and limbs can affect the eternal destiny of their souls.

We must not fall to smugness or self-righteous conceit just because we have not committed the act of adultery. But we must recognize and admit that we have adulterous hearts. We must never suffer the preacher's delusion that "this can never happen to me." We must never let our piety and spiritual accomplishments dull us to our potential for sin. We must mortify the very members of our bodies. If our eyes, hands, and feet are causing us to stumble, we must take desperate measures to keep that from happening. If we are stumbling because of what we are seeing, we must make a covenant with our eyes to stop, to leave the scene if necessary. We must not give in to what others will think. We must expect some misunderstanding and even ridicule when we make godly choices. "You have to be kidding! You mean you haven't seen such and such? You haven't read that best seller? You're culturally deprived. Go on like this and you'll be an intellectual dinosaur." But Jesus says it's better to be a cultural amputee than for our whole body to go to Hell.

If God is speaking to you about some things that need to be put out of your life, do what he says today. If God is telling you to change your visual habits, then do it for your soul's sake and that of your family. If God is saying that a relationship must end, then do it today. Or perhaps there is some pleasure that is okay for others but is causing you to stumble, and you know it must go. If so, get rid of it right now. You cannot do it through your own willpower. Obey God with humility and prayer. Ask him for strength, and then do what he says.

14

Jesus' Teaching on Divorce

MATTHEW 5:31-32

The February 1973 issue of *McCall's* magazine carried an article entitled, "Is Anyone Faithful Anymore?" in which the author included the following story. A young wife was at lunch with eleven of her friends, who had been meeting together regularly to study French since their children had been in nursery school. As they conversed, one of the women, the group's leader, asked, "How many of you have been faithful throughout your marriage?" Only one woman at the table raised her hand. That evening when the young wife told her husband about the conversation, she revealed that she was *not* the one who had raised her hand. He was shocked and devastated. "But I *have* been faithful," she added. "Then why didn't you raise your hand?" She replied, "I was ashamed."[1]

Times have changed, have they not? It used to be that most people would go to extremes to hide their infidelity, but today many people are ashamed of their fidelity. We live in a day when some experts speak of "healthy adultery" and the married faithful are less vocal than the unfaithful in promoting their ways.

I think no one would disagree that our contemporary culture is not intrinsically receptive to Biblical teaching regarding sexual relationships, marriage, and divorce. Because of this hostility, some preachers seem reluctant to speak out on these issues. Other ministers hesitate to address these topics because there is major disagreement about divorce in the church. Because there are numerous opinions as to what the Bible means, because the subject is complex, and because contemporary marital relationships are often incredibly tangled mazes, the subject becomes overwhelming. Sadly, we sometimes find it easier to just leave it unaddressed.

Some surveys indicate that eight of ten people are either directly or indirectly affected by divorce. The mere mention of the word *divorce* is painful to some. Many have been deeply wounded by broken marriages, and a discussion of the subject brings up memories and feelings they would like to forget. For these reasons preachers find little joy in preaching on the subject. But since Jesus brought it up right in the middle of the Sermon on the Mount, the greatest sermon ever preached, he obviously thinks it is an important subject, one we dare not ignore. To see this matter through Jesus' eyes is good for us as individuals, good for the church, and good for society.

What is to be the Christian's attitude regarding divorce? Is divorce always forbidden? Or is it sometimes allowable? What is the Christian position amidst the marital tragedy that surrounds us? As we answer these questions, I will try to be sensitive to those who are hurting. But at the same time I will do my best to be Biblical. The bottom line in all of this is, what does God's Word say?

To understand our Lord's statements on divorce, we must know something of the controversial social and theological context in which he made them. The controversy centered over the interpretation of a phrase in Deuteronomy 24:1, the stated ground of divorce: "If a man marries a woman who becomes displeasing to him because he finds something indecent about her, and he writes her a certificate of divorce . . ."

That verse taught that a husband could divorce his wife if he found "something indecent" in her, and that is where the controversy lay. The burning question in Jesus' day was, what does "something indecent" mean?" Those in the very liberal rabbinical school of Hillel interpreted "indecent" in the widest manner possible. They said a man could divorce his wife if she spoiled his dinner! They also extended "indecent" to mean a wife's walking around with her hair down, speaking to men in the streets, or speaking disrespectfully of her husband's parents in his presence. A wrong word about a mother-in-law and a woman could be out on the street! Rabbi Akiba, who was of this school of thought, went even further, saying that the phrase "becomes displeasing to him" ("she find no favor in his eyes," KJV) meant that a man could divorce his wife if he found a woman who was more beautiful. Such husbands were bigoted and arrogant.

Fortunately, they were opposed by the school of Shammai, which limited "indecent" to offenses of marital impropriety short of adultery. "Indecent" did not refer to adultery, which was punished by execution, but rather suggested other types of sexual misconduct such as shameful exposure.[2]

This conservative-liberal controversy over the meaning of "indecent" as a grounds for divorce was the backdrop of the Pharisees' coming to Jesus about this matter. Matthew 19:3 describes the situation: "Some Pharisees came to test him. They asked, 'Is it lawful for a man to divorce his wife for any and every reason?'" They were obviously trying to draw Jesus into the long-standing debate and then exploit his response for their own ends. Some even think they were hoping to use Jesus' answer to get him in trouble with Herod because a negative answer would publicly align him with the point of view that caused John the Baptist to be beheaded. Significantly, Jesus did not begin by directly answering their question but took the conversation back to God's creation design, giving us the most extensive teaching on divorce in the New Testament.

JESUS' TEACHING ON DIVORCE (MATTHEW 19:4-12)

Jesus began by stating the ideal:

> *"Haven't you read," he replied, "that at the beginning the Creator 'made them male and female,' and said, 'For this reason a man will leave his father and mother and be united to his wife, and the two will become one flesh'?" (vv. 4, 5)*

In the beginning divorce was inconceivable — and impossible. Jesus quoted lines from Genesis 2:23, 24 to emphasize two things. First, the *intimacy* of the marriage relationship. He says "the two will become one flesh." There is no other intimacy like it. It is deeper than one's relationship to one's own children. When my children were born, there was an amazing bonding that took place when I saw those babies. In the ensuing months and years the bonding increased, and my wife and I are close to our children, interwoven with them. But we are not one flesh with them. The Scripture says that a man becomes "one flesh" with his wife. Marriage is the deepest human relationship.

After intimacy, the emphasis is on *permanence*. There was no thought of divorce — ever! God's ideal was, and is, monogamous, intimate, enduring marriage. This is what he approves of. Anything less is a departure from the divine model. And the Fall did not change that ideal. We all know that some things possible before the Fall were not possible afterward. But regarding divorce, God's standard did not change. We not only see this in the very first book of the Old Testament but also in the very last one:

> *"Why has God abandoned us?" you cry. I'll tell you why; it is because the Lord has seen your treachery in divorcing your wives who have been faithful to you through the years, the companions you promised to care for and keep. You were united to your wife by the Lord. In God's wise plan, when you married, the two of you became one person in his sight. And what does he want? Godly children from your union. Therefore guard your passions! Keep faith with the wife of your youth. For the Lord, the God of Israel, says he hates divorce. . . . (Malachi 2:14-16,* TLB*)*

God hates divorce! Whenever divorce occurs, it is an aberration. It is something that was not meant to be. All of this talk about "creative divorce" is pseudoscientific and pseudo-liberated baloney. Those who become tired of their marriage because it is solid, predictable, and not very exciting should cast away their fantasies. Besides, there is nothing more boring than evil and its fruit.

The conversation between the Pharisees and Jesus is most enlightening. The Pharisees have alluded to the controversy in Deuteronomy 24, asking if a man may divorce his wife for any reason at all. Jesus has responded by saying divorce is not God's ideal. Now the Pharisees respond with another reference to Deuteronomy 24: "'Why then,' they asked, 'did Moses command that a man give his wife a certificate of divorce and send her away?'" (Matthew 19:7). The idea is this: "Moses made provision for divorce in Deuteronomy 24:1. How then can you say it is not part of the ideal?" Note Jesus' answer in verse 8: "Jesus replied, 'Moses permitted you to divorce your wives because your hearts were hard. But it was not this way from the beginning.'"

Jesus' answer corrects the Pharisees, for Moses only permitted divorce — he didn't command it as the Pharisees asserted. What Moses did command was the granting of a divorce certificate for the woman's protection. Without a certificate she could be subject to exploitation, even recrimination. The certificate also prevented the man from marrying her again. Thus she could not be treated like chattel. Marriage was not something one could walk in and out of. The reason God allowed divorce was the hardness of heart to which the men of Israel had succumbed. It was a divine concession to human weakness — reluctant permission at best!

Understanding this, we come to the very center of Christ's teaching and the heart of our study — Jesus' explanation as to when and why divorce is permitted: "And I say to you, whoever divorces his wife, *except* for *immorality*, and marries another woman commits adultery" (Matthew 19:9, NASB, emphasis mine).

Here everything rests upon the correct interpretation of the phrase "except for immorality" — and especially the single word, "immorality." The Greek word here is *porneia*, from which we derive the English word *pornography*. The Greek dictionaries tell us that *porneia* means unchastity, fornication, prostitution, or other kinds of unlawful intercourse. When *porneia* is applied to married persons, it means marital unfaithfulness, illicit intercourse that may involve adultery, homosexuality, bestiality, and the like. We should note (and this is very important!) that all these offenses were originally punished by death under Mosaic Law. These sins terminated marriage not by divorce but by death. However, by Jesus' time the Roman occupation of the country and its legal system had made the death sentence very difficult to obtain. Jewish practice had therefore substituted divorce for death. Thus the rabbinical schools of Hillel and Shammai were not discussing whether divorce was permissible for adultery. That was taken for granted by everyone. The point is, Jesus was far stricter than Hillel and Shammai because he superseded the teaching of Deuteronomy 24 and said that the *only* ground for which one may divorce his or her spouse is marital unfaithfulness.[3] This is the simple, plain meaning of Jesus' words in verse 9: "And I say to you, whoever divorces his wife, except for immorality, and marries another woman commits adultery." That is, divorce is allowed if your mate is guilty of marital unfaithfulness. But if you divorce for any other reason and remarry, it is you who commits adultery. This is likewise the meaning of Jesus' similar statement in the Sermon on the Mount:

> *"But I tell you that anyone who divorces his wife, except for marital unfaithfulness, causes her to become an adulteress [if she remarries], and anyone who marries the divorced woman [a woman who has been divorced for something short of unchastity] commits adultery." (Matthew 5:32)*

Jesus' teaching is clear. Some of the interpretations of these texts are unbelievably convoluted, but we must hold to the plain, unadorned sense of the text. Jesus meant what he said!

Some object that these exception clauses don't jibe with Jesus' teaching in two other Gospel passages, Mark 10:11, 12 and Luke 16:18, which contain no exception clauses. For instance, Mark records:

> *He answered, "Anyone who divorces his wife and marries another woman commits adultery against her. And if she divorces her husband and marries another man, she commits adultery."*

No exception clauses! Because of this, some have argued that Mark represents the earlier and pure teaching of Jesus, but Matthew contains a scribal addition of the exception clause and is thus unauthentic. However, we must hold that it is authentic because none of the ancient manuscripts omit it — all of them have it. Why the difference between the Gospels of Matthew and Mark then? John Stott gives the answer:

> It seems far more likely that its [the exception clause's] absence from Mark and Luke is due not to their ignorance of it but to their acceptance of it as something taken for granted. After all, under the Mosaic Law adultery was punishable by death (although the death penalty for this offense seems to have fallen into disuse by the time of Jesus); so nobody would have questioned that marital unfaithfulness was a just ground for divorce.[4]

The Lord Jesus Christ permitted divorce and remarriage on one ground and one ground only — marital unfaithfulness.

But notice that he *permitted* it — he did not command it. If you learn that your mate has been having an adulterous affair, it does not follow that you have license to seek a divorce. Too often men and women eagerly pounce on the infidelity of their mates as the opportunity to get out of a relationship they wanted to end anyway. It is so easy to minimize one's own behavior and to maximize the sins of the other party. Many look for a way out instead of a way *through* the problems. I want to be careful not to minimize the sin of adultery like the man who said to his wife, "I don't understand why you're so disturbed. All I did was have an affair." Yet I believe (this is my personal opinion) that we should not regard a one-time affair in the same way as a mate who persists in his or her adulterous ways and refuses to repent. Jesus' exception clauses should be viewed like this: No matter how rough things are, regardless of the stress and strain, whatever is said about compatibility and temperament, nothing allows for divorce except *unfaithfulness* — and even then it is not to be used as an excuse to get out of the relationship.

THE RADICALNESS OF JESUS' TEACHING (MATTHEW 19:10-12)

Jesus' teaching was radical. He had done away completely with the Mosaic divorce provision (Deuteronomy 24:1). This was revolutionary. The disciples' response indicates just how radical Jesus' teaching was: "The disciples said to him, 'If this is the situation between a husband and wife, it is better not to marry.'" They were blown away. If the only ground for divorce was unfaithfulness, if none of the exceptions suggested by Hillel and Shammai were valid, it was better to stay single! The radicalness of what Jesus taught is further underlined in Matthew 5 by its being one of the six statements that begin with variations of "You have heard it said, but I tell you," demonstrating the superior righteousness of Christ. The point of these statements is: This is the way a righteous person lives! Thus his or her marital relationship is supremely sacred. Nothing can sever it but unrepentant unfaithfulness — and then it is not an excuse for ending the marriage but is the sorrowful ground of divorce.

Such teaching is radical today. It is out of sync with our culture. Today even Christian counselors are recommending divorce and remarriage on grounds that are in opposition to the clear teachings of Christ. The sanctity of marriage has been corrupted by Christ's own church and his authority flouted. Marriage has been trivialized into a provisional sexual union that dissolves when our puny love gives out. But this is not the way the righteous person approaches marriage. According to Christ, marriage demands total commitment that only death or the most flagrant, ongoing sexual infidelity can bring to an end.

Having seen Christ's teaching, the question now is, does the Bible say anything else about divorce? The answer is yes.

JESUS' TEACHING AND PAUL'S (1 CORINTHIANS 7:8-16)

In 1 Corinthians 7:8-16 the Apostle Paul gives consecutive advice, first to the unmarried (vv. 8, 9), then to married believers (vv. 10, 11), and finally to those who have mixed marriages — when one's spouse is not a believer (vv. 12-16). It is on this final category that we will focus.

Paul begins his teaching by saying in verse 12, "To the rest I say this (I, not the Lord) . . ." which has been misunderstood by some as meaning that Paul is saying that his teaching is not as authoritative as Christ's. What he really means, however, is that what he is going to say was not said by Jesus in his earthly ministry but is now being said by Paul as part of his apostolic teaching. "He is saying in effect, 'I am now going to deal with cases on which the Lord Himself did not give a verdict.'"[5] Paul speaks with full apostolic authority. Notice what he says:

> *To the rest I say this (I, not the Lord): If any brother has a wife who is not a believer and she is willing to live with him, he must not divorce her. And if a woman has a husband who is not a believer and he is willing to live with her, she must not divorce him. (vv. 12, 13)*

Paul knew that in Corinth there were many marriages in which either the husband or wife had become a Christian after marriage, thus producing a spiritually mixed marriage. His advice was that the Christian must not leave his or her pagan spouse — it was not permitted. Then in verse 14 he gives the reason:

> *For the unbelieving husband has been sanctified through his wife, and the unbelieving wife has been sanctified through her believing husband. Otherwise your children would be unclean, but as it is, they are holy.*

The reason for staying together is that the unbeliever and the children will be influenced toward Christ by the life of the believer. I find this fascinating because we often think of the believer being corrupted by the unbeliever, and indeed sometimes this happens. But Paul lays down that it is generally otherwise! If you are in an unequal union, take heart! The general thrust is that you and your faith will prevail — though, sadly, not always.

Then in verse 15 we have Paul's new teaching: "But if the unbeliever leaves, let him do so. A believing man or woman is not bound in such circumstances; God has called us to live in peace."

The sense is, if the unbeliever deserts and is determined not to come back, let him or her go. The Christian is "not bound in such circumstances," which means that the believer is free from the marriage because the unbeliever has broken the marriage bond. The result is that the believer is free to divorce and remarry. The consistent use of the word "bound" in this passage and others means "is not bound in marriage."[6] There is no need to seek some other interpretation. This is the plain sense — this is what it means.

A SUMMATION OF BIBLICAL TEACHING

So we see that the Bible allows divorce for two reasons — marital unfaithfulness such as adultery and homosexuality, and the desertion of a believer by an unbelieving spouse.

As to the question of remarriage, the Scriptures allow it in three instances. First, if one's mate is guilty of sexual immorality and is unwilling to repent and live faithfully with the marriage partner, divorce and remarriage are permissible. Second, when a believer is deserted by an unbelieving spouse, divorce and remarriage are again permitted. And third, as an extension of the allowance for divorce and remarriage when deserted by an unbeliever, I personally believe that when someone has been married and divorced before coming to Christ, remarriage is allowed. Second Corinthians 5:17 says, "Therefore, if anyone is in Christ, he is a new creation; the old has gone, the new has come!" "New" here (*kainos*) means new in quality. "New" means what it says — really new, as contrasted to the old. The same word is used of the "new man" in Ephesians 2:15 and the "new self" in Ephesians 4:24. Not only are believers really new, but Paul says that "the old has gone, the new has come." A new believer is completely forgiven. I believe that among the old things that have passed away are all sins, including divorce prior to salvation. If it were otherwise, divorce would be the only sin for which Christ did not atone, and that would be inconceivable.

I hope no one misunderstands me, for divorce is not the ideal. It is a divine concession to human weakness. God hates divorce! We must realize that divorce (and remarriage) according to the Biblical guidelines is not sin — though it is due to sin. We must mourn every divorce!

How foreign to the Biblical mind are phrases like "creative divorce" or "the magic of divorce" or the ad that appeared on the back of a *TV Guide*: "Order your DIVORCE RING BAND today. . . . *Now* is the time to celebrate your new beginning."[7]

We have discussed the issues primarily with the non-offending party in view. What advice is there for the offending party? Here I can do no better than quote the concluding words of Dr. Martyn Lloyd-Jones:

> "Have you nothing to say about others?" asks someone. All I would say about them is this, and I say it carefully and advisedly, and almost in fear lest I give even a semblance of a suggestion that I am saying anything that may encourage anyone to sin. But on the basis of the gospel and in the interest of truth I am compelled to say this: Even adultery is not the unforgivable sin. It is a terrible sin, but God forbid that there should be anyone who feels that he or she has sinned himself or herself outside the love of God or outside His kingdom because of adultery. No; if you truly repent and realize the enormity of your sin and cast yourself upon the boundless love and mercy and grace of God, you can be forgiven and I assure you of pardon. But hear the words of our blessed Lord: "Go and sin no more."[8]

Finally, what do we say to the church, to ourselves? First, we must resist the permissiveness of our culture and solidly take our stand against divorce or remarriage on any grounds other than those taught in God's Word. Next, we must refrain from self-righteous judgmentalism. All of us are adulterers in heart. We must exercise our dealings with those who have fallen, realizing that we are ourselves under Christ's omniscient dictum: "But I tell you that anyone who looks at a woman lustfully has already committed adultery with her in his heart" (Matthew 5:28). Finally, toward those who have fallen to or suffered divorce, we must be forgiving, like our Lord. We must not call unclean that which he has called clean (Acts 10:15). We must endeavor to share the suffering of those ravaged by divorce. And lastly, the church should make provision for the remarriage of those who have Biblically divorced.

15

Radical Truthfulness

MATTHEW 5:33-37

This passage gives the fourth of six illustrations that Jesus used to depict a "righteousness [that] surpasses that of the Pharisees and the teachers of the law" (v. 20). Jesus here speaks of truthfulness and integrity of speech, a subject that is eminently relevant for us today because we live at a time when "truth [is] forever on the scaffold," to use James Russell Lowell's phrase. We see this internationally in news coverage of smiling diplomats shaking hands as they sign treaties they will almost certainly not keep. Most people believe nations will honor their word only when that serves their best interest. International politics seems to be the art of lying.

Things are not much different within our own land. Some years ago UPI reported this prayer by the Chaplain of the Kansas Senate:

> Omniscient Father:
>
> Help us to know who is telling the truth. One side tells us one thing, and the other just the opposite.
>
> And if neither side is telling the truth, we would like to know that, too.
>
> And if each side is telling half the truth, give us the wisdom to put the right halves together.
>
> In Jesus' name, Amen.

Perhaps that was (and is) a necessary prayer, but nevertheless it was a desperate expression of cynicism!

This cynicism regarding truth extends to the literature of our day as well. University of Chicago professor Mortimer Adler, editor of *The Encyclopedia Britannica* and the Great Books of the Western World series, says in his classic *How to Read a Book*:

> The question, Is it true? can be asked of anything we read. It is applicable to every kind of writing. . . . No higher commendation can be given any work of the human mind than to praise it for the measure of truth it has achieved; by the same token, to criticize it adversely for its failure in this respect is to treat it with the seriousness that a serious work deserves. Yet, strangely enough, in recent years, for the first time in Western history, there is a dwindling concern with this criterion of excellence. Books win the plaudits of the critics and gain widespread popular attention almost to the extent that they flout the truth — the more outrageously they do so, the better.[1]

Today there is an urgent truth shortage! There was a time when western culture was distinguished from other cultures by at least a conventional outward sense of obligation to tell the truth. But now there is a pervasive indifference to truth-telling, and this has not only infected day-to-day conversation but the most solemn pledges of life. Perjury under solemn oath is epidemic. The sacred vows of marriage are broken almost as often as repeated. God's name is invoked by blatant liars who purport to be witnesses to the truth.

There is, indeed, a crisis, but we must not make the mistake of thinking it occurs only out there because it happens among us too. It is difficult to always tell the truth. The great preacher and writer George Macdonald wrote to his son on December 6, 1878, "I always try — I *think* I do — to be truthful. All the same I tell a great many lies."[2] I identify with that. I am speaking to someone and suddenly realize that what I am saying is not the truth. Perhaps you have experienced the same. The difficulty comes from the combination of my own deceitful nature and the pervasive deceptiveness of the surrounding culture.

This drought of truth is what makes Jesus' teaching in the Sermon on the Mount so meaningful and refreshing. Our text tells us how to build radical truthfulness into our lives — how to tell the truth in a truth-perverting world.

THE OLD TESTAMENT'S TRADITIONAL TEACHING REGARDING TRUTH (v. 33)

Our Lord approached this subject of truthfulness by introducing the subject of the use of vows and oaths among his people in swearing that they were going to do something or that such-and-such a thing was true by employing phrases such as "as God lives, it is true." In verse 33 he perfectly summarized the traditional Old Testament teaching: "Again, you have heard that it was said to the people long ago, 'Do not break your oath, but keep the oaths you have made to the Lord.'"

From this and the rest of the Old Testament we understand two things about swearing vows and oaths. First, *vows were encouraged!* Deuteronomy 10:20 says, "Fear the LORD your God and serve him. Hold fast to him and *take your oaths in his name*" (emphasis mine). Not only were they encouraged to make vows and oaths, but they were encouraged to do so in God's name! Jeremiah 12:16, 17 mentions that having to swear in God's name will be a sign of grace:

> *And if they learn well the ways of my people and swear by my name, saying, "As surely as the LORD lives" — even as they taught my people to swear by Baal — then they will be established among my people.*

Swearing in God's name was not only presumed but encouraged in the Old Testament!

Secondly, what was discouraged was making a vow, swearing to do something, and then not doing it. Moses repeatedly emphasized this:

> *Do not swear falsely by my name and so profane the name of your God. I am the LORD. (Leviticus 19:12)*

> *When a man makes a vow to the LORD or takes an oath to obligate himself by a pledge, he must not break his word but must do everything he said. (Numbers 30:2)*

> *If you make a vow to the LORD your God, do not be slow to pay it, for the LORD your God will certainly demand it of you. (Deuteronomy 23:21)*

In summary: Vows were assumed, even encouraged. But once made, they were not to be broken under any circumstances. The Bible taught that they were very serious business.

The problem was that in Jesus' time the traditional, Biblical teaching had come under massive abuse. Somewhere along the line some rabbis (but not all rabbis) began to teach that an oath was not binding if it did not include God's name or imply it. Therefore, if you swore by your own or someone else's life or the life of the king (as Abner did in 1 Samuel 17:55) or by some object, but did not mention or allude to the name of God, you were not bound. The *Mishna* devotes one whole section called *Shebuoth* ("Oaths") to an elaborate discussion of when oaths are binding and when they are not.[3] The swearing of oaths had degenerated into a system of rules as to when you could lie and when you could not. The results were incredible. There was an ongoing epidemic of frivolous swearing, and oaths were continually mingled with everyday speech: "By your life," "by my beard," "may I never see the comfort of Israel if . . ." There was an inevitable trivialization of everyday language and integrity. It became common practice to convince another that you were telling the truth (while lying) by bringing some person or eminent object into reference. The deception was very subtle.

For instance, one rabbi taught that if one swore *by* Jerusalem one was not bound, but if one swore *toward* Jerusalem, it was binding — evidently because that in some way implied the Divine Name.[4] All of this produced in its adherents a profound spiritual schizophrenia: "I'm not telling the truth, but I'm really not lying." Their use of oaths was like children saying, "I have my fingers crossed, so I don't have to tell the truth."

CHRIST'S RADICAL TEACHING CONCERNING TRUTHFULNESS

The situation was utterly fantastic. So Jesus gave them a piece of his divine mind:

> *"But I tell you, do not swear at all either by heaven, for it is God's throne; or by the earth, for it is his footstool; or by Jerusalem, for it is the city of the Great King. And do not swear by your head, for you cannot make even one hair white or black." (vv. 34-36)*

Jesus rules out making vows using references to people or objects as backup. The reason is, God stands behind everything. The entire creation is God's, and you cannot refer to a part of it without referring ultimately to him. (Matthew 23:16-22 says the same thing in stronger language.) All such oath-taking, vowing, and swearing is wrong! It is sin!

But there is even more here. Jesus began by saying, "But I tell you, do not swear at all . . ." (v. 34a). Then he gave parenthetical information regarding evasive swearing (vv. 34b-36) and concluded with verse 37, saying, "Simply let your 'Yes' be 'Yes' and your 'No,' 'No'; anything beyond this comes from the evil one." (Compare the similar statement in James 5:12.)

Jesus' opening and closing teachings taken together state his radical superseding will: "But I tell you, do not swear at all. . . . Simply let your 'Yes' be 'Yes' and your 'No,' 'No'; anything beyond this comes from the evil one." Our Lord is saying that the radically righteous men and women of God's kingdom do not need to swear that they are telling the truth and in fact should refrain from using oaths and vows. Here again Christ surpasses and supersedes the requirements of the Law. The radically righteous do not need oaths. Their word is truth!

Here we must pause and note what we all know is true: The need for oath-taking and swearing comes from the fact that we earthlings are liars. Dr. Helmut Thielicke puts it like this:

> Whenever I utter the formula "I swear by God," I am really saying, "Now I'm going to mark off an area of absolute truth and put walls around it to cut it off from the muddy floods of untruthfulness and irresponsibility that ordinarily overruns my speech." In fact, I am saying even more than this. I am saying that people are expecting me to lie from the start. And just because they are counting on my lying I have to bring up these big guns of oaths and words of honor.[5]

Christ calls us away from such cheapening of language, instead giving ourselves to radical truthfulness.

THE RADICAL IMPLICATION OF CHRIST'S TEACHING FOR HIS FOLLOWERS

What are the implications of our Lord's radical teaching for our lives? Are we never supposed to take any personal oaths? What about public oaths we are asked to take in court? Some, like the Reformation's Anabaptists, and later the Moravians and Quakers, have taken an absolutist interpretation of Jesus' teaching. They refuse to take an oath or swear that something is true or not true any time anywhere. George Fox, the great founder of the Quakers, provided this famous rejoinder to the judges at Lancaster who sentenced him to prison for refusing to swear over a Bible that he would tell the truth:

> You have given me a book here to kiss and to swear on, and this book which ye have given me to kiss says, "Kiss the Son," and the Son says in this book, "Swear not at all." I say as the book says, and yet ye imprison me; how chance ye do not imprison the book for saying so?"[6]

Today because of George Fox's stand you do not have to lay your hand on a Bible in a court of law and swear to God that you are telling the truth. You may simply say, "I affirm that I am telling the truth."

Having come from a Quaker background, I especially admire George Fox and his followers, but I do not think they are correct. The context itself argues against such an absolutionist understanding because Jesus' illustrations of abuses are from everyday common speech. Jesus' prohibitions are in regard to everyday conversations. But even more decisive is the fact that Jesus honored the official oath of adjuration from Caiaphas by breaking his silence and speaking up in response.

> *But Jesus remained silent. The high priest said to him, "I charge you under oath by the living God: Tell us if you are the Christ, the Son of God." "Yes, it is as you say," Jesus replied. (Matthew 26:63, 64a)*

Not only do we have Jesus' example but also repeated examples by Paul — for example, "I call God as my witness that it was to spare you that I did not return to Corinth" (2 Corinthians 1:23). This is equal to saying, "I swear before Almighty God." Also, "God, whom I serve with my whole heart in preaching the gospel of his Son, is my witness how constantly I remember you" (Romans 1:9).

Obviously Paul did not believe he was going against Jesus' teaching when he appealed to God as his witness under the pressure of defending his pioneer ministry.

How does this translate into life? What deductions can we draw concerning our speech? Simply this: Oath-taking is permitted, but it is not encouraged. In civil life oath-taking, as in the courtroom, is permitted, and when one does so, he does not sin against Christ's teaching. Also, on rare occasions it may be necessary, as it was for Paul. However, oaths are not to be a normal part of our everyday conversation. In normal relations oaths should never fall from our lips. Kingdom men and women do not need such devices. Their commitment to truthfulness should be evident to all.

THE RADICAL CALL TO TRUTHFULNESS

Christ calls us to a life of profound truthfulness. Our problem is that we live in a radically deceptive world, a world that is deceitful at its very roots. We are awash in a sea of media deception. Men are told that if they dye the gray out, they will be handsome and virile and attractive to women everywhere. Rivers of hyperbole and exaggeration flow through advertising, political campaigning, and much more. Language has devolved to the extent that we do not know what the other person is saying. Studied ambiguities are the order of the day.

We embellish the truth without even realizing that we are doing so. One summer I caught a nice smallmouth bass that I then had stuffed. The taxidermist weighed it at three and three-quarters pounds, but he told me it looked like a four-pounder. It was so easy to brag about my great four-pound smallmouth bass! In fact, the more I talked about it, the more I was sure that it probably *was* four pounds! Fish get bigger, profits greater, boy friends more handsome, and strength greater in our world of "newspeak" and exaggeration — even in our own words. It is hard to tell the truth! Listen to George Macdonald's admission in full:

> I always try — I *think* I do — to be truthful. All the same I tell a great many petty lies, e.g. things that mean one thing to myself though another to other people. But I do not think lightly of it. Where I am more often wrong is in tacitly pretending I hear things which I do not, especially jokes and good stories, the *point* of which I always miss; but, seeing every

> one laugh, I laugh too, for the sake of not *looking* a fool. My respect for the world's opinion is my greatest stumblingblock I fear.[7]

It is not easy to be a totally truthful person today, but it is necessary for the church and the world. The world longs for freedom from dishonesty! Sure, it cultivates deception and promotes it, but deep down people long to escape the show and pretense. Many look eagerly to believers to display the honesty and integrity for which they so long. Our integrity as followers of Christ can make all the difference to a dying world. "The avoidance of one small fib . . . may be a stronger confession of faith than a whole 'Christian philosophy' championed in lengthy, forceful discussion."[8] When people know that you do not lie, your testimony will have more effect than all the theology you could ram at them. What a difference a truthful life can make!

A radical truthfulness is also greatly needed in the church. An act of deceit done to another brother or sister is a deceit done to all, for we are all members of one another. The Lord Jesus Christ prayed that his body would be unified, but a body that is not truthful is a body filled with distrust and is therefore not unified. Radical truthfulness is one of the greatest needs of the church today.

What can we personally do to promote Jesus' call to radical truthfulness? Remember that for Jesus, words were sacramental, for they were outward signs of an inward condition. Jesus said in Matthew 12:34, "Out of the overflow of the heart the mouth speaks." We need a truthful spirit that brings forth an increasing veracity of speech. We also need to remember that our Lord hears every word, not just the oaths, and that we will give account of all our words (see Matthew 12:36). Our words are freighted with eternity. We would do well to take this seriously.

Samuel Johnson wrote:

> Accustom your children constantly to this [the telling of the truth]; if a thing happened at one window, and they, when relating it, say that it happened at another, do not let it pass, but instantly check them; you do not know where deviation from truth will end. . . . It is more from carelessness about truth than from intentional lying, that there is so much falsehood in the world.[9]

Jesus minced no words with his friends, and neither does he with us. "But I tell you, do not swear at all. . . . Simply let your 'Yes' be 'Yes' and your 'No,' 'No'; anything beyond this comes from the evil one" (vv. 34a, 37). Let us be radically truthful!

16

Wrongs and Rights

MATTHEW 5:38-42

At this point in Jesus' Sermon on the Mount, we come to the fifth example of how the righteousness that Jesus demands supersedes and surpasses that of the scribes and Pharisees. This example has to do with the proper response when one is personally wronged. How is a person who has the surpassing righteousness of Christ supposed to react to personal offenses? Here, as before, Jesus' teaching can only be described as revolutionary. In fact, if it were not from him, we would be prone to dismiss it as coming from some out-of-touch visionary who did not really understand the human predicament. But the teaching is from the lips of our Lord, and Jesus knew more about human nature than anyone else. His words are immensely important today because we are continually beset with opposing teachings and examples. Retaliation is not only considered normative but indispensable to leadership. Moreover, we all know that beneath our genteel veneers is an apparently inexhaustible capacity for cultured anger and vengeance.

Jesus began characteristically by presenting the traditional Old Testament teaching: "You have heard that it was said, 'Eye for eye, and tooth for tooth'" (v. 38). That is an exact quotation from three Old Testament passages (Exodus 21:24; Leviticus 24:20; Deuteronomy 19:21) and represents the oldest law in the world — the law of retaliation, technically known as *Lex* (Law) *Talionis* (retaliation). The earliest reference to *Lex Talionis* comes from the Code of Hammurabi in the second millennium B.C. Far from being savage legislation, it was intrinsically merciful because it limited vengeance. The typical primitive blood feud knew nothing of equity. A small infraction by one tribe against another — for instance, trespassing — was met with a beating, which was returned by homicide, which was then countered by genocide. *Lex Talionis* did away with this — on paper at least.

Today we recognize *Lex Talionis* as foundational to all justice. The whole system of civil, penal, and international law is based on the idea of reparation and equity that has its roots in *Lex Talionis*. As it exists in the Bible, *Lex Talionis* was given to the judges of Israel as a basis for adjudication, as Deuteronomy 19:16-21 makes so clear. Individuals were *not* permitted to use this law to settle disputes with others. Only the courts were permitted to do so. Moreover, it was not literally carried out by the Jewish legal system because they correctly saw that in some cases to do so would result in injustice. For instance, a good tooth might be removed for a bad tooth! Thus they assessed damages just as we do in our courts today. The *Mishna* devotes an entire section entitled *Baba Kamma* to assessing proper damages.[1] So we have the traditional Old Testament teaching regarding one's response to personal wrong in the principle of exact retribution. There was nothing intrinsically wrong with that, apart from man's manipulation of it. It brought equity and stability to human relations.

Now comes Jesus' revolutionary new teaching: "But I tell you, Do not resist an evil person" (v. 39a). What does Jesus mean? Some believe he is teaching absolute nonresistance under any circumstances. Leo Tolstoy, the great Russian novelist, in his book *What I Believe* tells how in an intense time of soul-searching he read and reread the Sermon on the Mount and then in one life-changing moment came to understand that Christ meant exactly what he said in his command, "Do not resist an evil person." On the basis of this understanding he came to believe that no Christian should be involved in the army, the police force, or the courts of law. Christ's way, he argued, is not to resist evil in any way. And, he said, that teaching is absolute and unconditional.[2] I personally have seen this lived out, for I know a man who was present when his daughter and son-in-law were attacked physically by some thugs over a legal dispute, and the man did nothing to help or protect them. So some believe Jesus outlaws all force in any form. Not all pacifists, however, hold to this view.

Some believe force is just and necessary for the police and courts but disavow killing and war. Other Biblical pacifists would not isolate and absolutize this verse but base their beliefs on other Biblical passages, from which a far stronger case can be made. I personally believe this verse does not have anything to do with pacifism as it relates to the killing and taking of life, for that is not what the passage is about. The question of pacifism must be settled, one way or another, on other Biblical grounds.

The fact is, Jesus' statement — "Do not resist an evil person" — cannot be interpreted as an absolute prohibition of the use of all force, such as the police and court system, unless the Bible contradicts itself. Romans 13:1-7 teaches that the state is a divine institution that has the power to punish wrongdoers. This is impossible without force. The problem comes when we isolate and absolutize Jesus' words without giving due attention to the context, the flow of the argument, and the specific social implications of the time. Jesus clarified what he meant by providing four one-sentence illustrations of what it means to "not resist an evil person." Each of the illustrations is culturally specific, but they give us general principles for today's living. The principles are not for everyone, but only for those who follow Christ.

RESPONDING TO INSULT (v. 39b)

"If someone strikes you on the right cheek, turn to him the other also." What is Jesus describing here? Contrary to what we might think, he is not describing a physical attack, but rather a very traditional, calculated insult. Notice that Jesus specifically mentions "the right cheek," which tells us he is describing a backhanded slap (since most people are right-handed, this is surely what Jesus had in mind). According to rabbinic law, to hit someone with the back of the hand was twice as insulting as hitting him with the flat of the hand. The back of the hand meant calculated contempt, withering disdain. It meant that you were scorned as inconsequential — a nothing. Imagine how you would respond. My blood would boil. Not only was it a calculated insult, but it was here, as the great German scholar Jeremias argues, a slap given because of Jesus — a heretic's slap.[3]

When Jesus spoke of being slapped on the right cheek, he was describing an insult that comes because of one's faith. It was an insult for which a Jew could seek legal satisfaction according to the law of *Lex Talionis*. That is, he could seek damages. But Jesus says, do not do it! "If you are dishonored as a heretic, says Jesus, you should not go to law about it; rather you should show yourselves to be truly my disciples by the way in which you bear the hatred and the insult, overcome the evil, forgive the injustice."[4] In short, though you could take your opponent to the cleaners, do not do it! Lovingly absorb the insult.

What this means for us is that when we are insulted or abused for Christ's sake (whatever form that insult may take), we must not respond by getting even, by getting our legal pound of flesh according to the *Lex Talionis*, but must turn the other cheek. Jesus calls us to swallow our pride and give up our "rights" to reparation and fairness. That is the basic, essential interpretation. But there is another level of application that really gets down to where we live: We are to set aside our petty ways of getting even — the kind of living that punishes others by returning their own sins to them. If your spouse is messy, you leave things messy in return. If your friend is late, you will be late next time yourself. In effect Jesus asks us, in turning the other cheek, to make the other person and his or her well-being the center of our focus. We think of them and adjust our actions according to what we think will point them to Christ. And when we really do this, we begin to affect them. Such vulnerable love brings them to spiritual awareness. Evangelist Tom Skinner often told about the time after he was converted when he was playing football with some of the Harlem Lords, members of the gang he had formerly led. During the game someone took advantage of his Christianity and punched, kicked, and insulted him. After the game Tom said, "You know, because of Jesus, I love you anyway." That is what Jesus was talking about.

Jesus taught us how a righteous person should respond to personal wrong. This first illustration shows us how to respond to personal insult.

RESPONDING TO A RIP-OFF (v. 40)

"And if someone wants to sue you and take your tunic, let him have your cloak as well." It was possible in that day to sue others for the very shirt on their backs. However, no one could take another's cloak for a permanent, twenty-four-hour-a-day possession. A cloak or outer robe was indispensable for living in Palestine. So even if you lost your shirt (or tunic) in court, and your opponent asked for your cloak and won it, he had to return it every evening for you to sleep in. That was the law. What was the situation here? Evidently Jesus was giving advice to the poor among his followers — those who had been reduced to the garments on their backs because of persecution for their faith. His teaching is simply this: "As they sue you (no doubt falsely) for your shirt and win it, give them your cloak too, even though they cannot legally take it." This is supremely radical, and it is meant to point one's persecutors to Christ. Romans 12:17-21 describes the same call and potential effect:

> *Do not repay anyone evil for evil. Be careful to do what is right in the sight of everybody. If it is possible, as far as it depends on you, live at peace with everyone. Do not take revenge, my friends, but leave room for God's wrath, for it is written: "It is mine to avenge; I will repay," says the Lord. On the contrary: "If your enemy is hungry, feed him; if he is thirsty, give him something to drink. In doing this, you will heap burning coals on his head." Do not be overcome by evil, but overcome evil with good.*

This is the radical call of those who are suffering persecution for Christ. It is extreme advice for extreme circumstances.

We should note here that our Lord is not referring to the average lawsuit so characteristic of our litigation-happy society. Wrongly applied, this would do away with the possibility of law or legal redress. Rather, it is advice for the righteous who are pushed against the wall for the name of Christ. We should listen well, because someday we may need it!

RESPONDING TO FORCED LABOR (v. 41)

"If someone forces you to go one mile, go with him two miles." The indignity that Jesus described here had its origin with the Persians. In fact, the Greek word translated "forces" is of Persian origin. The Persians initiated a kind of Pony Express in which the mail-carrying rider simply "borrowed" horses. He started off with his letter riding one pony, and when that pony got tired he borrowed another, and when that one got tired he borrowed another, and when . . . He sort of rustled his way across the land. During Roman times this custom was common. Also, whenever a Roman official or soldier asked anyone within the Empire to carry a burden a mile, that person had to do it regardless of who he was or what the circumstances were. Almost all Jews had been subject to this, and they hated the very mention of it.

As in the previous examples, this form of persecution fell upon a believer because of his identification with Christ. Some think that may be why Simon of Cyrene was made to carry Christ's cross. The Roman soldiers knew he loved Jesus, it is surmised, so they said, "You carry the cross!" (See Matthew 27:32).

What Jesus was enjoining here was willing cheerfulness for any of his followers who would come under this form of persecution. There are two ways to do any task. You can mow the lawn with a hangdog expression, like you are mowing the Mojave desert. Or you can mow it and say, "There are birds in the sky, there are clouds above, it is not raining — this is a great day!" When you wash dishes, you can water them with your tears or you can sing hymns. Jesus calls for a revolutionary response in a difficult situation — cheerfulness. The kind that would cause a hardened soldier to say, "What's with him? This person has something I do not understand." Ridiculous? Impractical? Pollyannaish? I do not think so! This is the way Rome was won! Revolutionarily righteous people possessing revolutionary joy even when treated unfairly call everyone's hearts upward.

RESPONDING TO BORROWING (v. 42)

Finally, there is the matter of the believer who is being persecuted through others' borrowing. The Lord's advice is: "Give to the one who asks you, and do not turn away from the one who wants to borrow from you." Does this mean we are to give to every freeloader and panhandler who comes our way? I do not think so. I read about a Cambridge research student who thought otherwise — and ended up bankrupt as he went without while he supplied half a dozen men with the money for alcohol that they would have been better off without.[5] Jesus is not recommending that his followers give to every open hand, though, of course, he calls us all to deep generosity.

What then does he mean? He means that the righteous are to give to those who are attempting to hurt them through borrowing. Luke refers to this kind of persecution when he says, "But love your enemies, do good to them, and lend to them without expecting to get anything back" (6:35).

We must realize that Jesus' advice is for a specific situation in which a believer is being persecuted. Moreover, Jesus does not say how many times one is to loan to his persecutors. Nor does he mention the restraint that love will impose on one's generosity. As Alexander Maclaren wisely said:

> If turning the cheek would make the assaulter more angry, or if yielding the cloak would make the legal robber more greedy, or going the second mile would but make the press gang more severe and exacting, resistance becomes a form of love and duty for the sake of the wrongdoer.[6]

Jesus' advice is not a set of mechanical rules, but principles for meeting the personal wrongs that come to those who follow him. In the matter of loaning, the Lord wants his followers to reject a tightfisted, penny-pinching attitude that says, "This is mine and I'll never share it!"

Consider just how superseding this new teaching of Jesus was and is. Under the Old Testament, the believer thought in terms of *Lex Talionis* and its idea of equity. But then Jesus came and changed everything. Dr. Martyn Lloyd-Jones, who was for thirty years the great pastor of Westminster Chapel in London, preceded that ministry with eleven years in a place called Sandfields in Wales. His wife Bethan tells the story of the remarkable conversion of a man named Mark McCann. McCann was the meanest man in town, and he loved to fight. Although he was sixty years old, he was not known to have ever lost a scuffle. When he would go to a fair, he would always take two friends with him because when he got into a fight he would go so out of his mind that he would kill the other person if his friends did not restrain him. One time his wife fixed his dinner, and the dog got into it while McCann was washing his hands. He took a bread knife, took the dog into the kitchen, and cut his head off. Then that man met Jesus. He was barely literate, and as Bethan Lloyd-Jones tells the story, when he first saw the name of Jesus in Welsh in the Bible, he wept and kissed the name. He was completely changed from a vengeful, hateful, "these-are-my-rights," *Lex Talionis*, law-of-the-jungle sort of man to a man who was loving and kind.

Jesus changes our lives! We no longer consider it our duty to get even. "Eye for eye, tooth for tooth" is fine for the court, but not for our relation to others — even our enemies. Thanks to Jesus, we have let go of our legalistic obsession with fairness. We are glad that Jesus was not fair with us, for if we were to have gotten what was coming to us, it would not have been good. As Jesus' followers we give ourselves to the highest welfare of others, even our enemies. We put up with the sins and insults of others for

Christ's sake and theirs. Though hurt many times before, we refuse to withdraw into the shell of self. We do not run from hurt. We appear weak, but we are strong, for only the most powerful can live a life like this. But the power is not ours, but Christ's.

Everything comes from Christ. Jesus' sayings are hard — in fact, impossible! I am so glad that the Sermon on the Mount is impossible because then we have to depend on Jesus. May the Lord Jesus work in us a surpassing righteousness so that we do not hold on to our rights, so we do not always insist on others being fair to us, so we are willing to be hurt, so we are willing to be vulnerable, because then, just as in the ancient world, people will notice and will come to Jesus.

17

Superseding Love

MATTHEW 5:43-48

In a 1958 issue of *Christian Century*,[1] Dr. Normal Pittenger published "A Critique of C. S. Lewis." Among his criticisms was the accusation that Lewis did not care much for the Sermon on the Mount. In Lewis's "Rejoinder to Dr. Pittenger," he responded:

> As to "caring for" the Sermon on the Mount, if "caring for" here means "liking" or enjoying, I suppose no one "cares for" it. Who can like being knocked flat on his face by a sledge hammer? I can hardly imagine a more deadly spiritual condition than that of a man who can read that passage with tranquil pleasure.[2]

As we would expect from Lewis, it was a perfect comeback. But it is also an accurate statement of how the Sermon on the Mount affects any serious, believing reader. The Beatitudes, carefully examined, descend upon us with eight successively humiliating blows. Perhaps they even make us question the genuineness of our faith. Next come the stunning metaphors of salt and light. Who can say he has fulfilled such a dynamic witness? And if that is not enough, then comes the statement, "Unless your righteousness surpasses that of the Pharisees and the teachers of the law, you will certainly not enter the kingdom of heaven" (v. 20), followed by six stringent illustrations of what our righteousness should be like, each of them incredibly demanding, each impossible in our own strength. Almost every line of the Sermon, taken to heart, will flatten us! It seems impossible!

The classic preacher Alexander Whyte almost lost his arm when he was a little boy. He would have been taken to the hospital to have it amputated if it were not for a neighbor lady who said she would nurse him back to health, and she did. As the arm was healing, Whyte went through intense pain. But the woman would say, "I like the pain. I like the pain . . ." because that meant he had feeling in his arm and it was healing. As a result, when Whyte preached he often would say, "I like the pain. I like the pain."[3] In a similar way we should like the pain of the Sermon on the Mount.

Yes, it can be immensely discouraging, but at the same time there are few portions of Scripture more encouraging than the Sermon on the Mount, for it pays us an immense compliment. The fact that Jesus commands us to live it means that it is possible in some sense. It is possible for all of us to so progressively grow in our faith that all of the characteristics of the Sermon on the Mount become progressively evident in our lives. Jesus believes we can consistently reflect the Sermon's extraordinary level, with his help.

We come now to the Sermon's finale — the great commandment of love (5:43-48). Here our Lord gives instruction for building an expansive love into our lives. It is the most concentrated expression of the Christian love ethic in personal relations found anywhere in the New Testament. And again, though it is initially discouraging, it is ultimately encouraging. How does a believer love others? Jesus typically began by restating the traditional teaching about love.

THE TRADITIONAL TEACHING ABOUT LOVE: LIMITED LOVE (v. 43)

"You have heard that it was said, 'Love your neighbor and hate your enemy'" (v. 43). That was the traditional teaching as the religious establishment understood it and as the man on the street was taught to think. But that is not what the Old Testament actually said. If you look closely at verse 43, you will note that the sole Old Testament quotation is "You shall love your neighbor," a direct quotation from the Septuagint rendering of Leviticus 19:18. The phrase, "and hate your enemy" is not found in the Old Testament. It was added.

Why did the Israelites make such an addition? Primarily because they were convinced that the context of Leviticus 19:18 confines the definition of neighbor to a fellow Israelite, and thus they would not tolerate any extension of the term to anyone else. Moreover, they felt that God's direction of their historic relations with other peoples, such as his command to exterminate the Canaanites and the imprecatory Psalms, supported (even called for!) this hatred of others. What they failed to take into account was the fact that those and similar commands, including the imprecatory Psalms, were judicial — never individual.

Another reason, I think, that they added "and hate your enemy" is the natural human perversity that tends to counter a strong positive statement with a negative counterpart. That is, the sublimely elevated statement "You shall love your neighbor," stated categorically, invites a negative corollary

— "Yeah, and hate your enemy." In adopting this negative teaching, they had to set aside the implications of other Old Testament passages that taught kindness toward one's enemies — passages such as Exodus 23:4, 5:

> *If you come across your enemy's ox or donkey wandering off, be sure to take it back to him. If you see the donkey of someone who hates you fallen down under its load, do not leave it there; be sure you help him with it.*

See also Deuteronomy 22:1-4, and Proverbs 25:21, which Paul quotes in Romans 12:20 as a reason to show love: "If your enemy is hungry, give him food to eat; and if he is thirsty, give him something to drink."

By Jesus' time, this hatred of foreigners was so institutionalized that the Jews thought they were honoring God by despising anyone who was not Jewish. They had come a long way — *down*! The Qumran sect was typical, for they said, "Love the brother; hate the outsider." The standard love in Jesus' day was a limited love. "I will love only my neighbor [fellow Israelite], and I will hate everyone else. It is my duty." Perhaps the local Jerusalem Chamber of Commerce had this motto:

> *Believe as I believe, no more, no less;*
> *That I am right, and no one else, confess;*
> *Feel as I feel, think only as I think;*
> *Eat what I eat, and drink but what I drink;*
> *Look as I look, do always as I do;*
> *Then, and only then, will I fellowship with you.*
> — SOURCE UNKNOWN

Not too many Gentiles were vacationing in Palestine.

THE LORD'S NEW TEACHING ABOUT LOVE: UNLIMITED LOVE (vv. 44-47)

"But I tell you: Love your enemies and pray for those who persecute you" (v. 44). This is supremely radical! "To return evil for good is devilish; to return good for good is human; to return good for evil is divine."[4] That is true! To love an enemy is divine, and to pray for an enemy — a persecutor — is supremely divine! The fact that the text mentions "enemies" (plural) suggests that Jesus means personal enemies who are presently doing us harm. This is amazing teaching. To the man on the street, the mere idea of loving his enemies is absurd and offensive and beyond his capability. It offends his natural sense of right and wrong. To those under the Old Testament Law, the idea of loving one's enemies was completely contrary to their perception of God's Law, which they thought required rejection and hatred of enemies — a limited love.

Jesus commanded a love without limits, that loves everyone regardless of what they say or do to us. This is revolutionary, whatever one's culture. In fact, if practiced by you and me, it would change our entire community. We will return to this verse in a moment, but first let us find out why Jesus ordered us to love like this. He gives us two reasons.

The first, recorded in verse 45, is that it makes us like God: "that you may be sons of your Father in heaven [which is the Hebrew way of saying that you will be like your heavenly Father]. He causes his sun to rise on the evil and the good, and sends rain on the righteous and the unrighteous." In other words, if you impartially show love to your enemies as well as to friends, you will be like God, who shows the impartiality of his love by sending the sun and rain on both the righteous and unrighteous. A certain Rabbi Joshua ben Nehemiah noticed this and wrote, "Have you ever noticed that the rain fell on the field of A, who was righteous, and not on the field of B, who was wicked? Or that the sun rose and shone on Israel, who was righteous, and not upon the Gentiles who were wicked? God causes the sun to shine both on Israel and on the nations, for the Lord is good to all."[5] When we love without limits, we are like God.

The second reason for such love is that it distinguishes us from the world. Our Lord gave a negative example to make his point: "If you love those who love you, what reward will you get? Are not even the tax collectors doing that?" (v. 46). No one could miss the point of Jesus' example. Tax collectors may have it bad today, but it is nothing like the reputation they had in Jesus' time. The Roman Empire used a tax system in which the government would designate how much money was to be collected from a specific area, then hire a man to collect it. Each tax gatherer had to turn in that amount but could keep whatever else he could get. Tax gatherers were crooks, rich crooks, and they were loathed by everyone — especially the Jews, because the collectors were employees of the Gentiles. Jesus' point is that even those disgusting, double-crossing tax collectors loved their own tax-gathering buddies! So if a person loves only his friends, he is doing no better than a swindling tax collector. So you love your friends who reciprocate your love — big deal! Jesus underscored his point with his next statement in verse 47: "And if you greet only your brothers, what are you doing more than others? Do not even pagans do that?"

In other words, followers of Jesus should do *more* than what is common among nonbelievers in the way they show love. It is this "more" that is the distinctive quality of the Christian's love. Dr. Lloyd-Jones expresses it like this:

> We can emphasize that by putting it like this. The Christian is the man who is above, and goes beyond, the natural man at his very best and highest. . . . There are many people in the world who are not Christian but

> who are very moral and highly ethical, men whose word is their bond, and who are scrupulous and honest, just and upright. You never find them doing a shady thing to anybody; but they are not Christian, and they say so. They do not believe on the Lord Jesus Christ and may have rejected the whole of the New Testament teaching with scorn. But they are absolutely straightforward, honest and true. . . . Now the Christian, by definition here, is a man who is capable of doing something that the best natural man cannot do. He goes beyond and does more than that; he exceeds. He is separate from all others, and not only from the worst among others, but from the very best and highest among them.[6]

The question we must each ask is, is there a "more" in my love? Is there something about my love that cannot be explained in natural terms? Is there something special and unique about my love to others that is not present in the life of the unbeliever? These are important questions because if there is not a "more" to our love, if we love only those with whom we have something in common and who treat us well, if there is nothing more than that, we are perhaps not Christians at all. Notice, I did not say we must perfectly exhibit the "more" of his love. But is there a "more"? The call is to practice unlimited love.

PRACTICING UNLIMITED LOVE (v. 44)

We must love our enemies. "But I tell you: Love your enemies." How are we to do this? We must first notice that Jesus does not ask us here, nor has he ever asked us, to love our enemies in the same way that we love our loved ones — our nearest and dearest. There are people for whom we have a spontaneous, natural, instinctive love. We do not have to make any effort to love them — we just do. Jesus is not asking us to have a romantic love or a buddy love or a family love or an emotional love for our enemies. What he commands is an *agape* love — that is, a deliberate, intelligent, determined love — an invincible goodwill toward them.

The best illustration I know of to explain what Jesus is talking about comes from the life of one of my wife's dearest friends. She and her family had just returned from the mission field and had rented a rather nice townhouse — at least it was very nice compared to what they'd had on the mission field. She is a very creative person and did a wonderful job of decorating the place, and they settled in. Only one thing was wrong — the family who moved in next door. They turned the front yard into a desert, broke the windows out of their house, were always using foul language, urinated in the front yard, and generally caused havoc in the neighborhood. The final straw was when one of the boys climbed into our friends' yard and threw a whole can of orange paint over the patio walls. My wife's friend was really angry.

She did not like her neighbors. She was not happy with the Lord for putting her where he had put her. Realizing that her heart was not right, she got down on her knees and said, "Lord, you know that I do not like these people at all. God, help me to love them." She did not feel any different, but she resolved to exercise love. She baked her neighbors a pie and took it to them, thus beginning a caring relationship. Those neighbors did not change, but she did. She had begun to love them. When those neighbors moved away, she wept. What an example of intelligent, volitional love that says, "I will love by the grace of Christ within me."

C. S. Lewis wrote in *Mere Christianity*:

> The rule for all of us is perfectly simple. Do not waste your time bothering whether you "love" your neighbor; act as if you did. As soon as we do this we find one of the great secrets. When you are behaving as if you loved someone, you will presently come to love him. If you injure someone you dislike, you will find yourself disliking him more. If you do him a good turn, you will find yourself disliking him less. . . . The difference between a Christian and worldly man is not that the worldly man has only affections or "likings" and the Christian has only "charity." The worldly man treats certain people kindly because he "likes" them; the Christian, trying to treat every one kindly, finds himself liking more and more people as he goes on — including people he could not even have imagined himself liking at the beginning.[7]

That is something of the "more" that makes the true believer different from the world. It is within reach of everyone who is indwelt by the Spirit of Christ. If you are a believer, you can do it. If you are a believer, you are commanded to love like this. Where do you need to show the "more"?

The first command is to love our enemies. The second is to "pray for those who persecute you" (v. 44). This, too, is an exceedingly high call, taking us to the pinnacle of selfless love. Jesus is our greatest example, for while he was being crucified, possibly even while the nails were being driven through his hands, he prayed repeatedly (as the Greek imperfect tense indicates), "Father, forgive them, for they do not know what they are doing" (Luke 23:34). When you pray for someone while they are persecuting you, you are assaulting the throne of God on their behalf: "God, help this person." That is supernatural! If you do that, you are walking in the heavenlies with Jesus. One of the benefits of praying for our enemies is that it changes *us*. It is impossible to go on praying for another without loving him or her. Those for whom we truly pray will become objects of our conscious love.

18

Christianity Without Hypocrisy

MATTHEW 6:1-8

The Russian author Turgenev wrote, "I do not know what the heart of a bad man is like, but I do know what the heart of a good man is like, and it is terrible."

The Sermon on the Mount exposes the state of the heart of the believer. First, the Beatitudes (vv. 3-12) provide us with a description of the ideal character of the true believer. Then after two convicting metaphors (vv. 13-16) we are given six illustrations of the surpassing righteousness to which we are called (vv. 20-48), a righteousness that supersedes and fulfills that of the scribes and Pharisees — and indeed that of the Old Testament. This exposé of the heart brings us to an honest admission of what we really are, and it is not a pretty picture.

However, that is ultimately good because seeing ourselves as we are opens us up to God's grace. That is precisely the significance of the first Beatitude: "Blessed are the poor in spirit [the spiritually bankrupt who realize they have nothing to commend them to God], for theirs is the kingdom of heaven" (5:3). When we see our spiritual wretchedness, we are candidates for spiritual greatness. Or as Pascal said, "Man is great insofar as he is wretched."

Expanding this positive perspective, we should notice that the Sermon on the Mount not only exposes the believer's heart but defines it. None of us completely meets the standard of the Sermon on the Mount. But at the same time, if we are true believers, something of the character of the kingdom, something of each of the Beatitudes, will be authentically present in our lives — spiritual poverty, humility, spiritual thirst, mercy, peacemaking. Along with this, there will be the presence of the surpassing righteousness of Christ. We may fall at times, but we will practice righteousness. Anger, adulterous thoughts, insincere talk, and retaliation will progressively vanish from our lives. *Agape* love will become characteristic of us. When we are filled with the Holy Spirit and with his Word, including the explicit teaching of the Sermon on the Mount, we will practice righteousness.

However, *this is where the danger lies*. For once you begin to fulfill the righteousness of God, once you are flying spiritually, once you are living a life full of good deeds, it is very easy to begin "do[ing] your 'acts of righteousness' before men, to be seen by them."

JESUS' WARNING TO THE RIGHTEOUS (v. 1)

Being well aware of our danger, Jesus issued a warning at the beginning of chapter 6: "Be careful not to do your 'acts of righteousness' before men, to be seen by them. If you do, you will have no reward from your Father in heaven."

In normal, everyday conversation most of us have learned to use absolute words such as *always* and *every* sparingly. We know that statements such as "You always leave your dishes on the table" or "Every time I want to talk to you, you're watching television" or "You always want to be in control" can get us into hot water. This is also true regarding Biblical statements. We must be careful not to absolutize them if they are not absolute. But Jesus' words here *are* absolute. Jesus is saying, "Anyone who does a good deed so as to be seen and appreciated by others will lose his or her reward, no matter how 'good' and beneficial the deed is. Absolutely no exceptions!" It is possible for a believer to take a leper's ulcerated limb in his hands and caress it and gently speak words of comfort and have no reward from God. It is possible to pray for your enemies and have no reward. It is possible to preach like an angel and have no reward. Why? Because it is possible to do all these things for the recognition of men and not of God.

I find this terrifying, for it means that my life, which is ostensibly given to God, can in the end count for nothing. The outwardly most self-effacing saint in our congregation may have all his "good deeds" rejected. Jesus does not want that to happen. He is aware that those who have begun to fulfill his Word can be in great danger. So he gives this advice, supported by two immediate illustrations of the proper motivation in serving him.

JESUS' FIRST ILLUSTRATION: ALMSGIVING (vv. 2-4)

The first of our Lord's illustrations has to do with almsgiving, giving to the needy as an act of mercy (the actual Greek word has within it the root word for mercy). In verse 2 Jesus tells us there is a wrong way to give alms:

> *"So when you give to the needy, do not announce it with trumpets, as the hypocrites do in the synagogues and on the streets, to be honored by men. I tell you the truth, they have received their reward in full."*

The wrong way to give is to blow your own horn, which is precisely what Jesus was saying if he was using symbolic language. If he was speaking of a literal practice, he was probably describing the sound of the temple trumpets that called citizens to come and give. What a great opportunity to show off! The trumpets would blare, and people would be seen scurrying along the streets toward the temple with pious looks on their faces. "Hey, folks, look at *my* zeal! Big giver on the way to the temple here!" They thought they were really something, but Jesus called them "hypocrites." *Actors* was Jesus' idea. They were pretending to be something they were not. They were assuming a false identity, putting on a theatrical display. The truth is, they were not giving for the glory of God, or even for benefit of the needy. They were giving for the praise of men. This abuse is as common today as it was then. I wonder what would happen to our great national charities if there were no celebrity benefits or published subscriber lists or bronze plaques or rooms to be named for major donors or pictures to be taken with crippled children. The same question can be asked of the church, with much the same result. Giving so others will think we are good and generous is hypocrisy!

And the personal result is less than enviable: "I tell you the truth," says Jesus, "they have received their reward in full." Our Lord's language here is decisive, for the word translated "reward" (*apecho*) is a technical term for commercial transactions and means to "receive a sum in full and give a receipt for it."[1] Men's praise is all they will ever get. That is all they are capable of receiving. The truth is, they were not giving but buying, and they got what they paid for. It is possible to be the most generous Christian around, both in the amount and proportion you give, and yet have no reward except what you immediately receive.

Next Jesus describes the right way to be charitable:

> *"But when you give to the needy, do not let your left hand know what your right hand is doing, so that your giving may be in secret. Then your Father, who sees what is done in secret, will reward you." (vv. 3, 4)*

Our Lord uses an extreme, absurd illustration to emphasize the intense privacy that should be present when we give to help others. The right hand is the one we normally use in giving because most of us are right-handed. Thus when we give, our giving must be so hidden that the left hand does not even see what is happening. The idea is, not only are we not to tell others of our giving — we are not to make a big deal of it to ourselves. We are so subtly sinful that we will refrain from an outward show in giving and then pat ourselves on the back for our profound humility. We must guard against this. Do not keep a diary in which you jot down your good deeds, assuming that is so spiritual because you did it privately. Do not keep track. Do not give yourself merit marks. Forget your goodness. Follow God. Do it, and forget it.

What are the guiding principles we can draw from this? The true believer gives and serves to please God — not for the fleeting approval of man. Also, our lives are to be given to uncalculating generosity. And as we help others we must guard our eyes from wandering from those we are helping to the observers.

Regarding this matter of rewards, we are in error if we believe we must never seek rewards. Some think that serving with an eye to a reward is crass and mercenary, even when the reward comes from God. Why not give just to give? Such a view comes from a mistaken understanding. The rewards that God gives are not ribbons or medals but actually something of himself. C. S. Lewis explained it perfectly:

> We must not be troubled by unbelievers when they say that this promise of reward makes the Christian life a mercenary affair. There are different kinds of reward. There is the reward which has no natural connexion with the things you do to earn it, and is quite foreign to the desires that ought to accompany those things. Money is not the natural reward of love; that is why we call a man a mercenary if he marries a woman for the sake of her money. But marriage is the proper reward for a real lover, and he is not mercenary for desiring it. . . . The proper rewards are not simply tacked on to the activity for which they are given, but are the activity itself in consummation.[2]

Men who do works so they will be seen by men receive the applause of men. Those who do works for God's glory receive God's smile. The reward for the latter is overwhelming — and always will be.

JESUS' SECOND ILLUSTRATION: PRAYING (vv. 5-7)

In verse 5, Jesus describes the wrong way to pray:

> *"And when you pray, do not be like the hypocrites, for they love to pray standing in the synagogues and on the street corners to be seen by men. I tell you the truth, they have received their reward in full."*

These hypocrites liked to engage in ostentatious public prayer in two places — at street corners and in the synagogues. Opportunities for their street corner performances came at the time of the daily afternoon temple sacrifice and during public fasts when the trumpets were blown as a sign that it was time to pray. Wherever a devout man was on the street, he stopped, faced the temple, and prayed. It was a perfect opportunity to let everybody see your stuff. You could time your afternoon stroll so that when the trumpet sounded, you were on a very prominent corner where you could lift your hands and pray for all to hear — just as the Pharisee did in Luke 18:11, 12:

> *"God, I thank you that I am not like other men — robbers, evildoers, adulterers — or even like this tax collector. I fast twice a week and give a tenth of all I get."*

Synagogue prayer was led by a member of the congregation who stood before the Ark of the Law, raised his hands, and held forth. It was easy to become preachy, using all the right clichés, dramatic pauses, and voice variations to impress the crowd. The ecclesiastic exhibitionists loved it!

But Jesus had other ideas.

> *"But when you pray, go into your room, close the door and pray to your Father, who is unseen. Then your Father, who sees what is done in secret, will reward you."* (v. 6)

Jesus was not condemning public prayer. He was condemning the desire to be *seen* praying publicly. The early church thrived on public prayer, as the opening chapters of Acts so beautifully attest (see 1:24; 3:1; 4:24ff.). Jesus was emphasizing that prayer is essentially a conversation between the believer and God. It is intrinsically private, not exhibitionist. Man is to shut out every distraction and focus on God. In verse 7 Jesus added further advice: "And when you pray, do not keep on babbling like pagans, for they think they will be heard because of their many words." Our Lord was not and is not impressed with a lot of words. He is impressed with what the *heart* is saying.

This comes right down to where we live. Our Lord shows us here just how terrible and entrenched our sin is. We tend to regard sin as something that affects us when we are far away from God, like the prodigal son. But sin is far more subtle and ingrained than that. It intrudes into the very highest and holiest of acts. It is understood by all that when believers are engaged in prayer, that is the ultimate activity in which their souls can be engaged. A telling photograph of sin is that of someone on his knees in prayer pouring his soul out to God in worship, only to have the prayer dissolve into preoccupation with self so that he is really worshiping himself. Sadly, innumerable prayers, public and private, never rise beyond self.

James Montgomery Boice abandoned his characteristic optimism on one occasion when he told his congregation:

> I believe that not one prayer in a hundred of those that fill our churches on a Sunday morning is actually made to Almighty God, the Father of our Lord Jesus Christ. They are made to men or to the praying one himself, and that includes the prayers of preachers as well as those of the members of the congregation.[3]

Even if this statement is only partially correct, we all need to do what we can to keep our own prayers free from vain repetition and self-promotion. Our responsibility is not to monitor our brother's and sister's prayer life but our own.

Perhaps a few questions would help us. Do I pray frequently or more fervently when I am alone with God than when I am in public? Is my public praying an overflow of my private prayer? What do I think of when I am praying in public? Am I looking for "just the right" phrase? Am I thinking of the worshipers more than of God? Am I a spectator to my own performance? Is it possible that the reason more of my prayers are not answered is because I am more concerned about bringing my prayer to men than to God?[4]

We can be sure that Jesus meant exactly what he said: "Be careful not to do your 'acts of righteousness' before men, to be seen by them. If you do, you will have no reward from your Father in heaven" (v. 1).

When we honestly face the truth of this, it is sobering, even terrifying. When we do works of mercy, do we play to the crowd, however small it may be? When we pray, do we pray to God or to men? Asking ourselves these questions can be painful. But I am also reminded of Pascal's paradox: "Man is great insofar as he is wretched." If we see our problem in all its wretchedness, then we are in a position to receive grace.

What is the answer? First, absolute honesty. Second, we need to remember that God sees all. The psalmist in Psalm 139 says, "If I make my way to the heavens, you are there; if I make my bed in the depths, you are there" (v. 8). He sees and knows all. He knows the words that are forming on our lips. Each day we should pray something like this: "God, because you know all things, you know my motivations. God, help me to live my life for you."

Martyn Lloyd-Jones writes:

> He is everywhere. "Take heed that ye do not your righteousness before men." Why? "Else ye have no reward with your Father which is in heaven." He sees it all. He knows your heart; other people do not. You can deceive them, and you can persuade them that you are quite selfless; but God knows your heart. . . I sometimes feel that there is no better way of living, and

trying to live, the holy and sanctified life than just to be constantly reminding ourselves of that. When we wake up in the morning we should immediately remind ourselves and recollect that we are in the presence of God. It is not a bad thing to say to ourselves before we go any further: "Throughout the whole of this day, everything I do, and say, and attempt, and think, and imagine, is going to be done under the eye of God. He is going to be with me; He sees everything; He knows everything. There is nothing I can do or attempt but God is fully aware of it all. 'Thou God seest me.'" It would revolutionize our lives if we always did that.[5]

19

The Lord's Prayer: The Father

MATTHEW 6:9

The Lord's Prayer has been and remains the greatest prayer of the church. The church's greatest minds have consistently treated it so and have used it to preach thousands of sermons on prayer and basic Christian doctrine. In the early church such notables as Origen, Gregory of Nyssa, Tertullian, Cyril of Jerusalem, and Cyprian published expositions of the Lord's Prayer. Later the greatest of the ancient theologians, Augustine, followed suit. Dante devoted the eleventh canto of the *Purgatorio* to the Lord's Prayer. Meister Eckhart, the medieval Dominican mystic and theologian, used the categories of the Lord's Prayer to sum up scholastic theology. Martin Luther preached a volume of exposition on the Lord's Prayer. And the famous *Westminster Catechism* of the Presbyterian churches bases its last nine questions on the Lord's Prayer.[1] The Lord's Prayer is without a doubt the greatest prayer of the Christian church.

Because this great prayer has been called the Lord's Prayer for almost 2,000 years, it would be futile to attempt to change its name, though the best title would be "the Disciples' Prayer" because that is what it really is. At the disciples' request (Luke 11:1), Jesus provided it for them as a pattern for prayer. Strictly speaking, it is a prayer that the sinless Christ could never pray in its entirety because the last part includes a petition for the forgiveness of sins: "Forgive us our debts, as we also have forgiven our debtors." But the prayer's six petitions are absolutely perfect for every man or woman who has ever lived. Its initial focus is upward, with its first three requests having to do with God's glory. The remaining three requests are for our well-being.

God first, man second — that is the ideal order of prayer. His glory before our wants. This is parallel to the Ten Commandments, the first four of which have to do with God's glory and the last six with man's well-being. This prayer is the perfect prayer. Of its perfection Bonhoeffer said, "The Lord's Prayer is not merely the pattern prayer, it is the way Christians must pray. . . . The Lord's Prayer is the quintessence of prayer."[2]

It is the perfect pattern for the followers of Christ, and its depth cannot be exhausted by exposition. No matter how one advances in the matter of prayer, it remains the model and the challenge.

Sadly, it is more often mindlessly repeated than genuinely prayed. This is especially ironic because the context that introduces the Lord's Prayer in Matthew 6:7, 8 warns against meaningless repetition. "And when you pray," Jesus says, "do not keep on babbling like pagans" ("do not use meaningless repetition," NASB). The obvious problem for all of us is that "familiarity breeds contempt," in this case "surface familiarity." Some of us learned the Lord's Prayer at our mother's knees. We cannot count the times we have repeated it. We said it again and again as children. We repeat it today as adults. But there is a danger in our familiarity with its beauty — it can become just beautiful words, so that we "say" the Lord's Prayer without praying it.

Some who live in the mountains of Colorado rarely see the incredible scenery that occupies their every glance, while flatlanders like me travel a thousand miles just to see the mountains' beauty for a few days — and we really see them! Those who have been dulled to beauty need to see things in a new way, and in respect to the Lord's Prayer we may need to see it anew — not necessarily discovering new truth, but seeing the old truth for what it is. An in-depth study of the Lord's Prayer can help us pray with greater singleness and greater power, just as it has done for thousands through the centuries.

"OUR FATHER"

That God should be personally addressed as "Father" may not seem out of the ordinary to those of us who frequent the church and regularly repeat the Lord's Prayer, but it was absolutely revolutionary in Jesus' day. The writers of the Old Testament certainly believed in the Fatherhood of God, but they saw it mainly in terms of a sovereign Creator-Father. In fact, God is only referred to as Father fourteen times in the Old Testament's thirty-nine books, and even then rather impersonally. In those fourteen occurrences of *Father* the term was always used with reference to the nation, not to individuals. You can search from Genesis to Malachi, and you will not find one individual speaking of God as Father. Moreover, in Jesus' day, his contemporaries had so focused on the sovereignty and transcendence of God that they were careful never to repeat his covenant name — Yahweh. So they invented the word *Jehovah*, a combination of two separate names of God. Thus the distance from God was well guarded.

But when Jesus came on the scene, he addressed God only as Father. He never used anything else! All his prayers address God as Father. The Gospels (just four books) record his using *Father* more than sixty times in reference to God. So striking is this that there are scholars who maintain that this word *Father* dramatically summarizes the difference between the Old and New Testaments. No one had ever in the entire history of Israel spoken and prayed like Jesus. No one!

But this amazing fact is only part of the story, for the word Jesus used for *Father* was not a formal word, but the common Aramaic word with which a child would address his father — the word *Abba*. The German New Testament scholar Joachim Jeremias, perhaps the most respected New Testament scholar of his generation, has argued convincingly that *Abba* was the original word on Jesus' lips here in the Lord's Prayer and indeed in all of his prayers in the New Testament, with the exception of Matthew 27:46 when he cried out from the cross, "My God, my God, why have you forsaken me?" But there, Jeremias explains, Jesus was quoting Psalm 22:1.[3] Of course, Jesus reverted to *Father* with his final words before his death: "Father, into your hands I commit my spirit" (Luke 23:45, quoting Psalm 31:5). The word *Abba* was the word Jesus regularly used to address his father Joseph from the time he was a baby until Joseph's death. Everyone used the word. But as a careful examination of the literature of that day shows, it was never used of God — under any circumstances. *Abba* meant something like Daddy — but with a more reverent touch than when we use it. The best rendering is "Dearest Father."

To the traditional Jew, Jesus' prayer was revolutionary. Think of it! God was referred to only fourteen times in the Old Testament as Father, and then it was always as the corporate Father of Israel — never individually or personally. And now as his disciples ask him for instruction on how to pray, Jesus tells them to begin by calling God their Father, their *Abba*! As Jeremias says:

> . . . in the Lord's Prayer Jesus authorizes His disciples to repeat the word *abba* after Him. He gives them a share in His sonship and empowers them, as His disciples, to speak with their heavenly Father in just such a familiar, trusting way as a child would with his father.[4]

When we say *Abba* today in our prayers, as we sometimes do, we are making the same sound that actually fell from Jesus' lips — and from the lips of his incredulous disciples. Jesus transferred the Fatherhood of God from a theological doctrine into an intense, practical experience, and he taught his disciples to pray with the same intimacy. And that is what he does for us. "Our Father" — "Our Abba" — "Our dearest Father" — this is to be the foundational awareness of all our prayers. Does it undergird your prayer life? Is a sense of God's intimate Fatherhood profound and growing in your life?

Addressing God as *Abba* (Dearest Father) is not only an indication of spiritual health but is a mark of the authenticity of our faith. Paul tells us in Galatians 4:6, "Because you are sons, God sent the Spirit of his Son into our hearts, the Spirit who calls out, 'Abba, Father!'" The impulse to call on God in this way is a sign of being God's child. Romans 8:15, 16 says the same thing: "you received the spirit of sonship. And by him we cry, 'Abba, Father!' The Spirit himself testifies with our spirit that we are God's children." True believers are impelled to say this.

This is precisely what happened to me when I came to faith during the summer before my freshman year in high school. Before that I had a cool theological idea of the universal paternity of God as the Creator of all mankind. His Fatherhood was there, but it was not personal. But with my conversion, God became warm and personal. I now knew God, and I knew he was my Father! This realization is one of the great and primary works of the Holy Spirit. He makes Christians realize with increasing clarity the meaning of their filial relationship with God in Christ. He keeps enhancing this "spirit of sonship" in us and is ever integrating it into our lives.

Do you know that God is your Father? Do you think of him and address him as your "Dearest Father"? If you cannot answer in the affirmative, it may be that he is not your spiritual Father and you need to heed the words of Scripture and come into relationship with him through Christ. "Yet to all who received him [Christ], to those who believed in his name, he gave the right to become children of God" (John 1:12).

Dr. J. I. Packer considers one's grasp of God's Fatherhood and one's adoption as a son or daughter as of essential importance to spiritual life. He writes:

> If you want to judge how well a person understands Christianity, find out how much he makes of the thought of being God's child, and having God as his Father. If this is not the thought that prompts and controls his worship and prayers and his whole outlook on life, it means that he does not understand Christianity very well at all. For everything that Christ taught, everything that makes the New Testament new, and better than the Old, everything that is distinctively Christian as opposed to merely Jewish, is summed up in the knowledge of the Fatherhood of God. "Father" is the Christian name for God.[5]

That God is our *Abba*-Father is a truth we must cultivate for the sake of our soul's health.

The child-*Abba* understanding brings wholeness to spiritual life. First, it brings a sense of being loved. Missionary Everett Fullam was a missionary to a remote tribe of people in the interior of Nigeria. The tribe was so isolated that it had never heard the word *Africa*, must less *America*. They had a pagan, prescientific view of creation, so simplistic that when Fullam mentioned to the chief the then-recent phenomenon of two Americans walking on the moon, the old chief looked hard into Fullam's face, then up at the moon, and exclaimed in an angry tone, "There's nobody up there! Besides, it is not big enough for two people to stand on." The old chief meant it. He had absolutely no idea of the size of the moon or its distance from the earth. But there in the forgotten wilds of west Africa, Fullam had a memorable experience that drove home to him what it means to know God as Father. He baptized three people who had come to know the love of the Father through faith in Jesus Christ, and Fullam describes the experience this way:

> There were two men and one woman. We stood on the banks of a muddy river, wet and happy. I had never seen three more joyful people. "What is the best thing about this experience?" I asked. All three continued to smile, the glistening water emphasizing the brightness of their dark-skinned faces; but only one spoke, in clear, deliberate English: "Behind this universe stands one God, not a great number of warring spirits, as we had always believed, but one God. And that God loves me."[6]

How beautiful! Separated by millennia of cultural development, men and women through faith in Christ found the same spirit of adoption and sense of God's fatherly love that we have found. Those three Africans prayed "Our Father" and experienced the same sense of love that we know.

Next, the sense of God's Fatherhood helps drive home the reality of our forgiveness. It is significant that the first word to fall from the prodigal son's lips when he returned home was "Father": "Father, I have sinned against heaven and against you" (Luke 15:21). And those words were followed by forgiveness. The more deep-seated our sense of God's Fatherhood, the deeper will be our sense of forgiveness — the wholeness that comes from being loved and being forgiven.

Knowing God as Father also brings confidence, security, and wholeness into our lives. When I was a young father and my children were small, my younger son hid on top of the refrigerator one day. As I walked by, with no warning, he suddenly dove off the refrigerator onto my back. I did not see him, I did not feel him coming, but he just tackled me and held on. Carey felt that if he jumped in the direction of his father, he would certainly be safe. It never occurred to him that I would not catch him. And that is the way it is with our *Abba*, our heavenly Father. He gives us a great sense of security and confidence — and we know he will not disappoint us.

So the idea that God is our Father, our *Abba*, is not only a sign of our spiritual health and of the authenticity of our faith, it is one of the most healing doctrines in all of Scripture. Some grew up only with a mother and no father. Others grew up in conventional homes where the relationship with the father was negative at best. But whatever our background, we need the touch of a father, and our God wants to provide that. Some of us need to bow before God and simply say, "Dearest Father, *Abba*" and so find the wholeness and healing that he wants to give us.

"*OUR FATHER* IN HEAVEN"

As we have seen, Jesus' use of *Father* and *Abba* to address God was revolutionary because Jewish theology of the time stressed the transcendence and sovereignty of God. The problem among some evangelical Christians today is the opposite — they have sentimentalized God's fatherhood so much that they have little concept of his holiness. Many Christians are flippantly sentimental about God, as if he is a celestial teddy bear. Such flip familiarity outwardly suggests super-intimacy with God but actually hides a defective knowledge of God.

Jesus provides the remedy to both errors with his opening words, "Our Father in heaven." "Father" stresses his immanence — that is, that he is involved in our lives and is to be intimately approached as *Abba*. "In heaven" stresses God's transcendence. Sovereign and reigning, he surpasses all that is human. He is our Father and our King! We can affectionately call him "Abba," "Dearest Father," but we do it with a deep sense of wonder and reverence.

He is our Father, but he exceeds our earthly fathers in every way because he is "our Father in heaven." He always understands. He is always caring and loving. He never forgets us. And he always comes through for us.

I well remember the day that one of my boys came in with his little buddy Greggie Salazar, saying, "You can beat up Mr. Salazar, can't you, Dad? Greggie says you can't." He kept repeating this while I kept saying, "Now don't talk so loud — shh!" I didn't want Mr. Salazar to hear. Every boy *knows* his father is the strongest. There is no doubt about our heavenly Father because he is "our Father in heaven." He exceeds all of our earthly fathers' virtues a billion-fold. Oh, what tenderness and power the opening lines of the Lord's Prayer evoke!

"OUR *FATHER*"

The prayer begins with the word "Our" — "Our Father." While it is okay and beneficial to say "My Father, My dear Father," Jesus purposely said, "Our" because he wanted to stress the identity that God's Fatherhood brings. When we pray the Lord's Prayer, we are affirming that all of us who are Christians are brothers and sisters, and that if we love God, we will love one another. There is no place in God's family for the much-glorified American individualism that says, "I do not need anyone else — and they do not need me." "Our Father" calls us not only upward but outward to minister to our brothers and sisters. The Fatherhood of God enriches life vertically and horizontally. How beautiful his ways and his words are!

All this suggests how we ought to pray. First, we should approach God with confidence. When my children would come to me saying, as my girls sometimes did, "Daddy dear," they made my day. It was (and is) my delight to do anything for them within reason. Brothers and sisters, God delights to answer our prayers. We can be confident as we come to him.

Second, we must pray with simplicity. God does not ask for eloquent rhetoric from his children — just simple, direct, heart-felt conversation. Let us honor him with our simplicity.

Last, we ought to pray with love. The words "Dearest Father," "*Abba* Father" are words of love, and our prayer ought to overflow with love. "Our Father who is in heaven, we love you."

20

The Lord's Prayer: The Name

MATTHEW 6:9

Those who have the occasion to visit Hawaii learn a new word, if they do not already know it. The word is *haoli*, the word Hawaiians use for those from the mainland. Though often used without any malice, it can be used with withering disdain. Alice Kaholuoluna gives us the derivation of the term:

> Before the missionaries came, my people used to sit outside their temples for a long time meditating and preparing themselves before entering. Then they would virtually creep to the altar to offer their petition and afterwards would again sit a long time outside, this time to "breathe life" into their prayers. The Christians, when they came, just got up, uttered a few sentences, said Amen and were done. For that reason my people call them haolis, "without breath," or those who fail to breathe life into their prayers.[1]

In its original sense *haoli* was a term of biting religious reproach. Just how deserved it was is subject to question because missionaries often get a bum rap from their would-be converts and from unsympathetic historians. However that may be, *haoli* well describes the condition of multitudes of today's Christians who live life in the fast lane — dashing into God's presence, uttering some empty conventionalities, pausing to make a few requests (unless they are *really* in trouble!), then stepping back into the rush. This problem is extensive, undoubtedly one of the great sins of modern Christianity. We are spiritual *haolis* if we do not take time to breathe life into our prayers.

The remedy for this is found in Christ's pattern for prayer as he gave it to the disciples in what we call "The Lord's Prayer." The foundational awareness that the opening words — "Our Father in heaven" — impose on us demands that we take time to breathe life into our prayers. We are praying to "our Father," an ascription that was only made possible by the Lord Jesus, who broke with all tradition and called God his Father.

Moreover, the word he used was *Abba*, the Aramaic word for "dearest father" — a term of deepest intimacy. Perhaps even more cause for amazement is that he enjoined his followers to pray in the same way — "our Father." To the traditional Jew, this was incomprehensible. How could any mortal address deity in such a way? But that was the foundational awareness that Jesus advocated.

The other part of that basic awareness is the rest of the balancing clause, "who is *in heaven*." Though God is our Father, he is also transcendent and sovereign. He is both our Father and our King and is to be approached intimately, but with deepest awe and respect. Such an awareness is the remedy for the breathless impiety of so many twentieth-century Christians. We would do well to follow the custom of saints who have gone before us and prepare ourselves before prayer by reflecting on the One to whom we are going to speak. If we think about him, his Fatherhood, his omnipresence, his omniscience, his love, it will make a great difference in the way we pray.

Having considered the *foundational awareness* contained in the words, "Our Father in heaven," we now move to the *foundational petition*: "Hallowed be your name." As we have seen, the prayer is divided into six petitions. Three are for God — "your name," "your kingdom," "your will." And three are for us — "Give us," "forgive us," "lead us not . . . but deliver us." God intends for this foundational petition — "Hallowed be your name" — to interpret and control what follows.

THE UPWARD, GODWARD ASPECT OF THE FOUNDATIONAL PETITION

It is highly significant that this first, foundational petition is upward — "Hallowed be your name." The God-given order for prayer is to have regard for God first. To be sure, there are times when prayer in regard to our own needs is all we can do, as when Peter cried, "Lord, save me!" (Matthew 14:30) as he was sinking below the waves. That was not the time for worship! Worship came soon afterward, however. To insist that all prayers must begin with the pattern of the Lord's Prayer is in fact a denial of what "Our Father" means to us. We can come to him any time with any need. Nevertheless, prayer normally begins with a loving upward rush of the heart to God.

The meaning of "hallowed be your name" rests on two words — "hallowed" and "name." We will consider "name" first. Today names don't mean much more to us than convenient labels to identify people by. We commonly say, "A rose is a rose by any other name" or "a thorn is a thorn by any other name." We rarely even think about what a name means when we name our children. Our biggest concern is that the name be euphonious or that it honor some relative. But for the Jew a name was anything but a convenient label because names were considered to indicate character. This especially applied to the name of God. The psalmist said, "Some trust in chariots and some in horses, but we trust in the name [the character] of the LORD our God" (20:7). God's names revealed aspects of his being. For instance, Jehovah Shalom — "The Lord Our Peace" — was a name that Gideon hallowed by raising an altar to God by that name. Jehovah Jireh — "the Lord will provide" — was the name by which Abraham came to know God on Mt. Moriah when God provided a ram in place of Isaac. Jehovah Tsidkenu — "the Lord our Righteousness" — is the name by which God revealed himself to Jeremiah during the Captivity. The list of God's names in the Old Testament is quite long, including Jehovah-nissi, El Shaddai, El Elyon, Adonai, and all reflect his character. The book *Names by Which We May Praise the Lord* by GenEva Carlburg is full of names with which the author praised the Lord in prayer. What is the name that is prominent in the Lord's Prayer? Very simply but profoundly it is "Father" — "*Abba* Father" — "Dearest Father."

What does it mean to *hallow* God's name? The root word means "to set apart as holy," "to consider holy," "to treat as holy." The best alternate term is reverence. "May you be given that unique reverence that your character and nature as Father demand." St. Chrysostom had the same idea when he said it included the idea of honor, and Calvin agreed, saying it called for the greatest veneration.[2]

This petition that God's name as "Dear Father" be made holy or be reverenced has two distinct times in mind. First, eternity when in a final event his Fatherhood will be fully revealed before all creation. The aorist tense makes this primary, as Ernst Lohmeyer shows in his book *Our Father*.[3] Second, the Father's name is be hallowed in the present fallen age. This is exactly what Jesus did as he told the Father about his own ministry in John 17:25, 26a: "O righteous Father, although the world has not known You, yet I have known You; and these have known that You sent Me; and I have made Your name known to them, and will make it known" (NASB). Jesus manifested the *Abba*-Fatherhood of God.

So the divinely given pattern for prayer is first upward to God, not outward to mankind or inward to our needs. The modern mind, which never truly thinks of God first, cannot make anything out of these words, for they sweep the soul upward past what we can touch and taste to the adoration of

God. "*Abba*, Father, may your name as Father be reverenced among men now and at the end of time — for all eternity!"

Does this petition simply focus upward, leaving our faces pointing toward the sky? Does it have nothing to do with our life and walk now? Indeed it does.

THE MANWARD ASPECT OF THE FOUNDATIONAL PETITION

In one of the questions of his Greater Catechism (*Grosser Katechismus*) Martin Luther asked: "How is it [God's name] hallowed amongst us?" Answer: "When our life and doctrine are truly Christian." God's name as Father is reverenced when we lead lives that reflect his Fatherhood. We cannot truly pray "Hallowed be your name" without dedicating ourselves to him. If we pray this without commitment, it is just idle talk. Jesus himself is the example *par excellence*. As the cross grew near, he prayed, "Father, glorify your name" (John 12:28), but he knew what that meant in terms of his own commitment. He gave his own life so the Father's name would be glorified.

How then do we, God's children, hallow his name in our own lives? There are at least four ways: First, negatively, we are careful not to profane God's name with our mouths. We avoid swearing or taking his name in vain. We speak of him with great reverence. This is perhaps the least requiring aspect of hallowing his name. Second, we begin with the positives: We reverence him as Father with acts of public and private worship. I personally consider the morning worship at the church I pastor to be the most important aspect of my life and ministry (apart from my personal devotion). I do not consider my sermon to be the most important part of the service but the worship. Is God's name truly being lifted up? Do the hymns, Scriptures, and prayers lift up his name? We hallow his name when we worship.

There is a third way: We reverence God or hallow his name when our beliefs concerning him are worthy of him. We cannot hallow his name if we do not understand it. Specifically, in the Lord's Prayer we must understand his *Abba*-Fatherhood. The deeper our understanding, the more depth there will be to our reverence. It is all the work of the Holy Spirit, of course, but we must yield to that work. We understand the depth and wonder of saying, "*Abba* Father" only through the Holy Spirit. Is God your Dearest Father?

And fourth, we hallow his name by living a life that displays that he is our Father. This text has been applied in this way for hundreds of years, by men like Cyril, Cyprian, Augustine, Gregory of Nyssa, Martin Luther, John Calvin, and scores of others. Gregory offered this prayer in his exposition:

> May I become through thy help blameless, just and pious, may I abstain from every evil, speak the truth, and do justice. May I walk in the straight path, shining with temperance, adorned with incorruption, beautiful through wisdom and prudence. May I meditate upon the things that are above and despise what is earthly, showing the angelic way of life. . . . For a man can glorify God in no other way save by his virtue which bears witness that the Divine Power is the cause of his goodness.[4]

The reason the Church Fathers so strenuously stressed the quality of one's life is that they lived in a hostile environment, and the only way they could spread Christianity was by living a life of such devotion and certitude that others would thirst for the Father.

For us too this demands that our lives show that we really do have a heavenly Father. It demands that we display security and confidence in our Father when those who do not know Christ are overcome with fears and despair. It demands that we radiate the self-esteem that comes from knowing we are loved by our *Abba*-Father. It demands that we manifest the beautiful loyalty of a child toward his Father in our devotion to God the Father. But there is even more. We are not only to model that we have a Father in heaven — we must also model his fatherliness toward others.

Psychologically speaking (though not denying God's obvious arrangement of my life), I think this is one of the reasons I came so wonderfully to Christ as a child. My father had died when I was four, but at the age of twelve I met a man, a pastor (the one who led me to Christ), who modeled God's Fatherhood to me. He was like God the Father in that he was gentle and patient, like God because he was interested in me, like God because he was willing to be inconvenienced, like God because he cared about the smallest details in my life, and like the heavenly Father because he was concerned about what was best for me and believed in me. When I met a man like that after being without a father for eight years, I was ready to go to God as *Abba*. It is no wonder that when I came to Jesus at the age of twelve, "Dearest Father" became the refrain of my heart.

Luther was right. We best hallow God's name when our life and our doctrine are truly Christian. When we pray, "Our Father in heaven, hallowed be your name," we are dedicating ourselves to lead lives that reverence all that he is.

A friend of mine once told me about one of the most memorable days in his life. His newly-adopted five-year-old son, who had come from an overseas orphanage, was riding next to him in the car and suddenly placed his hand on his new father's leg and said with great thought, "Father, son." It was a wonderful day for that father, but even more significant for that little boy. The day that you and I come to see that we are truly "Father, son" or "Father, daughter" is certainly one of the banner days of our lives.

Let's not be *haolis* — those who fail to breathe life into their prayers. Let's learn to take time to reflect on the great foundational realities of true prayer, especially the truth that God is our dear Father. Let's take the time to breathe it in.

From a foundational awareness comes our foundational petition, "Hallowed be your name as *Abba*-Father."

God, may all historical differences and language vanish as all men bow to you as Father in the consummation of all things. And, God, may our lives hallow your name. May others see that we live as your children. May others find us to be fathers like you. Our Father who is in heaven, hallowed be your name. Amen.

21

"Your Kingdom Come"

MATTHEW 6:10A

As we have seen, the opening line of the Lord's Prayer, "Our Father in heaven," provides us with the foundational awareness with which all prayer should be offered. Healthy, God-pleasing prayer begins with the blessed realization that God is our "*Abba*-Father" — our Dearest Father. This foundational awareness leads to the foundational petition, "Hallowed be your name" — "Hallowed be your name as *Abba*-Father." Anyone who begins his or her prayer with this sublime upward realization and petition will pray in a manner that is pleasing to the Father.

With this in mind, we now take up the second petition, "your kingdom come" (v. 10a), which extends the upward rush of the prayer. In fact, the Hebrew thought structure here demands that we understand both "your kingdom come" and "your will be done" as enlargements on "hallowed be your name." The proper hallowing of God's name as Father includes praying that his kingdom will come and his will be done. Prayer for the kingdom is to be part of the pattern of our prayer life.

Over the years conflicting interpretations have been given to the meaning of "your kingdom come." Some have argued this is a prayer for the Second Coming of Christ and that is all — it has nothing to do with present life. Others have seen "your kingdom come" as a call to social action and nothing else — a mandate to bring in the kingdom now through good works. And then there are those who have seen "your kingdom come" as spiritually fulfilled in the salvation of souls. Actually the correct interpretation and application contains elements of all these views.

"YOUR KINGDOM COME" RECOGNIZES THE PAST

Praying "your kingdom come" does not suggest in any way that God has not been or is not presently sovereign King, that his reign is only future. "As He is already holy so He is already King, reigning in absolute sovereignty over both nature and history."[1] "The earth is the LORD's, and everything in it, the world, and all who live in it" (Psalm 24:1). God is already King, and his kingdom spans the entire universe. "Your kingdom come" is a call for a new and unique manifestation of his kingdom in the future.

"YOUR KINGDOM COME" IS FOR THE FUTURE

Though God is already King, his reign is also future. The verb "come" refers here to a decisive time in the future when the kingdom will come once and for all — an event that will happen only once.[2] This event is the second advent of Christ when he will return, judge the world, and set up his eternal kingdom. This idea in the Greek translated "your kingdom come" is so strong that Tertullian changed the order of the prayer, placing "your will be done on earth as it is in heaven" before "your kingdom come." He reasoned that after the kingdom came, there would be no need to pray, "your will be done" — everyone would be doing it! Tertullian's reasoning was wrong, but he did accurately understand that "your kingdom come" is a prayer for the final kingdom when, under Christ's rule, our evil hearts will be pure, our lying and deceit, distrust and shame banished, our asylums and penitentiaries gone, and all our words and actions done to the glory of God.

Men and women have longed for this since the Fall. We yearn for the time when there will be "righteousness, peace and joy in the Holy Spirit" as Paul describes the kingdom (Romans 14:17). Someone on the outside may say that such thinking is utopian, and in the general sense of the word they may be right. But it is not utopian in the strict sense because the word *utopia* comes from the Greek *ou* (not) and *topos* (a place), signifying an impossible dream.[3] The coming advent of the kingdom of God is no pipe dream! It is as sure as any established fact of history, and in it our greatest dreams will come true!

The ultimate perfection of the kingdom can happen universally only in the eternal state, not in this world. In the nineteenth century many Christians ignored this truth amidst the characteristic optimism of that age, when it was commonly taught that the gospel would keep spreading until the kingdom would be ushered in. For example, toward the end of that century Sidney Gulick wrote a book entitled *The Growth of the Kingdom of God*, which was subsequently translated into Japanese in an attempt to persuade Japanese students to become Christians. The book's argument was that Christianity is inexorably spreading and will ultimately take over the world, so why not convert now. He reasoned:

> The Christian powers have increased the territory under their rule from about 7 percent of the surface of the world in 1600 to 82 percent in 1893, while the non-Christian powers have receded from about 93 percent to about 18 percent during the same period. At present the Protestant nations alone rule about twice as much territory as all the non-Christian nations combined. . . . During the [first] ninety years of the religious history of the United States more persons have come under the direct influence of the Christian Church than during the first thousand years of Christianity in all lands combined.[4]

The Japanese were not convinced of the argument, as seen, for example, by their attack on Pearl Harbor. Those who taught that the kingdom would be brought in by the preaching of the gospel neglected the teaching of the Mystery Parables of Matthew 13, including "the Sower" and "the Tares." Those parables demonstrate that the church and its rule will be neither universal nor perfect.

What really put an end to such un-Biblical dreams were the great wars and sins of the so-called "Christian nations." In 1945 Helmut Thielicke, the great theologian and preacher at the University of Hamburg, stood before his congregation, their church having been reduced to ruins by air raids, and spoke these words:

> We must not think of it as a gradual Christianization of the world which will increasingly eliminate evil. Such dreams and delusions, which may have been plausible enough in more peaceful times, have vanished in the terrors of our man-made misery. The nineteenth century, which brought forth a number of these dreams and dreamers, strikes us today as being an age of unsuspecting children.[5]

He went on:

> Who can utter the word [progress] today without getting a flat taste in his mouth? Who can still believe today that we are developing toward a state in which the kingdom of God reigns in the world of nations, in culture, and in the life of the individual? The earth has been plowed too deep by the curse of war, the streams of blood and tears have swollen all too terribly, injustice and bestiality have become all too cruel and obvious for us to consider such dreams to be anything but bubbles and froth.[6]

Extreme pessimism? I do not think so. Actually, the sermon is one of remarkable optimism and encouragement, for in it Thielicke cries, "In the world of death, in this empire of ruins and shell-torn fields we pray: 'Thy kingdom come!' We pray it more fervently than ever."[7]

That is our ultimate hope. The kingdom of God is coming. Then the angels will sing, "The kingdom of the world has become the kingdom of our Lord and of his Christ, and he will reign for ever and ever" (Revelation 11:15). His reign will be universal, as Jesus himself tells us:

> *"I say to you that many will come from the east and the west, and will take their places at the feast with Abraham, Isaac and Jacob in the kingdom of heaven." (Matthew 8:11)*

Then all the world will own him not only as sovereign but as *Abba*-Father, and that will be an eternal refrain!

"Your kingdom come" is to be part of the ground and foundation of our prayers. We are to pray for the kingdom and eagerly await it with the same passion that Pastor Thielicke did as he stood in his worn boots in the rubble of 1945. The next to the last verse in the book of Revelation, the final book of the Bible, says, "Amen. Come, Lord Jesus" (22:20). That is a stupendous prayer. Are we bold enough to pray it?

In view of all this, it might be easy to conclude that "your kingdom come" promotes a laissez-faire, otherworldly attitude. Nothing could be more mistaken.

"THY KINGDOM COME" IS FOR THE PRESENT

When Jesus came to earth, he brought the kingdom of God in his own person. When he began his public ministry, the very first words from his mouth after reading from Isaiah were, "Repent, for the kingdom of heaven is near" (Matthew 4:17). Later he said of himself, "The kingdom of God is in your midst" (Luke 17:21, NASB). We can say that Jesus *was* the kingdom because he was the only person who ever fully accepted and fully carried out the will of the Father.

Jesus' passion was the kingdom. It was the major theme of his preaching. The word *kingdom* occurs forty-nine times in Matthew, sixteen in Mark, and thirty-eight in Luke — 103 times in those three Gospels! Before he went to the cross Jesus said, "I must preach the good news of the kingdom of God to the other towns also, because that is why I was sent" (Luke 4:43). After the Resurrection the kingdom was still his passion as he appeared to his disciples "over a period of forty days and spoke about the kingdom of God" (Acts 1:3). Preaching the kingdom was his consuming passion.

How did Jesus Christ bring the kingdom? Primarily by bringing men and women into obedient conformity to the Father's will. This is the meaning of "your kingdom come" in its context because the immediately following and parallel words are, "your will be done on earth as it is in heaven." Those who are in God's kingdom strive to do God's will. In fact, they *do* it.

When we see this, the kingdom becomes very personal for several reasons. First, my will wants to go its own way, but being in the kingdom means my will is bent to God's will. It means *repentance*. Jesus often said, "The kingdom of God is near. Repent and believe the good news" (see Mark 1:14; cf. Matthew 4:17). Being a Christian, a member of the kingdom, means that we do not just always do what we want but what God wants. To pray "your kingdom come" is to repent.

Second, this prayer demands *commitment*. Jesus was very direct when he said, "No one who puts his hand to the plow and looks back is fit for service in the kingdom of God" (Luke 9:62). The kingdom of God is for those who have decided to follow the Lord Jesus Christ and do not keep longingly looking back. To pray "your kingdom come" is to commit ourselves to him.

Third, the kingdom is to be *pursued above all else*. Jesus again gave the authoritative word: "But seek first his kingdom and his righteousness, and all these things will be given to you as well" (Matthew 6:33). Before all else we are to seek the kingdom in obedience to him. This dispels any idea of easygoing, do-nothing, armchair Christianity. We cannot pray the Lord's prayer with folded hands. To pray "your kingdom come" is to pursue it.

Fourth, the kingdom of God is for those who have *a profound dependence upon God*. We cannot overquote Jesus' words, "Blessed are the poor in spirit [the beggarly poor in spirit], for theirs [theirs alone!] is the kingdom of heaven" (Matthew 5:3). No one has the kingdom except those who have come to the end of themselves and have turned to God.

Praying "your kingdom come" demands a depth of commitment from us, and such a commitment produces a life that makes a difference in our society and world. Kingdom power impacts our most intimate relationships. Lives are influenced for Christ, and some are changed. We can make a difference in our schools. The ethics of those who rule our city can be touched by the kingdom. Sometimes whole societies are elevated. To pray "your kingdom come" is to reject the corrupt social structures of our day and to strive for a redeemed community. It is to work toward transforming our community and society. To pray "your kingdom come" is a commitment to live out the Beatitudes and the ethics of the Sermon on the Mount in dependence on God. That would be kingdom living now — a poverty of spirit, a mourning over the sins of the world, a requisite humility that springs out of those attitudes and actions, a hungering and thirsting after righteousness, a merciful, forgiving spirit — getting involved in society and life because of a singleness and commitment to God, even if that brings persecution.

Our vision for society should be the kingdom of God, and that is what we strive for. To be sure, we will never succeed in establishing a perfect kingdom as was supposed by some of our forebears. However, kingdom living has made and does make a difference in the world. Virtually all the great social reforms in history had their roots in kingdom living. The abolition of slavery came through the kingdom living of Christians such as William Wilberforce. Prison reform came from the kingdom living of Elizabeth Fry. Great advances in compassion and medical care came through Florence Nightingale. We do make a difference when we pray "your kingdom come."

In this vein Charles Colson has written:

> During a visit to London I asked a friend to take me to Clapham, the village where William Wilberforce lived almost two centuries ago. Wilberforce was the Christian member of Parliament who led the twenty-year fight, ultimately victorious, against the slave trade. He is one of my great heroes.
>
> Wilberforce was joined by a small band of like-minded Christians who lived, worked and prayed together in the Clapham home of Henry Thornton.
>
> We drove one night through London's crowded streets past block after block of Victorian row houses. A few miles from downtown we came upon a hill, then around a bend. "There it is," my host exclaimed. "That's where Henry Thornton's home used to be!"
>
> "Used to be?" I replied in disbelief. "Surely it has been preserved as an historic site!"
>
> "No," my friend responded, "leveled long ago."
>
> I was stunned. In the U.S., there are markers at the site of obscure battles, even the footprints of screen stars preserved in cement. But here there was nothing.
>
> We drove several blocks to the old church on Clapham Green.
>
> "Wilberforce once preached here," the old rector told me proudly, pointing to a painting in the center of the stained glass behind the altar — a "quite good likeness" of Wilberforce. I squinted but could barely make it out.
>
> "Is that all there is?" I asked, my disappointment deepening. "Oh, no," he replied, leading me to a small brass plaque and a pile of booklets about Wilberforce under a sign, "50 p each." That was it.
>
> We left the church and walked across Clapham Green. "After all these men accomplished," I mumbled, "surely more could have been done to honor them." But suddenly I stopped and stared across the soft grass. In my mind's eye I could see row upon row of men and women, freed from the laden slave ships; I could even hear the clanging chains falling from their arms and legs.
>
> *Of course, of course*, I thought. Clapham is just what Wilberforce and his colleagues would want. No spires of granite or marble, no cold statues and lifeless buildings. Rather, the monument to Wilberforce is the legacy of countless millions, once enslaved, who today live in freedom.[8]

When we pray "your kingdom come," we pray for three things. First, we pray for the final and ultimate establishment of God's kingdom. We pray for the day when all creation will freely call Him "Dearest Father" — "*Abba*." There is an almost martial, triumphant ring to "your kingdom come." *Come, O Lord!*

Second, we pray "your kingdom come" so we will be conformed to his will in this world. As we pray this, we hand ourselves over to the grace of God so he may do with us as he pleases. *Your kingdom come in my life. Use me for your kingdom.*

Third, "your kingdom come" is a prayer that God's rule will come to others through us. It is a prayer for Christ to work his revolutionary power in a fallen world. *Your kingdom come in my family, my job, my city, my nation.*

This is a big prayer that depends on a big God. And when truly prayed, it makes for a big life. Is your life, is my life, big enough to pray, "your kingdom come"?

22

"Your Will Be Done"

MATTHEW 6:10B

The Lord's model prayer is an outline of the elements that an ideal prayer should contain. Its simple structure is very specific. It begins with the foundational awareness that God is our "Dearest Father" with whom we have the intimacy of a father-daughter or father-son relationship. This is the distinctive ground of Christian prayer. From this intimate awareness flow six petitions. The first three concern the glory of God and are distinguished by the word "your." The second three concern our well-being and are distinguished by the word "us." Ideal prayer is first Godward for God's glory and then turns to man's needs.

"Your will be done on earth as it is in heaven" is surely the most abused of the Prayer's six petitions. The Lord's Prayer is repeated mindlessly thousands of times every week. Hollywood thinks it makes a perfect conclusion to a war movie. You know the story line. "The Terrible Ten" have been killing the enemy with ferocious joy and cohabiting with the local girls. The only time God has been mentioned is in their curses. But now the enemy has them encircled, their ammo is gone, and the situation is so desperate that they need to do something religious. So they begin to pray, "Our Father in heaven . . ." The Lord's Prayer is one of the most abused portions of Scripture in or out of the church. Not only is it abused through mindless repetition but in its being prayed by people who have never had any intention of doing God's will!

"Your will be done on earth as it is *in heaven*." Luther called this a "fearful prayer." If some people really realized what they were praying, their words would stick in their throats. Considering the petition's gravity, it is of the utmost importance that we understand what we are praying, then pray it with the utmost sincerity.

It is also important because submitting our wills to God is one of our greatest needs, though none of us finds it easy. We all like to be "captains of our souls" and often even retake the command we once humbly and wisely relinquished. Perhaps as children we were strong-willed, and our parents never succeeded in bringing us into line. Submitting to anyone's will is foreign to us. Whether or not that has been our experience, Jesus' words apply to us! Jesus tells us here that the ideal prayer should contain a section in which we bow before God saying, "Let your will be done in my life, in this situation, at this time, just as it is in heaven itself." Do we truly pray this? And if we do, what do we mean? What is Jesus asking us to pray for when he tells us to pray, "Your will be done on earth as it is in heaven"?

JESUS CALLS US TO PRAY FOR THE WORLD'S OBEDIENCE

This call is twofold. First, we pray for the universal obedience that will come at the end of history. In the final kingdom there will be no necessity for guidelines about divorce, retaliation, hate, lust, or hypocrisy because there will be no divorce or hatred or hypocrisy. God's will will prevail everywhere. "Your will be done on earth as it is in heaven" focuses on this final inevitable event and fills us with hope in this rebellious world.

Second, the prayer calls for God's will to be done right now in present history. To those who question how this is possible, Jesus answers with his life. Early in his ministry Jesus told his disciples, "My food is to do *the will* of him who sent me" (John 4:34). If I pray this petition rightly, my food — what I really live for — is not an extra dessert or a bit of religion to decorate my life, but doing God's will. Helmut Thielicke wrote:

> Just as I live by my daily bread, just as my heart and my eyes and my whole body are driven toward food by the spontaneous urge of hunger, so I live by the will of the Father, so I am driven to him and linked to him with every fiber of my being.[1]

Later Jesus again said, "I seek not to please myself but him who sent me" (John 5:30). And yet again in John's Gospel, "I have come down from heaven not to do my will but to do the will of him who sent me" (6:38). And in Gethsemane, in the midst of bloody sweat, he cried to his Father, "*Abba* Father, everything is possible for you. Take this cup from me. Yet not what I will, but what you will" (Mark 14:36).

We are to emulate our Lord's example. It is possible for men and women, despite their imperfections, to experience the working out of God's will. We are to pray that this will happen not only in regard to salvation, but so righteousness and justice will be brought about in this fallen world.

"Your will be done on earth as it is in heaven." This petition is stridently upward. "Father, *your* will (and no other) be done just as it is in heaven." This is a command (aorist passive imperative) and as such demands passionate expression. Pray it with all your heart, for it is also a prayer for individual obedience.

JESUS CALLS US TO PRAY FOR OUR OWN OBEDIENCE

"Your will be done [in me], on earth as it is in heaven." In praying this we invite God to conquer us, and that is why this petition is so scary. When we pray this prayer, we are asking God to do what is necessary to make his will prevail in our lives. And God then comes with gracious, kind violence to root out all impediments to our obedience. To pray this prayer may terrify us, but it will also deliver us from ourselves. It can truly be said that we have not learned to pray at all until every request in our prayers is made subject to this one. "Your will be done" is the petition that determines the authenticity of the other upward petitions, for if we do not mean it, we cannot truly pray, "hallowed be your name" or "your kingdom come." Truly praying "your will be done" is fundamental to all true prayer.

What else is our obedience to be like? The key is found in the second half of the petition: "as it is in heaven." Not only is God's will to be done by us, but we are to do it just as the believers are doing it in Heaven at this moment! How is it done in Heaven? Gladly, with no reservation. It is possible to say "your will be done" in a tone of bitter resentment, but that is not what God wants.

> Julian was the Roman Emperor who tried to turn the clock back. He tried to reverse the decision of Constantine that Christianity should be the religion of the Empire, and he tried to reintroduce the worship and the service and the ceremonies of the ancient gods. In the end he was mortally wounded in battle in the east. The historians tell how, when he lay bleeding to death, he took a handful of his blood and tossed it in the air, saying: "You have conquered, O man of Galilee!"[2]

We can say "your will be done" through angry, clenched lips, but that is not Heaven's tone. It is possible to say "your will be done" in a funereal tone of resignation and defeat, which goes well with sweet organ tones and the smell of flowers but not with Christian consecration. "God, I wanted things my way, but they are not turning out that way. So I shall turn them over to You, for Your competitive will has more power than mine and will probably have its way anyhow. So teach me not to grumble too much about how things are going against me."[3]

It is also possible to say "your will be done" with a note of cheer and buoyancy, for we know that is the way it is in Heaven! The glorified saints and angels find their greatest joy in doing God's will. They probably do it with singing, judging by the heavenly vignettes in the book of Revelation.

When we pray this third petition of the Lord's Prayer, we pray for two things. First, we pray that we ourselves will live in profound obedience, that his will may be the supreme desire of our lives. And second, we pray that our obedience may be "as it is in heaven" — joyous, bounding, and enthusiastic.

How can we attain this? Besides the obvious, which is to pray that his will be done and then consciously submit to it, we should keep foremost in our minds the fact that this entire prayer is controlled by the word "Father." Here "your will" is the Father's will — the will of One we call *Abba* — "Dearest Father." You and I are asked to do the will of our Father whose love is measured by the cross of Jesus Christ. The fact that his will issues from his Father-love ought to be the greatest encouragement to do his will.

Our father-love, as imperfect as it is, always desires the best for our children. All healthy fathers dream and even scheme to secure a happy and prosperous future for their sons and daughters. Over the years my wife and I went out for breakfast every Monday, my day off, and most of our conversation centered on our children. We did talk about other things, but our beginning conversation was always about our kids. We would talk about the pressure that one was under, the "good week" of another, what we thought was best for each, what we needed to pray about, lists of things they needed. The mental focus of a caring father (and mother) is incredible. If one of our children is having a difficult time, it affects us immensely. Our father-love for them (imperfect as it is) has only the best in mind for them.

To pray "your will be done" is to pray that the perfect, loving Father-will of our heavenly Father will be done in our lives. It is to pray that what is "good, pleasing and perfect" (Romans 12:2) will be done in our lives. This is what we need to keep in mind as we attempt to grow in obedience to God's will. What foolishness it is to resist his loving will for us. To do so is to resist the best, to resist love supreme.

Another thing that is helpful to keep in mind as we strive to grow in obedience is that in order to do God's will, we need to know God's will. Thus when we truly pray "your will be done," there must be a corresponding commitment to learn all we can about his will. This requires the continual study of the Scriptures, which are the main revelatory agency of his will. The Bible is infallible, but sadly, many believers are woefully ignorant of its contents. To truly pray "your will be done" is to commit oneself to knowing God's will as it is revealed in his Word, then to do it.

The last thing we must keep in mind if we want to grow in obedience is that in his will we find our greatest joy. Elisabeth Elliot once stayed in the farmhouse of a Welsh shepherd and his family high in the mountains of North Wales. She stood watching one misty summer morning as the shepherd on horseback herded the sheep with the aid of a champion Scottish collie named Mack. In her own words:

> Mack . . . was in his glory. He came of a long line of working dogs, and he had sheep in his blood. This was what he was made for; this was what he had been trained to do. It was a marvelous thing to see him circling to the right, circling to the left, barking, crouching, racing along, herding a stray sheep here, nipping at a stubborn one there, his eyes always glued to the sheep, his ears listening for the tiny metal whistle from his master that I couldn't hear.[4]

That day Mack assisted his master who had arranged to dip his struggling sheep. Mack was magnificent. As the sheep would attempt to escape the tub, he would snarl and snap at their faces to force them back in. Mack's every move in the pen or out in the pasture was perfect. He seemed as good as the shepherd himself. Amazed, Elliot asked the shepherd's wife if the sheep had any idea what was happening. "Not a clue!" was the answer. "And how about Mack?" The answer was unforgettable: "The dog doesn't understand the pattern — only obedience." Elisabeth Elliot reflected:

> I saw two creatures who were in the fullest sense "in their glory." A man who had given his life to sheep, who loved them and loved his dog. And a dog whose trust in that man was absolute, whose obedience was instant and unconditional, and whose very meat and drink was to do the will of his master. "I delight to do thy will," was what Mack said, "Yea, thy law is within my heart."
>
> To experience the glory of God's will for us means absolute trust. It means the will to do His will, and it means joy.[5]

She was right. Never are we greater, never do we know greater joy, than when we do God's will.

Here we have an advantage over Mack the collie, for we can understand something of the pattern and something of our Shepherd-Father. He is the Creator, the One who set the stars in their trajectories and put the shutter on the lizards' eyes. He is the God who in the Person of Jesus Christ created the universe with his own hands and then allowed those hands to be nailed to the cross. And we can trust him. Our greatest glory is to pray and live the prayer, "your will be done on earth as it is in heaven." What joy and glory come from absolute and unconditional obedience! Only he whose will is bound to God's is what he ought to be.

To glibly parrot this prayer does nothing, but to pray it sincerely is revolutionary. When we truly pray, "your will be done on earth as it is in heaven," we pray for the world's obedience — we pray for the final day when all will bow. And we also pray for the here and now. We pray for that which is surely coming, and we unite ourselves with future victory even while we reside in a disobedient world.

We also pray for our own obedience. "Your will be done" means that I want my submission to be like the submission in Heaven — eager, cheerful, buoyant. In his will is our greatest glory and joy.

We either line ourselves up with the Son of God and say to the Father, "Your will be done," or we give in to the principle that controls the rest of the world and say, "My will be done." Obedience to God is an act of the will. Put yourself in his hands. Choose to give yourself to him daily.

> *Therefore, I urge you, brothers, in view of God's mercy, to offer your bodies as living sacrifices, holy and pleasing to God — this is your spiritual act of worship. (Romans 12:1)*

23

The Lord's Prayer: The Bread

MATTHEW 6:11

When Jesus responded to the disciples' request that he teach them how to pray, he gave them the most perfect and comprehensive outline ever conceived in what we have come to call "the Lord's Prayer." The extraordinary comprehensiveness of its six petitions caused Helmut Thielicke to remark that they are like the colors of the spectrum into which light divides when it shines through a prism. The whole light of life is captured in the rainbow of these petitions, taking into account our every need. "Great things, small things, spiritual things and material things, inward things and outward things — there is nothing that is not included in this prayer."[1]

We will now begin to consider the last three petitions, which turn from praying for God's glory to praying for ourselves. How does one properly pray for oneself? The answer as we see it in the Lord's Prayer does away with some commonly held pious presuppositions and frees us to pray naturally from the heart.

The initial petition seems simple enough: "Give us today our daily bread." We may assume we understand this simple request, but there is more depth here than we realize. In addition, the word "daily" has been the source of a great controversy. The problem stems from the fact that this is the only occurrence of the word in all of Greek literature. It was found once in a nonliterary source on a papyrus fragment that contained a grocery list where it seemed to indicate the requirements of the day, though the meaning is not crystal-clear. Linguists today tell us the word can mean either "today's bread" or "tomorrow's bread," though many prefer the latter. So the Lord's Prayer probably literally reads, "Give us this day our bread for tomorrow," as the margins of the *Revised Standard Version* and *New English Bible* have it.[2]

If this prayer is offered in the morning, it is a prayer for the needs of the day. If it is prayed in the evening, it is a prayer for the needs of the next day. The basic, primary sense is the same. "Give us today tomorrow's bread" is a prayer for God to meet our daily physical needs. At the same time, praying for tomorrow's bread implicitly requests that God meet our needs with the bread of the ultimate tomorrow — the bread of eternity.

WE ARE TO PRAY FOR OUR **PHYSICAL** *NEEDS*

The basic meaning of "Give us today our daily [or tomorrow's] bread" is that we are to pray for our physical needs. The early church fathers rejected this plain meaning and spiritualized the bread to mean the bread of Communion. Jerome called this bread, in his translation of the Bible, *Panem nostrum supersubstantialem* or super-substantial bread — bread that is more than physical. The main reason he did this was because it just did not seem right after the first three upward petitions for God's glory to immediately switch to something so crass as asking for our material well-being. The first part of the prayer is completely selfless and now to pray for bread seemed so selfish and materialistic. However, despite all the fathers' rationalizing and theologizing, this petition means exactly what it says. God wants us to pray for physical provision. In fact, in the Lord's Prayer that is the first thing God tells us to pray for when we pray for ourselves!

That we should pray for our material well-being of course demands some thoughtful application. First, "Give us today our daily bread" is not *carte blanche* to pray for everything in the Sears catalog or the Nieman Marcus catalog. I once heard a minister who was later convicted by a grand jury for fraud tell a group of pastors that if we wanted Cadillacs or large wardrobes, it was God's will for us. His rationale was Psalm 37:4: "Delight yourself in the LORD and he will give you the desires of your heart." So if we are delighting ourselves in the Lord and our hearts desire Cadillacs and Gucci shoes, it must be God's will and we should believe God for them. Scripture does not teach or endorse such foolishness, and especially not the Lord's Prayer. The Lord's Prayer calls us to pray for "bread" — that is, the necessities of life, whether large or small, those things that are necessary for the life and health and well-being of ourselves and our families. We are to pray for bread, not dessert!

Second, "Give us today our daily bread" is an invitation to come to God with requests that others might call small. One of the precious realities of our Christian life is that God cares for the simple, ordinary, day-to-day things of life. Jesus taught us that even supposedly trivial matters are important to God. Our Lord took babies in his arms and loved them and blessed them when his disciples wanted to send them away. He bestowed his special love upon the seemingly worthless existences of those who were ignored and looked down on — the lepers, the lame, the mentally ill. God cares whether his people are warm, well-fed, and well-housed. And besides, these things are not so little when we lack them. "A Beethoven symphony . . . sounds quite different if we listen to it when we are shivering with cold. And a visit to an art gallery is less inspiring . . . when we undertake it on an empty stomach."[3] If you are freezing, a warm sweater has higher priority than a volume of C. S. Lewis's poems. God wants us to bring our everyday needs to him, even if they seem trivial. He does not demand that we approach him only when we have raised ourselves to some kind of spiritual elevation above the everyday things of life. The greatness of our God lies in his descending to meet us where we are. When we come to him with our "little things," we do him great honor.

Third, in commanding us to pray, "Give us today our daily bread" God is fostering in us a daily dependence upon himself. No other line in the Lord's Prayer so sharply challenges the direction of today's world. The man on the street wants to compound his security and his independence. To be sure, there is nothing wrong with planning for future rainy days, but it is wrong to make total independence your consuming goal. Whether we are rich or poor, God wants us to depend upon him "daily." He wants us all to pray for our daily needs, and he wants us to daily thank him.

Lastly, God wants to build a mutuality between us and our brothers and sisters through this prayer. He commands us to pray "give *us*," not "give me." Every time we pray this prayer from our heart, we are affirming our solidarity with our brothers and sisters. When we pray, "Give *us* today *our* daily bread," we are also making an implicit commitment to help provide bread for needy friends. The prayer is a stretching, broadening petition. We not only depend on God for practical provision — we commit ourselves to be part of God's answer for others in need.

God wants us to feel free to come to him with requests for even the tiniest needs — the bread we need, a coat, shoes, a car, books, a vacation, exercise, a bicycle, groceries . . .

> . . . he whose eye encompasses in its boundless reach the first day of creation and the last hour of judgment, reflecting all the eternities; he whose outstretched arm enfolds the oceans, islands, and continents, because all authority in Heaven and earth has been given to him, he occupies himself with the trivialities of humankind.[4]

WE ARE TO PRAY FOR OUR SPIRITUAL *BREAD*

The secondary meaning of this petition is the spiritual bread, which is characteristic of the eternal state. I see this dual interpretation for several reasons. First, the petition actually reads, "Give us this day our bread for tomorrow," pointing to the special bread of the future state. Second, the three preceding petitions of the prayer all refer ultimately to the final eternal state, when God's name is once and for all hallowed, his kingdom comes, and his will is perpetually done. So it follows that the bread of tomorrow is also eternal. Third, Jesus used only one symbol to describe the eternal state for believers, and he used it many times — a great, joyous feast.[5] Surely this is where the bread of heaven will be served. So when Jesus bids us to pray for the bread of tomorrow, he is bidding us to pray for the bread of eternity today.

Here in the Lord's Prayer the Lord Jesus tells us, his children, that through prayer we can grasp the glorious bread of eternity and feast upon it. The ultimate bread is, of course, Christ himself. Jesus said:

> *"I am the living bread that came down from heaven. If anyone eats of this bread, he will live forever. This bread is my flesh, which I will give for the life of the world." (John 6:51)*

And we say back in response:

> *By Thee the souls of men are fed*
> *With gifts of grace supernal;*
> *Thou, who dost give us earthly bread,*
> *Give us the bread eternal.*

Jesus never disappoints us. He always gives this bread to those who ask. I once read of a woman who in the Christmas rush purchased fifty greeting cards without looking at the message inside. She signed and addressed all but a few, then dropped them in the mailbox. A few days later, when things had slowed down, she finally read one of the cards. To her great embarrassment it said:

> *This card is just to say*
> *A little gift is on the way.*

Needless to say, about fifty disappointed families never received their presents. Jesus is not like that. He never disappoints us, never fails to give us all he has promised. He calls us to pray for the "bread of tomorrow," and he gives us himself.

When we pray, "Give us today our daily bread," we pray for physical bread *and* for spiritual bread — in both cases the "bread of tomorrow."

In the Lord's Supper, a privileged remembrance feast for Christ's followers, physical bread symbolizes the spiritual bread of the kingdom. It is a foretaste for us of the coming kingdom in all its fullness, when we will sit with one another with Jesus at the head of the table. The bread of Communion is real bread. It has the taste of the past when our blessed Lord's body was broken for us on the cross. But it also has the taste of tomorrow, when we will enjoy him forever.

Lord, give us this day the bread of tomorrow! Amen.

24

The Lord's Prayer: Forgiveness

MATTHEW 6:12

Robert Louis Stevenson in his *Picturesque Notes of Edinburgh* tells the story of two unmarried sisters who shared a single room. As people are apt to do who live in close quarters, the sisters had a falling out, "on some point of controversial divinity." In other words, they disagreed over some aspect of theology. The controversy was so bitter that they never spoke to one another again! Yet, possibly because of a lack of means or because of the innate Scottish fear of scandal, they continued to live together in the single room. They drew a chalk line across the floor to separate their two domains. It divided the doorway and the fireplace, so that each could go in and out and do her cooking without stepping into the territory of the other. For years they coexisted in hateful silence. Their meals, their baths, their family visitors were continually exposed to the other's unfriendly silence. And at night, each went to bed listening to the heavy breathing of her enemy.[1] Thus the two sisters (ostensibly daughters of the church!) continued the rest of their miserable lives.

No doubt when they attended church they were compelled often to "say" the Lord's Prayer, but they obviously never truly prayed it, for that would have brought their reconciliation. How could they truly pray "Our Father" and remain estranged? Or "Give *us* today *our* daily bread" and not reconcile? And what about the next petition — "Forgive us our debts, as we also have forgiven our debtors"? There is no way they could *truly* pray those words and remain bitter and unforgiving!

Seriously prayed, the petition we will now consider can be healing salve for a fractured spiritual life and broken human relationships. Our

Lord's second great instruction on how we ought to pray for ourselves, it tells us how to pray in the matter of forgiveness. It is an explicit prayer for forgiveness ("Forgive us our debts"), and it is also an implicit prayer for a forgiving spirit ("as we also have forgiven our debtors"). Jesus teaches us here that ideal prayer contains a request for personal forgiveness and a request for a forgiving spirit.

A PRAYER FOR A FORGIVING SPIRIT

St. Augustine called this request "the terrible petition" because he realized that if we pray "Forgive us our debts, *as we also have forgiven our debtors*" with an unforgiving heart, we are actually asking God *not* to forgive us, for "debts" here really means "sins." "Forgive us our sins, as we have forgiven those who sin against us." Jesus does not want anyone to misunderstand here, so he states it categorically in verses 14-15: "For if you forgive men when they sin against you, your heavenly Father will also forgive you. But if you do not forgive men their sins, your Father will not forgive your sins."

Shocking as Jesus' words are, they are really nothing new but were common to Jewish understanding. The author of Ecclesiasticus, The Wisdom of Jesus the son of Sirach, says, "Forgive your neighbor the wrong he has done, and then your sins will be pardoned when you pray." Then to drive home his statement, he asked three questions:

> 1. Does a man harbor anger against another, and yet seek for healing from the Lord?

The unspoken answer is, "Absurd!"

> 2. Does he have no mercy toward a man like himself, and yet pray for his own sins?
>
> 3. If he himself, being flesh, maintains wrath, who will make expiation for his sins?[2]

Thus we see that Jesus words were in accordance with the understanding of God's people.

The New Testament states this several times. In Matthew 5:7 Jesus says, "Blessed are the merciful, for they will be shown mercy." A merciless, unforgiving heart will receive neither forgiveness nor mercy. James 2:13 says the same: "Judgment without mercy will be shown to anyone who has not been merciful." And our Lord's powerful parable of the man who was forgiven 10,000 talents by his lord but refused to forgive his own slave a 100-denarii debt ends with this terrifying warning:

> *"Then the master called the servant in. 'You wicked servant,' he said, 'I canceled all that debt of yours because you begged me to. Shouldn't you have had mercy on your fellow servant just as I had on you?' In anger his master turned him over to the jailers to be tortured, until he should pay back all he owed. This is how my heavenly Father will treat each of you unless you forgive your brother from your heart." (Matthew 18:32-35)*

So there is no doubt that Jesus meant exactly what he said: "if you do not forgive men their sins, your Father will not forgive your sins" (Matthew 6:15b).

Awareness of this solemn truth occasioned one of John Wesley's famous statements. Wesley was serving as a missionary to the Colonies and was having a terrible time with General Oglethorpe, who was noted for his pride and unbending nature. In a particularly prideful moment Oglethorpe said, "I never forgive." To which Wesley replied, "Then I hope, sir, you never sin." Wesley knew that if we pride ourselves on never forgetting a wrong, if we make an unforgiving spirit a virtue, we cannot be forgiven. Thomas Watson, the great Puritan, said, "A man can as well go to hell for not forgiving as for not believing."[3] And Charles Spurgeon stated, "Unless you have forgiven others, you read your own death-warrant when you repeat the Lord's Prayer."[4] And in our own time C. S. Lewis wrote:

> No part of his teaching is clearer: and there are no exceptions to it. He doesn't say that we are to forgive other people's sins provided they are not too frightful, or provided there are extenuating circumstances, or anything of that sort. We are to forgive them all, however spiteful, however mean, however often they are repeated. If we don't, we shall be forgiven none of our own.[5]

Sometimes our unforgiving hearts make our prayers die on our lips. The Lord's Prayer can then be nothing more than a self-inflicted curse — a prayer of doom instead of blessing, for if we pray, "Forgive us our debts, as we also have forgiven our debtors" with unforgiving hearts, we are asking God not to forgive us!

Let me extend the principle even further. If we will not forgive, we are not Christians! This is a frightening statement, but it is true, for when God's grace comes into our hearts, it makes us forgiving. We demonstrate whether we have been forgiven by whether or not we will forgive. So if I refuse to forgive, there is only one reason — I am outside grace and I am myself unforgiven. These are hard words, but they are graciously hard, words especially needing to be heard by the religious person who can state all the answers, who attends church, who leads an outwardly moral life, but who holds a death grip on his grudges. He will not forgive his relatives for some infraction. He has no desire to pardon his former business associate. He nourishes hatreds, cherishes animosities, revels in malice. Such people had better take an honest inventory of their lives and see if they really know Jesus.

As mentioned earlier in our discussion of the Beatitude "Blessed are the merciful" (Matthew 5:7), a few words of qualification are in order. I am not referring to those who find that bitterness and hatred recur even though they have forgiven the offender. The fact that you have forgiven and continue to forgive is a sign of grace. We are not talking about people who are struggling with forgiveness. It is those who have no desire to forgive who are in soul danger. There may also be some who have been recently offended and are still in emotional shock and so have not been able to properly respond with forgiveness. The point is: If we are Christians, we can and will forgive!

Is "Forgive us our debts, as we also have forgiven our debtors" a curse upon us or a blessing? Are our most precious possessions our grudges? Do we pride ourselves on the fact that we never forgive? If so, the chances are very good that we are not truly believers. How good of God to put it this way. This requires no elaborate reasoning process to determine whether or not we know him — no special knowledge. All it requires is honesty. Does the state of your heart regarding forgiveness indicate grace or not?

This fifth petition of the Lord's Prayer not only helps us to understand whether or not we are believers, but if we are believers, it helps us to monitor our spiritual health. We all have the unhealthy tendency to be more conscious of the wrongs done to us than the wrongs we have done to others. When others are hurt, we credit it to their oversensitive feelings. But when we are wronged, we tend to exaggerate our own hurt and the evil of the offender. Lewis says of this:

> In our own case we accept excuses too easily, in other people's we do not accept them easily enough. As regards my own sins it is a safe bet (though not a certainty) that the excuses are not really as good as I think: as regards other men's sins against me it is a safe bet (though not a certainty) that the excuses are better than I think.[6]

Furthermore, our unhealthy tendencies to take offense and to offend take their toll on our relationships — oftentimes the relationships we most value. Our quickness to take offense and our reticence to forgive strain even our best relationships. An unforgiving spirit brings isolation and a compounding of our bitterness, and sooner or later it shows itself. Self-pity finds its roots here. Then comes depression as an unforgiving, offended self turns inward. We become even more fault-finding and hurt and unforgiving, then more depressed and emotionally unhealthy. Not only do friendships sour, but our own healthy relationship with God becomes insipid. The heavens seem as brass to the unforgiving heart, and they practically are so. We suffer from spiritual ill health.

On the other hand, the health benefits of a forgiving spirit are incalculable. The chief benefit is this: We are never closer to God, or more like God, than when we forgive! When we forgive, we are like the Father and like the Son, who prayed, "Father, forgive them, for they do not know what they are doing" (Luke 23:34). We say "to err is human," and that is true. But the last part of that couplet is, "to forgive is divine," and so it is. You are never more beautiful or noble or healthy than when you forgive, for then you are like God. It is too easy to agree with General Oglethorpe: "I never forgive. And I'm so proud of my hatreds, and no one crosses me, and I always pay accounts." To forgive is divine. To not forgive is demonic.

This fifth petition of the Lord's Prayer is, as Augustine said, "a terrible petition," but it is also a gracious prayer. And it monitors our spiritual health. Are we healthy, forgiving people?

A PRAYER FOR FORGIVENESS

The fundamental qualification for praying this prayer is that we are "debtors" — that is, sinners. Many people who repeat this prayer do not see themselves as sinners. People often pray the Lord's Prayer with a condescending tolerance that permits them to inwardly say, "I'm praying this along with the people who really need it." Thousands who say this prayer do not consider themselves guilty before God. Thus for them the Lord's Prayer is merely an empty repetition by self-satisfied souls. The fact is, it can be properly prayed only by "debtors." Are we debtors? If we are genuinely Christians, our sins have been paid for by the blood of Christ. But this prayer teaches that we are to engage in daily, ongoing confession of sin. In fact, to do so is a sign of spiritual maturity and health.

In sum, this fifth petition — "Forgive us our debts, as we also have forgiven our debtors" — tells us to do two things. First, we are to ask God to forgive us. This request for forgiveness follows the request for daily food in the Lord's Prayer, and numerous commentators have noted that it should surpass our craving for food. If you have not yet had your debts canceled and forgiven, ask God to forgive you by the grace and blood of Jesus Christ. Do it today!

The second thing this fifth petition tells us to do is to forgive those who have wronged us. Do this for the health of your soul. Do it for the health of the church, which is sick from a lack of forgiveness among God's children. Do it for the sake of the world, which has not yet discovered what Christ is like. But it can if you and I will truly forgive, for "to forgive is divine."

Do you need to forgive your spouse? Covenant to do so right now.

Have you been unwilling to forgive your parents? Promise God that you will do it. Have you forgiven that employer or neighbor or church member who wronged you? Do you have a grudge against your last church, or its pastor or elders? Forgive today!

Forgiveness is not a psychological trick. It is a miracle! And God can help you do it. Do it most of all for God's sake. "Be kind and compassionate to one another, forgiving each other, just as in Christ God forgave you" (Ephesians 4:32).

This "terrible petition" can curse us or bless us. Dare we pray it? Can we pray it? *Lord, forgive us our debts, as we also have forgiven our debtors.*

25

The Lord's Prayer: Temptation

MATTHEW 6:13

During the school year and summer of 1962 I shared an apartment with three of my good buddies. We were all vibrant Christians, and we all shared the same interest — serving Christ. We all entered the ministry, and all of us except one have remained in our work. It is the one who did not make it that I would like to tell you about. Of my three roommates, he and I had more in common. He actively and winsomely shared his faith with everyone, and for this I greatly admired him and sometimes imitated him. I especially remember us spending all night in prayer over a map of the world. We even liked the same girls! In fact, he really put our friendship to the test when one hour after I asked my wife-to-be, Barbara, out for our first date, he called and asked her out. When I did marry Barbara a year and a half later, he fell in love and married a terrific girl, and we all became very close friends. We had a great deal in common: We were poor, we shared similar dreams, and our children came about the same time. As we expected, our callings took us to separate places. He went to work as an evangelist for a national organization, and I pursued the pastorate. His was an especially difficult ministry, and we often prayed urgently for him and his family. We understood each other. We fought the same battles.

All went reasonably well until my friend parted ways with his organization, wounded and bitter. Things had not been going well for him and his wife — even while in the ministry — and their circumstances were worse than we knew. Taking a new job brought an unhealthy change in his lifestyle and the company he kept, especially in regard to the opposite sex.

After a while I heard he had left his family for a time but now was living with them though he was considering a divorce. The news was such a blow that I did something I had never done before. I scheduled a flight after a Sunday evening service, flew to the west coast, rang his doorbell at 7 A.M. on Monday morning, and spent most of the day and evening attempting to listen to and reason with my old friend. I flew back to Chicago that night with his promise that he "wouldn't do anything rash." A year later I received an engraved invitation to attend the wedding of my friend and his wife-to-be aboard the yacht *Mia Vita* in Huntington Harbor, California. *Mia Vita* means "my life," and as I read the invitation I imagined Frank Sinatra singing ". . . but, best of all, I did it my way." So long to twenty-two years of marriage! So long to the wife of his youth! So long to the call of Christ! So long to comfortable intimacy with his children and grandchildren! So long to a life of meaning!

All this goes to show, first, that *no one is above falling*. No one is above shelving his or her faith, family, and heritage. No one is above yielding to temptation in its multiple, variegated forms. No one! The pastor in his pressed suit and starched shirt who appears to have it all together is not above succumbing. None of us pastors are, regardless of our present spiritual temperature. Secondly, *we need to know how to pray for spiritual protection for ourselves*.

That is what the sixth and final petition of the Lord's Prayer is all about: "And lead us not into temptation, but deliver us from the evil one [some translations: "from evil"]" (Matthew 6:13). The six petitions of the Lord's Prayer are structured like a ladder. The top three rungs are in Heaven, having to do with God's Fatherhood — his name. The next rung down concerns God's kingdom, the third his will. The next three rungs descend to earth as we pray for daily bread, forgiveness, and finally protection from evil. On the ladder of the Lord's Prayer we descend from the contemplation of who God is — our Father — to who we are — sinful children. Proper prayer includes praying for spiritual protection. This final petition has two requests. The first is negative: "And lead us not into temptation." The second is positive: ". . . but deliver us from the evil one."

"LEAD US NOT INTO TEMPTATION"

What does "Lead us not into temptation" mean? Certainly it cannot mean (as some have wrongly thought) that God is the prime mover behind all temptations. James 1:13 makes this clear: "When tempted, no one should say, 'God is tempting me.' . . . nor does he tempt anyone." On the other hand, others have imagined that if Christians truly pray this prayer, they can be delivered from *all* temptation. But the Bible is clear that temptation is an inavoidable part of human existence. All the apostles and all the great saints have lived in continual temptation. The key to what "Lead us not into temptation" means is found in the fact that the word translated "temptation" has two meanings. It can denote an enticement that has the goal of causing one to sin, or it can refer to a test or trial of the validity of one's faith. The word occurs twenty-one times in the New Testament, and twenty of those appearances have the latter idea of testing or trial.[1] Thus the meaning of "Lead us not into temptation" is simply, "Do not allow us to come under the sway of temptation that will overpower us and cause us to sin." This meaning is supported by an ancient Jewish evening prayer that Jesus may well have known:

Lead me not into the power of transgression,
And bring me not into the power of sin,
And not into the power of iniquity,
And not into the power of temptation,
And not into the power of anything shameful.[2]

The idea is: "Lord, preserve me from temptation that will bring me under its sway and will cause me to fall." We cannot help being exposed to temptation, and we are not to pray that we will be spared being tempted at all. Rather, we are to pray that we will be spared those temptations from Satan that we cannot withstand.

The abiding reality is that temptation is good for us. Temptation molded the life and ministry of the Lord Jesus Christ himself. His ministry began with his epic temptations in the wilderness. Satan came at him with the most elaborate and insidious psycho-spiritual attacks ever made. Jesus withstood it all and with the temptation conquered went on to live his peerless life. Some three and a half years later in Gethsemane he triumphed again over temptation as he conquered the impulse to flee from the cross. The writer of Hebrews bears testimony to the molding effect of those and other sufferings in the earthly life of our Lord:

In bringing many sons to glory, it was fitting that God, for whom and through whom everything exists, should make the author of their salvation perfect through suffering. (2:10)

If temptations helped shape the life and ministry of the perfect Christ, much more do they do so for us! Temptation is necessary for the development of our moral character. "Temptation is not so much the penalty of manhood as it is the glory of manhood. It is that by which a man is made an athlete of God."[3] That was the way it was for Martin Luther. No one can doubt that Luther became stronger as he fought off the massive temptations of the world, the flesh, and the devil. Conquered temptation knits the fibers of our souls into muscular cords. The old belief that the strength of a slain enemy passes into the slayer is true in regard to a Christian's overcoming temptations. That is why the Scriptures urge the long view. "Consider it pure joy, my brothers, whenever you face trials of many kinds, because you know that the testing of your faith develops perseverance" (James 1:2, 3). That is why today we count among the great Christians of our time people like Dietrich Bonhoeffer, Corrie ten Boom, and Alexander Solzhenitsyn. Their great trials made them into spiritual giants.

So the proper prayer regarding temptation is not that we be delivered from all temptation, for facing and overcoming it is necessary for the health of our souls. But proper prayer does ask God to deliver us from overpowering temptations, recognizing that we are weak and liable to fold under severe testing. It was Peter's fleshly presumption that led to his terrible failure. Hours prior to his fall he said in effect, "I don't know about the rest of these others, but, God, when you look at me you are looking at a real man. All the rest of them might forsake you, but *I'll* never forsake you." But hours later he denied Christ in sweaty, sordid, foul language that had not come from his lips in years. Our presumption can take many forms. We need to see the weakness of our flesh.

History records the fate of two men who were condemned to die under Queen Mary. One of them boasted very loudly to his companions that he would be a man at the stake. He was so grounded in the gospel that he knew he would never deny Christ. He even said he longed for the fatal morning like a bride for her wedding. His prison companion was a poor trembling soul who, though determined not to deny his Master, was much afraid of the fire. He said he had always been very sensitive to suffering, and he was in great dread that when he began to burn, the pain might cause him to deny the truth. He urged his friend to pray for him and spent his time weeping over his weakness and crying out to God for strength. The other man continually rebuked him and chided him for being so unbelieving and weak. When they both came to the stake, he who had been so bold recanted at the sight of the fire and went back ignominiously to an apostate's life, while the poor trembling man whose prayer had been "Lead me not into temptation" stood firm as a rock, praising and magnifying God as he died a cruel death.[4] The proper prayer for protection is soaked with the awareness that we are profoundly weak and liable to fall. There is a danger in pious bravado that assumes we are too strong to stumble or fail.

"DELIVER US FROM THE EVIL ONE"

The Lord goes on to say, "Deliver us from the evil one." Though some versions render this, "Deliver us from evil," "the evil one" is a more accurate translation, referring to the devil. Proper prayer for spiritual protection understands that the devil is a real person, not an impersonal cosmic force. Believing in a real devil has not been in vogue for many years. Those who believe there is an utterly malignant being behind the universe's evil are sometimes classified as medieval fools who picture Satan as a green-eyed gnome with cloven hooves who smells like brimstone. It is still "in" to pooh-pooh his existence, which, as Lewis has said, is one of the best things the forces of evil ever pulled off for themselves. Fortunately, in recent years a return to Bible reading, books like *The Screwtape Letters*, and the manifestations of evil in modern history have done much to clear up people's thinking. As the great theologian Helmut Thielicke said in postwar, occupied Germany:

> There is a dark, mysterious, spellbinding figure at work. Behind the temptations stand *the* tempter, behind the lie stands *the* liar, behind all the dead and bloodshed stands *the* "murderer from the beginning."

And then a few lines later he added, "Dear friend, in our times we have had far too much contact with demonic powers."[5] The Scriptures call this malignant being Satan and the devil. *Satan* is the common Hebrew word for "adversary," as in 1 Samuel 29:4 where David is called a *satan* ("adversary," KJV) to the Philistines. *Devil* is the common Greek word for "slanderer," as in 1 Timothy 3:11 where Paul says women are to be serious-minded, not *diabolous*, "devils, slanderers." The evil one is both our real adversary and our real slanderer. Moreover, he is a being of cosmic intelligence and stealth. He is dangerous precisely because he does not have hooves and the smell of sulfur.

The point is, proper prayer acknowledges his amazing power. He is "the ruler of the kingdom of the air, the spirit who is now at work in those who are disobedient" (Ephesians 2:2). His agents are everywhere — in Washington, in Moscow, in seminaries, in pulpits. He is not omnipresent, but he tries to imitate the omnipresence of God by commanding a host of evil spirits that afflict the godly and the ungodly, even as God sends his ministering spirits to care for his elect. Second Corinthians 11:14, 15 says:

> *And no wonder, for Satan himself masquerades as an angel of light. It is not surprising, then, if his servants masquerade as servants of righteousness. Their end will be what their actions deserve.*

But we do not need to fear, for when we acknowledge our foe's cosmic power by correctly praying, "Deliver us from the evil one," we are in the same breath acknowledging that God's power is greater. God can deliver us! Luther was right when he sang:

The prince of darkness grim,
We tremble not for him —
His rage we can endure,
For lo! his doom is sure:
One little word shall fell him.

"Deliver us from the evil one" should be a part of our daily prayers. I pray regularly that God will put a hedge around my church and a hedge around my family. I also intercede for various ones who I know are undergoing attacks from Satan, praying they will be delivered from his power and his emissaries. It is imperative that this be part of the daily prayer life of believers.

Sadly, the story of my friend's fall is not unusual. The path from Christ's life in me to *mia vita* is well traveled. None of us is above succumbing to the trials and temptations that beset us. The assaults are incessant, and we need to ever recognize our frailty and weakness and to lean upon God's power, understanding that without it we cannot stand.

Acknowledging that temptation is necessary for our spiritual growth, we must pray that God will keep us from temptations that would destroy us. We must humbly pray, "Lead us not into temptation." We must empty ourselves of all spiritual presumption. We must also pray, "Deliver us from the evil one," acknowledging that victory over Satan can come only through God's power as we truly depend on him.

Being willing and able to authentically pray, "Lead us not into temptation, but deliver us from the evil one" is a key to spiritual health. It is part of our Lord's ideal pattern for prayer. Do we pray it? Is a prayer for deliverance from temptation and the power of the devil part of our everyday prayer life? Are we willing to make it so?

26

The Lord's Prayer: Glory

MATTHEW 6:13

In some Bible versions the Lord's Prayer closes with the doxology, "For yours is the kingdom and the power and the glory forever. Amen." However, many believe this doxology was probably not spoken by Christ and was not a part of the original Lord's Prayer, for several reasons. It does not appear in any of the oldest manuscripts for the Gospel of Matthew. It appears that it was added in at the time of the first or second century. The earliest references to this doxology are in the *Didache*, or *Teaching of the Twelve Apostles*, where it reproduces the Lord's Prayer and then adds the words, "for thine is the power and the glory for ever. Pray thus three times a day."[1] Ernst Lohmeyer, who has done one of the most scholarly and exhaustive studies of the Lord's Prayer, says this doxology was included because of the Jewish custom of ending all daily prayers with a brief doxology. He believes that the Jewish Christians in Syria began to repeat the Lord's Prayer daily with the customary addition of a doxology, finally adding it to their version of their New Testament, which then influenced other ancient versions.[2]

I think Lohmeyer's explanation makes good sense. From a literary point of view, one can also see why the doxology was naturally included, for it seems to add an appropriate conclusion to the prayer. It seems rather cold and cheerless to end the prayer with the words "the evil one." But of course the text of the Bible is not to be decided by one's feelings or notions of appropriateness but by the evidence. And the evidence does not allow us to imagine that this doxology was part of the original Lord's Prayer as it came from the lips of Jesus.

However, it does not follow that because Jesus did not use it, it is wrong to insert the early church's song of praise at the end of the Lord's Prayer when we pray it. The Lord's Prayer is an outline, a model, of what our prayers should contain, and there is nothing wrong with additional praise and doxology in keeping with the spirit of the prayer — as long as we do not imagine that Jesus said it. Actually, this doxology is Scriptural in the sense that variations of it are found numerous times in the Bible. The Old Testament contains what many believe is the model from which this doxology is condensed — 1 Chronicles 29:10, 11, where David gives thanks before the people, saying, "Praise be to you, O LORD, God of our father Israel, from everlasting to everlasting. Yours, O LORD, is the greatness and the power and the glory and the majesty and the splendor, for everything in heaven and earth is yours. Yours, O LORD, is the kingdom."

In the New Testament among the many parallel references are the words of the four living creatures in Revelation 5:13: "To him who sits on the throne and to the Lamb be praise and honor and glory and power, for ever and ever!" So the doxology here is Scriptural in content, and what we have in its un-Scriptural addition at the end of the Lord's Prayer is the church's proper reaction to praying the Lord's Prayer. This doxology is the joyous declaration of one who has truly prayed the Lord's Prayer.

For yours is the kingdom! — Lord!
Yours is the power! — God!
Yours is the glory forever! Amen!

This doxology is a model of the heart response of one who truly enters into the Lord's Prayer. It is the song of the heart that prays according to the Lord's pattern prayer.

THE DOXOLOGY DECLARES THE KINGDOM TO BE GOD'S

"Yours is the kingdom." Here the fundamental, underlying meaning is that God is King, carrying the traditional Jewish sense of "Thou art king forever."[3] No truth is more constantly reiterated in Scripture than this. "Yours is the kingdom" is a joyful affirmation of the sovereignty of God. It affirms that he is all-powerful, linking beautifully with the next declaration of the doxology. It also affirms that he is all-knowing.

> God knows instantly and effortlessly all matter and all matters, all mind and every mind, all spirit and all spirits, all being and every being, all creaturehood and all creatures, every plurality and all pluralities, all law and every law, all relations, all causes, all thoughts, all mysteries, all enigmas, all feeling, all desires, every unuttered secret, all thrones and dominions, all

> personalities, all things visible and invisible in heaven and in earth, motion, space, time, life, death, good, evil, heaven, and hell.
>
> Because God knows all things perfectly, He knows no thing better than any other thing, but all things equally well. He never discovers anything. He is never surprised, never amazed. He never wonders about anything. . . .[4]

The phrase also affirms that God is absolutely free, beyond human experience and understanding. Our earthly analogies fall short of describing this. We customarily describe someone who we think is free as "free as a bird," but as any naturalist knows, predators, food supplies, and natural fears keep birds in bondage. And man is no more free than a bird — in fact, less because of his sin. Only God is free! He can do what he pleases when he pleases as he pleases. He is King!

But "yours is the kingdom" not only affirms his sovereign kingship — it declares that he is King of this fallen, rebellious world. The world has trouble believing this. Everywhere one looks, it appears that only the strong and nasty prevail. As Napoleon said in a moment of vain cynicism, "I have observed that God is always on the side of the strongest battalions."[5] Pontius Pilate had the same perspective as he faced the mutilated visage of Christ standing on the pavement before his palace. The power of Rome stood with Pilate, and Jesus was to him no more than a twig on the unfortunate tides of history. Thus Jesus' words, "My kingdom is not of this world" (John 18:36) were incomprehensible to him. The truth is, Pilate was the captive and Jesus was the King, the only free man in history.

If you do not see Christ as King and have not experienced his kingdom, it is because you are standing in the wrong place.

> It is like the colored windows of a church. If you go around the outside of the church, you see nothing but gray monochrome and cannot tell whether they are merely dirty, sooty panes or works of art. In other words, you are seeing them from the wrong perspective. But the moment you enter the nave of the church, the windows begin to shine and the whole story of salvation, captured in color, rises up before you.[6]

The mystery of God's kingdom can be seen only from the inside. From within we joyously declare, "yours is the kingdom" and know that it is coming and that all will see it, even those on the outside when the Lord Jesus Christ comes riding on the white horse, his name emblazoned on his robe and thigh: "KING OF KINGS AND LORD OF LORDS" (Revelation 19:16).

This realization makes all the difference in the way we live! We believe that he is in control and that we will answer to him — and this belief influences everything. Over 350 years ago Lancelot Andrewes sat as bishop of the Church of England. He was a marvelous preacher, and on a memorable occasion in 1621 he had the opportunity to preach to the assembled House of Commons at their opening session in Westminster Abbey. He told his country's leaders that God was standing in the congregation and that God would judge among them, and that if they would see him standing they would never have to fear his judgment. He said they needed just four things:

> 1. "Set down this and believe it, that He is present;
> 2. So behave yourselves as if you did believe it;
> 3. Show yourselves well affected to His presence;
> 4. Do those things which may make Him rejoice to be among you.[7]

Andrewes called the politicians of his day to live what they publicly subscribed to — that God is King.

We must live as if God is King and that his kingdom is already present and is coming! "Yours is the kingdom."

> *Lord of every thought and action,*
> *Lord to send, and Lord to stay,*
> *Lord in speaking, writing, giving,*
> *Lord in all things to obey;*
> *Lord of all there is of me,*
> *Now and evermore to be.*[8]

That is the first thing we declare.

THE DOXOLOGY DECLARES THAT THE POWER IS GOD'S

"Yours is . . . the power." Sovereignty and omnipotence go together. One cannot exist without the other. To reign, God must have power; and to reign sovereignly, he must have all power. That God is omnipotent ought to be self-evident to anyone in the Judeo-Christian tradition, but unfortunately it is not so. Consider the best seller *When Bad Things Happen to Good People*, authored by Harold Kushner, a once obscure rabbi. The book deals with the age-old question, how can a loving God allow such horrible suffering and misery in the world? Kushner's answer is that God is indeed all-loving, but he is not all-powerful. So the bad things that happen are simply out of his control. Amazingly, thousands of readers have swallowed his answer hook, line, and sinker. "Now I can believe in a more realistic God," some have said. Molding God into our image is nothing new. What is amazing is that even Christians are buying into this! A well-known pastor endorsed the book! So you see, God is not dead — he is just sick and feeble!

Fortunately, there are better books on the subject, perhaps the best among them being Philip Yancey's masterful *Where Is God When It*

Hurts? The Christian, Biblical answer is far superior and better argued than Kushner's "sick God" theory or the popular dualism of others. One can get applause on a talk show for the latter views, but not from the Scriptures. "One thing God has spoken, two things have I heard: that you, O God, are strong . . ." (Psalm 62:11). The Old Testament refers to God as "Almighty" numerous times in the English Bible — and never once to an angel or to a human being. The New Testament is equally consistent and clear.

> *He is the image of the invisible God, the firstborn over all creation. For by him all things were created: things in heaven and on earth, visible and invisible, whether thrones or powers or rulers or authorities; all things were created by him and for him. He is before all things, and in him all things hold together. And he is the head of the body, the church; he is the beginning and the firstborn from among the dead, so that in everything he might have the supremacy. (Colossians 1:15-18)*

> *For since the creation of the world God's invisible qualities — his eternal power and divine nature — have been clearly seen, being understood from what has been made, so that men are without excuse. (Romans 1:20)*

> *Then I heard what sounded like a great multitude, like the roar of rushing waters and like loud peals of thunder, shouting: "Hallelujah! For our Lord God Almighty reigns." (Revelation 19:6, KJV)*

Since God is omnipotent, he can do anything as easily as anything else. All his acts are done without effort. He has unlimited strength. When we pray "Yours is . . . the power," we are declaring that he can do anything!

If we do not believe this, we have no reason to pray. If he is not omnipotent, our prayers are exercises in pious futility. All six petitions of the Lord's Prayer require an omnipotent God. "Yours is . . . the power," truly believed, brings a profound dependence upon him. The Second Person of the Trinity tells us, "Apart from me you can do nothing" (John 15:5). That is profoundly true. But the converse is true as well. With God we can do great things. The French painter Emile Renouf depicted an old man dressed in fisherman's garb, seated in a boat with a little girl beside him. Both the elderly gentleman and the child have their hands on a huge oar. He is looking down fondly and admiringly upon her. Apparently he has told her that she may assist him in rowing the boat, and the child feels she is doing a great share of the task. It is easy to see, however, that it is his strong, muscular arms that are actually propelling the boat through the waves. The painting, titled "A Helping Hand," is a parable of what a soul can do when it depends upon God. God's hand propels us through life, even through storms, and accomplishes great things for his glory. "Yours is the power. All power is yours. We are dependent upon you, God." That is the reflex of the heart that knows the reality of the Lord's Prayer.

THE DOXOLOGY DECLARES THE GLORY TO BE GOD'S

The doxology now rises to its final declaration: "Yours is . . . the glory forever." When we think of God's glory, we think, first, of his splendorous existence in light — the brightness of which no man can bear — the *Shekinah* glory of which Moses saw the afterglow as God covered him with his hand when his glory passed by — the glory that momentarily flowed through Jesus on the Mount of Transfiguration when his face shone like the sun and his clothing became white with light. Second, when we think of glory we think of honor. Both of these infinitely belong to God. "Your is . . . the glory" is a martial-like shout that all splendor and all honor belong to God.

This is intensified by the addition of the word "forever." How long is forever? If a dove were to fly to the moon and bring the entire moon to earth piece by piece, by the time the dove had finished its task, eternity would have just begun. When we say, "Yours is . . . the glory forever," we are not talking about a static existence. The Greek translated "forever" reads literally "into the ages." The Hebrew idea, as opposed to the Greek idea of a timeless state, is an eternity of unfolding ages.

We joyfully declare in faith, "Yours is . . . the glory forever," for it will be God's always. And amazingly, we will share in that glory!

> *Therefore we do not lose heart. Though outwardly we are wasting away, yet inwardly we are being renewed day by day. For our light and momentary troubles are achieving for us an eternal glory that far outweighs them all. (2 Corinthians 4:16, 17)*

As we remember that his is the glory, we are called to deny our material fixations and to seek the things that are eternal. The proper reflex of the heart that prays the Lord's Prayer is to declare "Yours is . . . the glory forever," and to then say, "Amen," which is the Hebrew way of saying, "Let it be so" — "so be it." But here it means even more. It is a confident expression that "Yours is the kingdom and the power and the glory forever" will indeed be so. It is a word of faith and conviction. *Amen.*

27

Lasting Treasure

MATTHEW 6:19-21

Mrs. Bertha Adams was seventy-one years old when she died alone in West Palm Beach, Florida on Easter Sunday 1976. The coroner's report read, "Cause of Death . . . malnutrition." After wasting away to fifty pounds she could no longer stay alive. When the state authorities made their preliminary investigation of her home, they found a veritable "pigpen . . . the biggest mess you can imagine." One seasoned inspector declared he had never seen a dwelling in greater disarray. Bertha had begged food at her neighbors' doors and had gotten what clothes she had from the Salvation Army. From all appearances she was a penniless recluse — a pitiful and forgotten widow. But such was not the case! Amid the jumble of her filthy, disheveled belongings were found two keys to safe-deposit boxes at two different local banks. The discovery was unbelievable. The first box contained over 700 AT&T stock certificates, plus hundreds of other valuable notes, bonds, and solid financial securities, not to mention cash amounting to $200,000. The second box had no certificates, just cash — $600,000 to be exact. Bertha Adams was a millionaire and then some! Yet she died of starvation. Her case was even more tragic if she was destitute spiritually.

Her life is an extreme parable of the lethal dangers of materialism, which promises so much but cannot give us what we need most. Our consumer society is constantly telling us that life at its best consists of having more and more possessions and pleasures. As Christians, we know this is patently false. But the tug is so strong that many of us try a balancing act between what the Bible teaches and what the admen say, between the spiritual riches God offers us in Christ and worldly treasures that cannot feed our soul. Sadly, some of us lose our balance, and the results are devastating.

In Matthew 6:19-21 our Lord tells us in easy-to-remember terms how we should relate to the world. In a world boobytrapped with snares even more subtle than materialism, the Lord provides wisdom that will guide us safely and profitably. Our Lord reveals his wisdom first in a negative command in verse 19: "Do not store up for yourselves treasures on earth, where moth and rust destroy, and where thieves break in and steal." Then he says positively in verse 20, "But store up for yourselves treasures in heaven, where moth and rust do not destroy, and where thieves do not break in and steal." He concludes with an axiom in verse 21 that he wants us to build into our lives: "For where your treasure is, there your heart will be also."

NEGATIVE WISDOM ABOUT TREASURE (v. 19)

When Jesus said, "Do not store up for yourselves treasures on earth, where moth and rust destroy, and where thieves break in and steal," he was speaking in terms that were highly relevant to his hearers. He was speaking of the ultimate futility of supposing that one can somehow amass wealth and keep it safe and referred to three things — one's clothing, one's food supply, and one's gems and precious metals. Garments were considered a part of one's wealth in the Middle East. That is why Achan found a beautiful Babylonian garment so tempting and sinned against the Lord, resulting in his destruction (Joshua 7:21-26). Jesus reminded his hearers that all garments will succumb to the moth, no matter how fine they are. The word "rust" is an approximate translation of a word that means "eating" and refers better to the spoiling action of worms upon food storage. Jesus is here reminding his listeners that regardless of how vast their grain supplies, those supplies will ultimately succumb to the rats, mice, worms, and vermin. Finally, one's gold and silver were never safe in the ancient world. There were no such things as banks or savings and loans. Valuables were generally stored or buried in one's house. But the problem was that thieves regularly dug through the soft clay walls of homes and departed with the family wealth. From the Lord's point of view, the accumulation of wealth was a very precarious pursuit due to natural laws of deterioration and the fact that we live in a fallen world. His advice still holds today, regardless of FDIC guarantees and guaranteed high-yield investments.

So we see the surface meaning of Jesus' words, but the question is, what did he really mean by his command? Was he condemning all wealth? No. The Scriptures nowhere contain a prohibition of private property. Nor is saving for rainy days forbidden. In fact, it is encouraged, as in the parable of the ant in Proverbs 6:6-8. We are to provide for our own (1 Timothy 5:8). Moreover, Paul tells us in 1 Timothy 4:3, 4 that we are not to despise the good things of life by becoming ascetics, but rather are to enjoy food and the comforts of life. What Jesus is prohibiting in Matthew's Gospel is the selfish accumulation of goods. In Luke 12:15 he puts it this way: "Watch out!

Be on your guard against all kinds of greed; a man's life does not consist in the abundance of his possessions."

Certainly this is a warning to those who are rich, but this teaching is not for the wealthy only. Our text does not say, "Do not lay up for yourselves money on earth." It says, "treasures," and the Greek word used here is an inclusive term. Certainly it refers to money, but it is not confined to money. What Jesus has in mind are people who get their entire satisfaction from things that belong to this world only. He warns us against focusing our ambitions, interests, and hopes on the things of this life. Even if you have not set your mind on the greedy accumulation of great wealth, something else — for example, a home — could be a sinful treasure. I have seen young couples purchase their first home and shrivel with their new blessing. All their thoughts and energies were spent dreaming of chairs and sofas, the right antiques, colors, carpets — what they do not have. This is not a unique malady of the rich. There is also the treasure of family. Some people put family before everything. Some mothers and fathers think only of their children — a form of narcissism and selfishness. When we give such primacy to our family, there is no time for our neighbors and our community. Though one may not have a fixation on wealth, he may have "treasures" that are just as deadly — perhaps a CD collection, a position in the workplace, a memory. If anything in this world is *everything* to you, it is an earthly treasure.

The reason Jesus gives for prohibiting the storing of such treasure is that it will be destroyed. You cannot take it with you. It is temporal, not eternal. An old miser called his doctor, lawyer, and minister to his deathbed. "They say you can't take it with you," the dying man said. "But I'm going to try. I have three envelopes with $30,000 cash in each one. I want each of you to take an envelope, and as they lower my casket, throw in the envelopes!" Each man tossed in his envelope as requested. But on the way home the minister confessed, "I needed the money for the church, so I took out $10,000 and threw only $20,000 into the grave." The doctor said, "I, too, must confess. I'm building a clinic. So I took $20,000 and threw in only $10,000." The lawyer said, "Gentlemen, I'm ashamed of you. I threw in a personal check for the full amount." The old miser's material fixation produced a futile scheme to take his wealth with him, but the scheme did not even survive his burial because of the materialism of his three friends.

None of us will take anything with us! Job understood this perfectly: "Naked I came from my mother's womb, and naked I will depart" (Job 1:21). Or as the Spanish proverb says, "There are no pockets in a shroud."[1]

There is a tale of an eminent man, full of love of letters and art, who drew near the end of his life. One day an old family servant found him moving slowly and with tottering steps through his splendid library. He touched many a treasured volume with sensitive, loving fingers. He laid gentle hands upon one after another of the exquisite bits of statuary with which the room was adorned. He gazed at the many beautiful paintings. And as he moved slowly about, he said over and over, "I must leave you, I must leave you."[2]

That is the truth! We can take none of our earthly treasures with us. No money, no fame, and no position will go with us. We would be wise to remember that Jesus' words of prohibition are a command, not an option.

POSITIVE WISDOM ABOUT TREASURE (v. 20)

We see the positive side of this matter in verse 20: "But store up for yourselves treasures in heaven, where moth and rust do not destroy, and where thieves do not break in and steal." It is important that we not misunderstand what Jesus is saying here. He does not mean that one can earn his own salvation, for that would deny the central doctrine of the New Testament of justification by faith alone.

What Jesus *is* saying is that believers are positively rewarded in eternity according to the way they live their lives here on earth.

> *For no one can lay any foundation other than the one already laid, which is Jesus Christ. If any man builds on this foundation using gold, silver, costly stones, wood, hay or straw, his work will be shown for what it is, because the Day will bring it to light. It will be revealed with fire, and the fire will test the quality of each man's work. If what he has built survives, he will receive his reward. (1 Corinthians 3:11-14)*

As to what this "reward" is, the Scriptures are basically silent, and that is probably best. Needless to say, the treasure in Heaven will be substantial and beyond our wildest dreams. The thing Jesus emphasizes for us is that treasure in Heaven will be eternal. Nothing will destroy it — not moth or rust or thieves. The question we should ask ourselves about our present pursuits is, how important will they be 100 million trillion years from now? How important will our wallpaper be? How important will our promotion be? How important will our fame be? Are we making the right investments now in our lives? Exchanging the eternal for the temporal is no bargain.

How should we live? Paul's words in 1 Timothy 6:17-19 are helpful for all of us:

> *Command those who are rich in this present world not to be arrogant nor to put their hope in wealth, which is so uncertain, but to put their hope in God, who richly provides us with everything for our enjoyment. Command them to do good, to be rich in good deeds, and to be generous and willing to share. In this way they will lay up treasure for themselves as a firm foundation for the coming age, so that they may take hold of the life that is truly life.*

A WISE SAYING FOR LIFE (v. 21)

Now Jesus gives us an epigram for life, a saying that ought to be branded upon our souls, for it is lifesaving: "For where your treasure is, there your heart will be also."

In order to get all the sweetness out of this verse, we need to understand that "heart" here means a great deal more than it means in modern usage. Generally we think of *heart* as a name for the affections. But the Bible uses it for the whole inner man, the core of our total being, the wellspring of all we do. This means that Christ is telling us that where our treasure is, there will be all our total being. Not only will our affections focus on our treasure, but our entire self will be entwined with it. And as a result, what happens to our treasure happens to us. "Where our treasure is, there will be our inner being — our total person."

This verse is a gracious mirror in which we can see where our heart really is. It is natural and right for our vocation, our education, or our home to occupy a large place in our thoughts, but Christ warns against a total earthbound absorption with them. Realizing that where our treasure is, there is our heart also, we would do well to ask ourselves:

1. What occupies our thoughts when we have nothing else to do? What occupies our daydreams? Is it our investments, our position? If so, those are the things we treasure, and that is where our hearts really are.

2. Similarly, what is it that we fret about most? Is it our home or perhaps our clothing? If so, then we know where our treasure lies.

3. Apart from our loved ones, what or whom do we most dread losing?

4. What are the things that we measure others by? (This question is a very revealing mirror because we measure other people by that which we treasure.) Do we measure others by their clothing? By their education? By their homes? By their athletic prowess? Do we measure others by their success in the business world? If so, we know where our treasure lies.

5. Lastly, what is it that we know we cannot be happy without?

Jesus' words are an axiom of life without exceptions. "Where your treasure is, there your heart [your being] will be also." Where is your heart? On earthly treasure? If so, your treasure will suffer attack by moth, rust, and thieves, and it will be destroyed. And there is a danger that your heart will become like your treasure. As George Macdonald says:

> One day you will be compelled to see, nay, to *feel* your heart as God sees it; and to know that the cankered thing which you have within you, a prey to the vilest diseases, is indeed the center of your being, your very heart.[3]

Or is your heart set on heavenly treasure? If so, your treasure is incorruptible, and so is your heart.

What a gracious mirror the Lord's words give us. The ancient Assyrians had a superstition that if a demon saw itself in a mirror, it would fly away. The idea was that the demon's ugliness would cause it to flee in terror. The superstition was baseless, of course. However, the mirror of Christ's Word does allow us to see ourselves as we really are and thus allows us to do something about it. What do we see in Jesus' epigram, "for where your treasure is, there your heart will be also"? What are we going to do about it?

What has Jesus been urging in these beautiful words? Simply this: We are not permanent residents of this world — we are sojourners. When we truly admit this, everything falls into place. That was the secret behind the great lives of the saints in Hebrews 11. They walked as "seeing Him who is unseen" (v. 27, NASB). They were looking for the city whose "architect and builder is God" (v. 10). This is how we must see ourselves, and when we do, we see that we are stewards of the things God has given us. Our money, our intellects, our education, our homes, our position, our personalities are to be used in the service of God. The worldly man thinks he owns them, but the Christian says, "I am not the owner of these things. I have them on lease — they do not belong to me. I am a custodian. I cannot take them with me. I can only use them for God's glory. I must be careful about my attitude toward what I have been given. I must do what he tells me to do."

This is not a call for a life of negation and asceticism. Believers are to enjoy life fully and authentically. But the Christian does not hold tightly to what he has in this world. His possessions and privileges, whatever they may be, are not his focus. Dr. Lloyd-Jones puts it this way:

> I do not cling to these things. They do not become the centre of my life and existence. I do not live for them or dwell upon them constantly in my mind; they do not absorb my life. On the contrary, I hold them loosely . . . I am not governed by them; rather do I govern them; and as I do this I am steadily securing, and safely laying up for myself, "treasures in heaven."[4]

28

Unclouded Vision

MATTHEW 6:22-24

The words of the Lord in Matthew 6:19-21, considered in the previous study, provide us with a graciously revealing mirror of God's will concerning our treasures as well as a reflection of the condition of our souls. In that passage Jesus tells us not to store up earthly treasures, which are transitory, but to lay up for ourselves treasures in Heaven. He then goes on to proclaim, "where your treasure is, there your heart will be also." If we want to know where the center of our being is, all we have to do is honestly admit where our treasure is. The image we see in this spiritual mirror may be terrifying, but the reflection is gracious, for then we can do something about the situation, with God's help. Today's church, which is riddled with materialism and narcissism, needs this mirror desperately. As Os Guinness says in his book *The Gravedigger Files*:

> *Firm Believer* says it all. With spiritual narcissism so well advanced, "firm believer" is a matter of aerobics rather than apologetics, of human fitness rather than divine faithfulness. Shapeliness is now next to godliness, and to judge by the new "shape-up centers" in Christian stores, training righteous character has given way to trimming the right curves.[1]

The church's laying up earthly treasures is further seen in the popular theologies of success and the proliferation of "Jesus junk" and "holy hardware." These commercial ventures with a veneer of Christian platitudes reveal the materialistic philosophies that have invaded the church. Luther's indulgence-peddling archenemy, Tetzel, would feel right at home with some of today's money-hungry Protestants who apparently will do almost anything for a buck.

> The Lord is my banker, my credit is good. . . . He giveth me the key to his strongbox. He restoreth my faith in riches. He guideth me in the paths of prosperity for his namesake.[2]

The church today urgently needs to hold itself up to the mirror of Jesus' words and take them to heart.

To establish and expand his point, the Lord uses two more metaphors — vision (physical sight) and the slave master. Verses 22, 23 tell of two kinds of vision — one clear and the other dark. And verse 24 tells of the possibility of two masters — God and money (mammon). This passage deals with developing and maintaining a spiritual vision that is unclouded by selfishness or covetousness.

THE MEANING OF CHRIST'S WORDS

> *"The eye is the lamp of the body. If your eyes are good, your whole body will be full of light. But if your eyes are bad, your whole body will be full of darkness. If then the light within you is darkness, how great is that darkness!" (vv. 22, 23)*

The idea here is simple but beautiful. The eye is pictured as the window through which light comes into the body. If a window is clean and the glass is clear, the light that comes in will properly light every part of the room. If the window is dirty, or if the glass is uneven or tinted or discolored, the light will be hindered, and the room will not receive the full benefit of the light. The amount and quality of the light that comes into a room depends on the condition of the window through which it comes. So it is with the eye. The condition of the eye determines the quality of the light that enters the body. If you are color-blind, all the reds and greens of Christmas decorations are lost to you. If you have cataracts, you may sit next to someone and perceive only a shadow. If your eye is blind, "how great is that darkness." There are no colors, no forms, no motion.

Of course, Jesus is not giving us a lesson on optics. He is saying that the light that comes into a man's soul depends on the spiritual condition of the eye though which it has to pass because the eye is the window of the body. That is the basic meaning. But there is a more specific and deeper meaning depending on the two words "clear" (NASB) and "bad." I believe that "clear" here means "generous," and "bad" means "ungenerous." The Greek word translated "clear" was often used to mean generous in the Greek translation of the Old Testament (for example, Proverbs 11:25: "A generous man will prosper"). The word carries the same meaning in the New Testament. For example, in James 1:5 God is described as one "who gives generously to all." The same idea is seen in Romans 12:8,

2 Corinthians 8:2, 9:11, 13. Here in our text the specific meaning is "the generous eye."

Likewise, the phrase "bad" eye or "evil" eye (KJV) regularly refers to an ungenerous spirit. The rabbis said that an evil eye indicated a grudging, cheap, ungenerous heart. Proverbs 28:22 says, "A man with an evil eye hastens after wealth" (NASB). Proverbs 23:6 says, "Do not eat the food of a stingy man" (literally, "a man who has an evil eye"). Consider also Deuteronomy 15:9: "Be careful not to harbor this wicked thought: 'The seventh year, the year for canceling debts, is near,' so that you do not show ill will toward your needy brother and give him nothing. He may then appeal to the LORD against you, and you will be found guilty of sin" (literal translation: "Beware that you do not harbor an unlawful thought in your heart . . . and your eye *become evil [ungenerous]* toward your brother who is in need"; cf. Sirach 14:10: "A stingy man's eye begrudges bread, and it is lacking at his table" (literal translation: "an evil eye [is] envious for bread").

> *"The eye is the lamp of the body. If your eyes are good [generous], your whole body will be full of light. But if your eyes are bad [ungenerous],* your whole body will be full of darkness."

That this is the Lord's meaning is substantiated by the fact that it fits perfectly within the context, for this text is framed on both sides with warnings against selfish materialism. The preceding words are, "Do not store up for yourselves treasures on earth." And the following words are, "No one can serve two masters. . . . You cannot serve both God and Money."

THE APPLICATION OF JESUS' WORDS

In Luke 16:19-31 Jesus tells a story about a rich man who refused to show any mercy to a beggar at his gate. His self-centered, stingy spirit never thought of aiding poor Lazarus, who longed to be fed with crumbs from the man's table. Ultimately death came to them both, and the rich man was plunged into the darkness that had long been in his soul. In torment, he begged for a messenger to go and tell his living relatives about the truths he had failed to see during his life. Materialism shuts out the light of Christ. Such was the case with Esau, Solomon in later life, and tragic Demas, who forsook Paul "because he loved this world" (2 Timothy 4:10). And it is the same for us. The increasing materialism of the church is shutting out the light of Christ. Some evangelicals know all the passwords and carry well-thumbed Bibles but are just as dark on the inside as the rich man in Jesus' parable. The effects of an ungenerous spirit are far worse than any of us really knows.

Such a spirit clouds the way we look at life. When the things of this world are our focus, we believe we cannot be happy without them. That's the unrelenting gospel of TV-land, and the majority of people believe it. Christians need to learn the lesson a certain unhappy king learned. That poor king was so discontented with life that he called in his wise men and asked if they could help. Their consensus was that if the king could find a happy man and borrow his shirt and wear it for his garment, he would be happy. A delegation was sent out to find a happy man. They searched and searched and almost gave up but at last found a happy man. There was only one problem — he had no shirt! Materialism clouds our vision of happiness.

It also clouds our vision of success. Because of our grasping spirits, some of us have defined success in financial terms and have thereby condemned ourselves to perpetual failure because we never quite reach our goal. What a tragedy!

A grasping spirit also clouds our vision of others' worth. If others do not join us in the scramble for the things of this world, we call them spiritless or lacking in ambition or worse. I have seen missionaries despised by Christians because of their choice to serve Christ in a way that means a lower income.

A grasping heart also keeps us from having a healthy vision for our children's lives. Their chosen profession must fit our economic and social criteria, we think. Never mind that Christ was a carpenter. And our sons' and daughters' future spouses had better move them toward our criteria too!

A grasping spirit also distorts our vision of God's will for our own lives. We selfishly assume God would never lead us onto a path that would involve a diminishing of our status, position, or bank account. How different are the Master's words:

> *"I tell you the truth, unless a kernel of wheat falls to the ground and dies, it remains only a single seed. But if it dies, it produces many seeds. The man who loves his life will lose it, while the man who hates his life in this world shall keep it for eternal life." (John 12:24, 25)*

Furthermore, and perhaps most seriously, a selfish fixation on things clouds our ability to understand and profit from the Scriptures. No wonder the Bible is so minimized and ignored by twentieth-century man.

So a grasping, ungenerous spirit darkens our inner lives. Very little spiritual light is able to penetrate the eye of the materialist. It also clouds and distorts our vision.

Such an attitude is indeed tragic, being fraught with a pervasive dissatisfaction. For such persons, nothing ever completely satisfies. There is always a desire for more and better. One of my past parishioners who did the electrical work on the mansion of a prominent California family told me that the lady of the house ordered the painter to repaint her bedroom fourteen times, finally deciding on one of the earliest shades! With that kind of mind-set, life is a like Chinese dinner. No matter how good and satisfying the meal is, you'll be hungry two hours later!

This dissatisfaction goes hand in hand with covetousness and envy.

Envy went to church this morning.
Being Legion, he sat in every other pew,
Envy fingered wool and silk fabrics,
Hung price tags on suits and neckties.

Envy paced through the parking lot
Scrutinizing chrome and paint.
Envy marched to the chancel with the choir
During the processional.

Envy scattered information
About better committees and better promotions
Through piously bowed heads. . . .

Envy thumped at widows and widowers,
Jabbed and kicked college girls without escorts,
Lighted invisible fires inside . . . jackets.

Envy conferred often this morning
With all of his brothers;
He liked his Sunday scores today
But not enough.

ELVA MCALLASTER

Compulsive ambition comes into the picture too because those filled with dissatisfaction and covetousness are always trying to "arrive" professionally and socially. Those who project the most security and élan are predictably the least satisfied and soon find themselves treating other people as things to be used to fulfill one's desires. During the last century we saw this in the use of child labor by British industry. Children seven or eight years of age (in one case *three* years old) were employed in the mines, working as much as sixteen hours a day. When Christians began to protest the situation, other believers actually complained, saying reform would bring economic chaos to the country. Of course, that was one of the motivations behind slavery in our own country as well. In less dramatic ways many of us have been treated as objects by those who are in the clutches of materialism, and that is never pleasant or right. As Jesus said:

> *"The eye is the lamp of the body. If your eyes are good [generous], your whole body will be full of light. But if your eyes are bad [ungenerous],* your whole body will be full of darkness. If then the light within you is darkness, how great is that darkness!"

Sadly, most of those who are in the darkness do not even know it. They are self-deceived. Many Christians are like this. They think their eye is good when it is bad. They think their loyalty to Christ and his values is deep and grounded, when in fact it is shallow and contrived. Greed reigns, not Christ! And "how great is that darkness!" How tragic this is! Thousands of Christians think they have it all together, but their eyes are clouded by materialism and their lives are inauthentic. How is your vision?

That is the dark side of Jesus' saying, but there is also a bright side: "If your eyes are good [generous], your whole body will be full of light." The believer who has a generous spirit, who is not tightly grasping the things of this world, maximizes the reception of light (divine truth) in his life. The Scriptures are open before such a heart, for he is seeking the things above. Then not only does the eye of such a person receive light, but it radiates light to those around. This person is "a city set on a hill [that] cannot be hidden" (Matthew 5:14). This person's light shines before others in such a way that they see his beautiful works and glorify his Father in Heaven (Matthew 5:16). And as we might expect, a person with a generous spirit holds the things of life loosely, bringing great joy to others and experiencing it himself.

This principle is illustrated in a story about Bismarck, the famous German general and chancellor:

> It was after one of the big battles of the Franco-German war. It had been a grim struggle, but at last the issue had been decided and victory won. And Bismarck — the tension over — took out a cigar, the last he had, happy in the thought of a smoke. But just as he was about to apply the match to it, he saw a wounded soldier looking at his cigar with longing eyes. Bismarck understood the appeal. He lit the cigar and gave it to the wounded soldier, and saw him in such enjoyment that he almost forgot the pain of his wound. "It was the best cigar I ever had," said the old warrior.[3]

How wonderful such "bests" are — the best meals, the best coats, the best beds, the best books. Jesus himself tells us in Luke 16:9, "Use worldly wealth to make friends for yourselves, so that when it is gone, you will be welcomed into eternal dwellings." Our wealth can be used not to buy friends, but to build friendships.

Now Jesus begins to explain that foundational to our choosing where we will lay up our treasures and which of the two visions we will set our eyes upon is an even more fundamental choice between two masters.

Before considering Jesus' words, we need to remind ourselves that money is non-moral. There is no inherent evil in it and no inherent good. The questions of right and wrong have to do with what we do with money. You put it to low uses or you can put it to good use, bringing eternal reward and riches. Furthermore, the amount you have is not the determining factor. A ditchdigger may be miserly and covetous, while a wealthy stockbroker may be generous. Now, what does Jesus say?

> *"No one can serve two masters. Either he will hate the one and love the other, or he will be devoted to one and despise the other. You cannot serve both God and Money." (v. 24)*

Love and hate are common Semitic idioms. Jesus' meaning is clear — you will always prefer one master over the other. (Cf. Luke 14:26 where the same language is used concerning one's family and Christ.) In the case of the opposing masters of God and Money (Mammon), we will *always* prefer one over the other.

Both these masters make total demands on us. Worldly things demand our entire devotion, but so does God. "Love the LORD your God with all your heart and with all your soul and with all your strength" (Deuteronomy 6:5). God wants our all!

Yet, how prone we are to compromise, to try to walk the fence. When we do this, we become like the Assyrians: "While these people were worshiping the LORD, they were serving their idols" (2 Kings 17:41). We are sometimes like that. "If then the light within you is darkness, how great is that darkness!" In the final analysis there is nothing so insulting to God as to say we are serving him but then to show by our lives that we are serving Mammon.

> The story is told as the actual truth which perfectly illustrates what we are saying: It is the story of a farmer who one day went happily and with great joy in his heart to report to his wife and family that their best cow had given birth to twin calves, one red and one white. And he said, "You know, I have suddenly had a feeling and impulse that we must dedicate one of these calves to the Lord. We will bring them up together, and when the time comes we will sell one and keep the proceeds, and we will sell the other and give the proceeds to the Lord's work." His wife asked him which he was going to dedicate to the Lord. "There is no need to bother about that now," he replied, "we will treat them both in the same way, and when the time comes we will do as I say." And off he went.
>
> In a few months the man entered his kitchen looking very miserable

> and unhappy. When his wife asked him what was troubling him, he answered, "I have bad news to give you. The Lord's calf is dead." "But," she said, "you had not decided which was to be the Lord's calf." "Oh yes," he said; "I had always decided it was to be the white one, and it is the white one that has died. The Lord's calf is dead."
>
> We may laugh at that story, but God forbid that we should be laughing at ourselves. It is always the Lord's calf that dies. When money becomes difficult, the first thing we economize on is our contribution to God's work.[4]

Where is your heart? Where is mine? Is the light within us still light, or has it become darkness? And which master do we serve — God or Money?

29

"Do Not Worry . . . But Seek First"

MATTHEW 6:25-34

In Matthew 6:19-24 Jesus warned us about the problem of materialism. In 6:25-34 he turns to its twin malady of worry. Jesus knew that a materialistic focus leads to anxiety regardless of whether one is rich or poor. Three times in this text the Lord tells us not to worry:

> *"Therefore I tell you, do not worry about your life." (v. 25)*
>
> *"So do not worry . . ." (v. 31)*
>
> *"Therefore do not worry about tomorrow." (v. 34)*

Here our Lord powerfully and memorably gives us his counsel regarding anxiety. It was needed then, and it is even more needed today. Anxiety is the universal disease of our age. Way back in 1961 *Time* magazine said:

> Not merely the black statistics of murder, suicide, alcoholism, and divorce betray anxiety . . . but almost any innocent everyday act: the limp or over-hearty handshake, the second pack of cigarettes or the third martini, the forgotten appointment, the stammer in mid-sentence, the wasted hour before the TV set, the spanked child, the new car unpaid for.[1]

And things have not gotten any better since then. Businessmen torment themselves with imagined scenarios of what could take place if X does so and so and Y counters. Mothers worry over the future of their children until it is *their* very future that is in question. Students worry over examinations and future interviews and dates and grad school and money. Kierkegaard said it well: "No Grand Inquisitor has in readiness such terrible tortures as anxiety." Today people consume tranquilizers and sedatives by the ton and are running to counselors by the millions. Christ's counsel is sorely needed, and what he says here can profit every one of us.

I do not believe Christ's intent here is to foster in us a detached "who cares" attitude. There is a type of good worry (or perhaps I should say good concern) that all healthy Christians have. For example, Luther says we are to be anxious about the spiritual well-being of others[2] and points to Paul as the example in 2 Corinthians 11:28, 29:

> *Besides everything else, I face daily the pressure of my concern for all the churches. Who is weak, and I do not feel weak? Who is led into sin, and I do not inwardly burn?*

We are also to be concerned about the state of our hearts and the incessant temptations to sin (see Psalms 38 and 51). And there is the care and concern that is inherent in any serious work for God. We are to think, plan, and anticipate any pitfalls (see Luke 14:28-32). Some concern is good, but Jesus is counseling us against worry that is self-centered and has at its root a lack of trust in God. No good architect does a good job of building a bridge without sometimes waking up at night and checking his figures, the quality of his metals, and the quality of his design. No great athlete performs to his or her best without some concern about what he or she is doing. The distinction is sometimes very subtle. A preacher might be honestly concerned about his sermon — that it be true to the text, practical, spoken in the power of the Holy Spirit and in love. Or he might simply be worried about his reputation. The first is healthy and godly, the second is not.

CHRIST'S COUNSEL: DO NOT BE ANXIOUS BECAUSE GOD IS THE KING OF LIFE (vv. 25-30)

> *"Therefore I tell you, do not worry about your life, what you will eat or drink; or about your body, what you will wear. Is not life more important than food, and the body more important than clothes?" (v. 25)*

Jesus' words here get our attention because he cites the world's trinity of cares — what we eat, drink, and wear. One glance at the TV or current magazines and we see how on target Jesus was.

An issue of *Accent* magazine some time back carried the normal alluring advertisements for champagne, cigarettes, food, clothing, antiques, and carpets, together with an "esoteric weekend's shopping in Rome." There were also articles on how to win a luxury cabin cruiser or 100 twelve-bottle cases of scotch. The following month's issue included articles on staying in bed, high-fashion underwear, and the "delights of reindeer meat and snow-berries" — everything needed for the welfare of the body and "how to feed it, clothe it, warm it, cool it, refresh it, relax it, entertain it . . . and titillate it."[3] Self-indulgence is what our culture is all about, and that is why there is so much anxiety. Such narcissism is obviously unhealthy, being built on a false reductionist view of humanity — the belief that we are just bodies that need to be fed, watered, clothed, and housed.

Jesus did not teach us to despise the pleasures of life, but he did say by implication that if we see life in this reductionist manner, we are bound to have anxiety. And frankly I believe that is where Christians' anxiety comes from. We say our values are above the world's, but in fact we often believe there is little more to life than what we eat, drink, or wear. Jesus' words in verse 25 are very convicting. They not only give us the diagnosis of our anxiety, but they also contain a subtle *a fortiori* argument (that is, an argument that proceeds from the greater to the lesser). The argument is found in the final line of the verse: "Is not life more important than food, and the body more important than clothes?" Since life itself comes directly from God, why should we worry and fret about his giving us the food and drink necessary for life? He will not go halfway. He gave you life, and he will maintain it as long as he wills. If there is a God who has given us the great gift of life (and he has!), we do not need to be anxious about the little things we need day by day.

Next Jesus gives us in verses 26-30 three illustrations of his care from the animate and inanimate world. These illustrations enforce what he has already said. The first has to do with food and the example of the birds:

> *"Look at the birds of the air; they do not sow or reap or store away in barns, and yet your heavenly Father feeds them. Are you not much more valuable than they?" (v. 26)*

This is a verse that John Stott loves to quote. He is Rector Emeritus at All Souls' in London and is one of the foremost Bible expositors in the world — and a zealous bird-watcher. He says:

> Some readers may know that I happen myself to have been since boyhood an enthusiastic bird-watcher. I know, of course, that bird-watching is regarded by some as a rather eccentric pastime; they view the likes of me with quizzical and patronizing amusement. But I claim Biblical — indeed dominical — warrant for this activity. "Consider the fowls of the air," said Jesus according to the AV, and this in basic English could be trans-

> lated "watch birds"! (Indeed I am quite serious, for the Greek verb in his command [*emblepsate eis*] means "fix your eyes on, so as to take a good look at."[4]

When we take a good look at the birds and verse 26, we see the obvious. There are millions and millions of birds, and by and large they are healthy and happy. None of them are suffering hypertension, none are suffering stress-related diseases, and certainly none of them are worrying. God takes care of them even though, unlike us, they do not sow or reap. And God will take care of us too. That is the obvious meaning.

But what Jesus did *not* mean needs to be said too. He was not calling us to laziness or indolence. Birds themselves instinctively make provision for the future. In fact, some argue that no creature works harder than the birds! Neither does the example of the birds teach us that if we trust God, every day will be smooth sailing. Sparrows sometimes starve, sometimes they are eaten by predators, and certainly they all die in a short span.

The specific application is this: The birds demonstrate God's care for the lower creation, and thus we who are a much higher creation can be assured of his great care.

Said the robin to the sparrow:
"I should really like to know
Why these anxious human beings
Rush about and worry so."

Said the sparrow to the robin:
"Friend, I think that it must be
That they have no heavenly Father,
Such as cares for you and me."[5]

Well said! But the truth is even stronger because the birds do *not*, in fact, have a father. Only we, his children, can call God our Father. What's more, the birds do not bear his image, but we do! Jesus' question, "Are you not much more valuable than they?" (v. 26) is an understatement! There is no reason for us to be anxious. We need not fret about the essentials of life.

Moreover, our anxiety will not lengthen our lives. Verse 27 says, "Who of you by worrying can add a single hour to his life?" Worry about clothing, food, and drink will not add to our quality of life, and it certainly will not lengthen our life span. In fact, anxiety not only inhibits our ability to enjoy the things of life — it shortens our time to enjoy them!

Regarding clothing, Jesus gave a beautiful teaching illustration:

> *"And why do you worry about clothes? See how the lilies of the field grow. They do not labor or spin. Yet I tell you that not even Solomon in all his splendor was dressed like one of these." (vv. 28, 29)*

In light of Solomon's great glory, some might think this illustration is overstated. Far from it! "Lilies of the field" are wildflowers, and a microscope applied to *any* of them reveals a magnificence that makes Solomon's robes look like rags! These wildflowers collectively decorate the green grass with exquisite beauty for a short time, but then they are mown down like mere weeds and are tossed into the furnace. We again see the divine logic:

> *"If that is how God clothes the grass of the field, which is here today and tomorrow is thrown into the fire, will he not much more clothe you, O you of little faith?" (v. 30)*

Since God takes care of inanimate flowers that cannot reason or toil, how much more will he care for us, his gifted creation, to whom he repeatedly gives his immediate and living presence. Luther says it for us all:

> It seems . . . that the flowers stand there and make us blush and become our teachers. Thank you, flowers, you, who are to be devoured by the cows! God has exalted you very highly, that you become our masters and teachers.[6]

How powerful Jesus' argument is! "Is not life more important than food, and the body more important than clothes?" (v. 25b). Since he has given us the great gift of life, will he not give us the lesser daily things? Consider the birds, consider the flowers, and rest in him!

CHRIST'S COUNSEL: DO NOT BE ANXIOUS BECAUSE YOU ARE THE KING'S CHILDREN (vv. 31-34)

> *"So do not worry, saying, 'What shall we eat?' or 'What shall we drink?' or 'What shall we wear?'" (v. 31)*

Here Jesus changes the argument to a more personal vein. We need not be anxious because we are the King's children. He will provide all we need.

He also tells us that if we are anxious about these things, we will be just like the secular world: "For the pagans run after all these things, and your heavenly Father knows that you need them" (v. 32).

The Gentiles, the secular world, seek material things because they overestimate their significance. The characteristic tendency of those without Christ is to be bound by the horizons of earth. Everything is crammed into the visible. This, in turn, promotes worry about secondary matters such as food and clothes.

Unbelievers' anxiety also rests on a misunderstanding of God's character. They naturally think of God as far removed from the complexities of life and ignorant of their struggles. What distinguishes our thinking as Christians from that of unbelievers is that we know our "heavenly Father knows that [we] need" all these things (v. 32b). God is our Father, and he wants us to trust in him.

How, then, as God's children should we live? Jesus gives his famous answer in verse 33: "But seek first his kingdom and his righteousness, and all these things will be given to you as well." Seeking his kingdom primarily means trying to spread the reign of Christ through the spread of the gospel. It involves a profound poverty of spirit. Seeking his righteousness involves making his righteousness attractive in all areas of life — personal, family, material, international. The Lord tells us that the one who does this is approved: "Blessed are those who hunger and thirst for righteousness, for they will be filled" (Matthew 5:6). Matthew 6:33 marvelously encompasses our evangelistic and social responsibilities, which we are to carry out with fervor one day at a time. "Therefore do not worry about tomorrow, for tomorrow will worry about itself. Each day has enough trouble of its own" (v. 34).

"Tomorrow," the future, will have trouble. It is unavoidable. No Christian should ever be caught in what I call the "then syndrome." "Then things are going to be trouble free." "When I get married, then I'll be beyond trouble." "When I have children . . . when I get a promotion . . ." It is futile to try to live a problem-free life. You can spend all your time and energy fortifying the castle of your life, but there is always a place that goes unguarded. Tomorrow will have its challenges and trials, no matter how hard you try to prevent them.

We are not to worry about tomorrow. Worry will not destroy tomorrow's trials, but it will sabotage our strength. George Macdonald put it this way: "No man ever sank under the burden of the day. It is when tomorrow's burden is added to the burden of today, that the weight is more than a man can bear."[7]

Worrying does not enable you to escape evil. It makes you unfit to cope with it. The truth is, we always have the strength to bear the trouble when it comes. But we do not have the strength to bear worrying about it. If you add today's troubles to tomorrow's troubles, you give yourself an impossible burden.

Also, worry makes us subject to miseries that we otherwise would never know. A line from Faust says it perfectly:

Each blow that falls not dost thou feel,
And what thou ne'er shalt lose,
That ever art bewailing.

The anxious heart receives all kinds of blows through anticipatory anxiety that will never happen. Some of us have suffered much more in this world than has ever happened to us. We fear everything because everything is possible. Such a heart possesses nothing, though it may have all. Its only real possessions are its fears.

Jesus' counsel is so beautiful: "Therefore do not worry about tomorrow, for tomorrow will worry about itself. Each day has enough trouble of its own."

Stop worrying. Anxiety is futile. Do not borrow trouble. How can we possibly do this?

Verse 33 is the answer! "Seek first" is in the present imperative, which means we are to be in a continual quest for God's kingdom and God's righteousness. When you and I do this, our focus is no longer on what we wear, eat, and drink, and we are thus liberated from the blight of anxiety. If we constantly seek him, there will be no room for lesser matters. If we seek his kingdom and his righteousness, the cares of the day will flee.

In summary: Reject the secular reductionist mind-set. You are more than a body. Along with this, refuse to focus on the world's trinity of cares.

Consider the birds and the flowers. If God cares for the lesser, what will he do for the greater — for us?

Do not live in the future. Live now. Put your arms around your wife right now. Take a walk with your child today. Enjoy the life God has given you.

"But seek first his kingdom and his righteousness, and all these things will be given to you as well."

30

The Speck and the Log

MATTHEW 7:1-5

Richard DeHaan, in his book *Men Sent from God*, lists some of the criticisms pastors receive. The list is written "tongue in cheek," of course. If the pastor is young, they say he lacks experience. If his hair is gray, he is too old for the young people. If he has five or six children, he is irresponsible; if he has no children, he is setting a bad example. If he uses a lot of illustrations, he neglects the Bible; if he does not use enough, he is not relevant. If he condemns wrong deeds, he's cranky; if he does not, he's compromising. If he drives an old car, he shames his congregation; if he drives a new one, he's setting his affection on earthly things.

DeHaan's point is that criticism is part and parcel of the public life of the ministry. In fact, criticism is part of living, period. You cannot do anything without being criticized by someone — whether you are selling newspapers, knitting a sweater, working your farm, or mowing your lawn. The ever-present fact is, people are by nature critical and condemning, as the experience of a certain young bachelor illustrates. Every time he brought a prospective wife home, his mother criticized her unmercifully. The young man was at his wit's end when a friend offered this advice: "Find someone like your mother." So he looked and looked until he found a clone. She looked like his mother, her gait was like his mother's, she talked like his mother, and she even thought like his mother. It was amazing! So he took her home. The next time he saw the friend who had given the advice and was asked how his mother liked the girl, the bachelor answered, "It went great. My mother loved her, but my father couldn't stand her."

A critical spirit, a judgmental, condemning spirit, is endemic to the human situation. The media, our social relationships, our schooling, and our work situations are immersed in it. And though we often joke about it, experiencing it is most unpleasant. Few things are more exhausting and debilitating than harsh, unloving criticism.

Even sadder, the church of Jesus Christ is itself full of those who make a habit of criticism and condemnation. Some seem to think their critical spirit is a spiritual gift. But the Lord does not agree. In the opening verses of Matthew 7 (the final chapter of the Sermon on the Mount), our Lord sets the record straight in no uncertain terms. He tells us how we should relate to our brothers and sisters in this matter of judgmentalism, especially in respect to the fact that we will all undergo a final judgment.

WE ARE NOT TO RELATE JUDGMENTALLY TO OTHERS (vv. 1, 2)

Our Lord minces no words in his opening statement in verse 1: "Do not judge, or you too will be judged." His words have been subject to much misunderstanding. These first three words, "Do not judge," have been taken by some to mean that good Christians must never exercise any critical judgment. Some believe model Christians are totally accepting, whatever the situation. Christlikeness is equated with a suspension of critical faculties — a pious, all-accepting blindness. Ironically, the world loves opinionated people. Its darlings are those who are articulate and dogmatic about their positions on politics, art, music, literature, culture — you name it! However, when it comes to matters of individual morality, the world abhors opinionated people, especially if they represent conventional morality. In these matters it adores the nonjudgmental person. The ideal Christian, and especially the ideal clergyman, is an undiscerning, flabby, indulgent, all-accepting jellyfish who lives out the misinterpretation of "judge not."

The reasons this text cannot be made to say that we are never to judge are quite simple and obvious. First, in verse 6, which immediately follows Jesus' teaching on judgment in verses 1-4, Jesus continues by saying, "Do not give dogs what is sacred; do not throw your pearls to pigs." We cannot obey Jesus' command here unless we must judge who are "dogs" and who are "pigs." Similarly, just a few verses later in verse 15, Jesus warns us to "Watch out for false prophets. They come to you in sheep's clothing, but inwardly they are ferocious wolves." This requires subtle, discriminating judgment on our part. Many additional Scriptures exhort us to exercise judgment.

> *Dear friends, do not believe every spirit, but test the spirits to see whether they are from God, because many false prophets have gone out into the world. (1 John 4:1)*

"Stop judging by mere appearances, make a right judgment." (John 7:24)

Christians have an obligation to exercise critical judgment! What Christ means when he says "Do not judge" is that we are to refrain from hypercritical, condemning judgment. There is a universe of difference between being discerningly critical and hypercritical. A discerning spirit is constructive. A hypercritical spirit is destructive. The person with a destructive, overcritical spirit revels in criticism for its own sake. He expects to find fault, like the man who sat watching his preacher neighbor nail up a trellis in his backyard. The preacher, seeing him watching intently from his yard, asked, "Trying to pick up some pointers on carpentry?" To which his neighbor replied, "Nope. Just waiting to see what a preacher says when he hits his thumb." When a critic discovers faults in another, he feels a malignant satisfaction and always sees the worst possible motives in the other's actions. The critical spirit is like the carrion fly that buzzes with a sickening hum of satisfaction over sores, preferring corruption to health.

One of the most prominent characteristics of this critical, fault-finding person is that he predictably focuses on things that are of little importance and treats them as matters of vital importance. Within the church this takes bizarre forms — judging the spirituality of a young couple by observing whether they spank their children with a bare hand or an implement, judging others by where they sit in church or the Bible version they carry or whether their theology agrees with the critic's point for point . . . and so it goes! This pettiness on secondary issues is condemned in Romans 14 in the strongest of terms.

> *Accept him whose faith is weak, without passing judgment on disputable matters. One man's faith allows him to eat everything, but another man, whose faith is weak, eats only vegetables. The man who eats everything must not look down on him who does not, and the man who does not eat everything must not condemn the man who does, for God has accepted him. Who are you to judge someone else's servant? To his own master he stands or falls. And he will stand, for the Lord is able to make him stand. (vv. 1-4)*

Paul adds in another passage:

> *You, therefore, have no excuse, you who pass judgment on someone else, for at whatever point you judge the other, you are condemning yourself, because you who pass judgment do the same things. (Romans 2:1)*

We set the standard and tone for our own final judgment by our judgmental conduct in life. And we prove by our judging of others that we know what is right. So if we do not do what is right, we condemn ourselves.

Perhaps the clearest statement of this is in James 3:1, "Not many of you should presume to become teachers, my brothers, because you know that we who teach will be judged more strictly." If you become a teacher, set yourself up as a religious authority over others, and act accordingly, you will be judged by the authority you claim. Do I claim to have an exceptional knowledge and grasp of Scripture? I will be judged accordingly. Do I claim to have been an especially wise and discerning servant? I will be judged according to the position I have assumed. If we set ourselves as authorities and judges over others, we should not be surprised or complain when we are judged by our own standard. "For in the way you judge, you will be judged; and by your standard of measure, it will be measured to you" (Matthew 7:2). We need to face and apply this text with all its fearful force.

How will this affect us eternally? There are two eternal judgments. One is the separation of believers and nonbelievers, "the sheep from the goats" (Matthew 25:31-46). True believers, of course, are the sheep who will go to be with God and who will appear before the Judgment Seat of Christ to receive their proper rewards. There God will judge us as we have judged others. Judgmental believers will still go to be with God forever, but they will have very little reward, for their hypercritical spirit will have vitiated much of the good they had done. Very few of us dare to pray, "God, judge me as I judge my fellow men and women." Our Lord means to put a holy fear in us so we will put away our critical hearts! God is going to judge us as we judge others. The tone of our life is going to become the tone of our judgment.

> *For we must all appear before the judgment seat of Christ, that each one may receive what is due him for the things done while in the body, whether good or bad. Since, then, we know what it is to fear the Lord, we try to persuade men. What we are is plain to God, and I hope it is also plain to your conscience. (2 Corinthians 5:10, 11)*

There is nothing more ungodly than a critical spirit, and nothing more un-Christlike than the false righteousness that is always looking for something wrong in someone else. Now our Lord extends his argument even further.

WE ARE NOT TO RELATE TO OTHERS HYPERCRITICALLY (vv. 3, 4)

> *"Why do you look at the speck of sawdust in your brother's eye and pay no attention to the plank in your own eye? How can you say to your brother, 'Let me take the speck out of your eye,' when all the time there is a plank in your own eye?"*

The picture Jesus gives here is as ludicrous and sarcastic as possible. The word translated "plank" ("log" in other translations) denotes a huge piece of wood, like a rafter in a house. "Speck" is a small piece of sawdust. With such a monstrous log in a man's eye, his vision would not be simply impaired — he would be absolutely blinded! The idea of his lending a helping hand to another man who has a speck in his eye would not only be comical but impossible! The tragedy is, the situation Jesus is portraying is common.

When King David was at the lowest point morally in his life, having taken Uriah's wife and committing adultery with her, discovering that she was pregnant and then having Uriah murdered, Nathan the prophet told him a story about a rich man with huge flocks of sheep who lived next door to a poor man. The poor man had only one little ewe lamb that he loved like a daughter. But the rich man, not wanting to take a lamb out of his own herds to feed some guests, took that little lamb and slaughtered it. David's response was basically, "That man deserves to die. He must repay everything fourfold." Nathan, pointing a prophetic finger at the king, pronounced, "You are that man." Forget someone else's speck — look at the log in your own eye, David!

We find it so easy to turn a microscope on another person's sin while we look at ours through the wrong end of a telescope! We use some strong term for someone else's sin but a euphemism for our own. We easily spot a speck of phoniness in another because we have a logjam of it in our own lives. Furthermore, we especially hate our own faults when we see them in others. Wrath toward the speck in someone else's life may come from the suppressed guilt over the same massive sin in our own lives. Log-toting speck inspectors are hypocrites, says Jesus (v. 5). They do not care at all about the speck in the other person's eye. All they really care about is building up themselves in their own eyes. The pattern is universal. Self-righteousness turns to censoriousness, which produces a false benevolence ("Let me help you with that speck"), which in turn produces contempt. I have seen the most unchristian aggression practiced by ostentatiously humble people who come with a "concern." What are we to do instead?

WE ARE RATHER TO BE BROTHERS AND SISTERS TO EACH OTHER (v. 5)

> *"You hypocrite, first take the plank out of your own eye, and then you will see clearly enough to remove the speck from your brother's eye." (v. 5)*

We are to judge ourselves — "take the plank out of your own eye." Both the Old and New Testaments call us to do this. And when we do it, we begin to see others as they are.

"Blessed are the poor in spirit, for theirs is the kingdom of heaven. Blessed are those who mourn, for they will be comforted." (Matthew 5:3, 4)

We then see ourselves as we are, and we see others as they are. Instead of being critical, we weep for ourselves and them. When we have removed the log from our own eye, then we can see clearly to take the speck out of our brothers' and sisters' eyes. Jesus does not encourage a laissez-faire attitude toward fellow believers. Jesus does want us to discern the sins and shortcomings in others, but he wants us to see them through clear, self-judged eyes — eyes that are tender and compassionate.

The procedure for removing a speck from an eye is very difficult and delicate. There is nothing in the human body more sensitive than the eye. The instant we touch it, it closes up. What is required in clearing an eye is gentleness, carefulness, patience, and sympathy for the other person. In the spiritual realm, the care is even more delicate, for we are handling a soul — the most sensitive part of a human being. We must be humble, sympathetic, conscious of our own sins, and without condemnation. We need God's mercy. We need to be people who speak the truth in love because the love of God controls us.

We see critical spirits all around us — in our media, in our schools, in our social relationships. But it should not be a part of the church. May God purge it from our lives and from our churches. We would each do well to ask ourselves, who have I been critical of this week? Has my focus on their faults blinded me to my own? Then we need to ask God to help us see ourselves as we are.

First Corinthians 13:4-8 is helpful in this regard. Verses 6-8 say, "Love does not delight in evil but rejoices with the truth. It always protects, always trusts, always hopes, always perseveres. Love never fails."

31

"Seek and You Will Find"

MATTHEW 7:7-11

There are two ways to approach the Sermon on the Mount. One is proudly, believing that the Sermon is simply a list of exalted, though humanly attainable, moral precepts. Some who hold this view have said that the Sermon on the Mount is the only really necessary part of Scripture, the rest can be discarded, and people just need to give moral adherence to the Sermon on the Mount. They say they love it because it is from Christ and therefore is not cluttered with Paul's theologizing as in the epistles. According to such persons, with some moral education and some discipline, the world will be revolutionized. This view, dominated with fleshly presumption about the goodness of man and an amazingly shallow view of the Sermon on the Mount, always brings failure.

The other (correct) view, approaches the Sermon on the Mount humbly, with a deep sense of the need for God's grace. Far from finding the Sermon untheological, those who hold this view see that the teachings of the Sermon are amazingly theological and profoundly requiring. In fact they require perfection, as Jesus says after its first great movement: "Be perfect, therefore, as your heavenly Father is perfect" (5:48). Those holding this view understand the first Beatitude though moralists do not. They know it teaches that poverty of spirit, a sense of moral bankruptcy, and the realization that one cannot live the Sermon on the Mount by oneself, is the key to living the Sermon on the Mount. Thus they approach God as beggars and receive grace to do the impossible — and they succeed!

In Matthew 7:7-11 Jesus describes the way a man or woman prays who understands what the Sermon on the Mount is all about. The instruction in this text should not be lifted from its context in the Sermon and abused. All of us have heard this done. "The Bible says, 'Ask, and it shall be given to you; seek, and you shall find; knock, and it shall be opened to you.' Therefore, all we have to do is ask for it with faith and persistence, and we *will* get it. 'You do not have because you do not ask' (James 4:2). So go for it! Name it and claim it!" This view sees God as a celestial slot machine. Pull the handle enough times in prayer, be persistent, and you will get what you want!

Such thinking is entirely wrong! A text without a context is a pretext. Isolating this text from its setting in the Sermon on the Mount is deadly. The broad context of the Sermon sets down the surpassing righteousness, humility, sincerity, purity, and love expected of those who are members of the kingdom of God. These virtues are beyond human attainment apart from God's grace. The broad context underscores our need. In the immediately preceding context (vv. 1-6) Jesus has shown us the danger of condemning other people as if we were judges. He also has told us to get the plank out of our own eye before we attempt to remove a speck from someone else's. His warning is, "For in the same way you judge others, you will be judged, and with the measure you use, it will be measured to you" (v. 2). This standard is terrifying. Who is adequate for such things? How can we live up to such a high standard? We need to be cleansed. We need help and grace, but from where? Jesus answers, "Ask and it will be given to you; seek and you will find; knock and the door will be opened to you" (v. 7).

This famous text is not *carte blanche* for our material desires. Rather, it tells us how to pray for the character of the kingdom in our lives. It instructs us how to pray the Lord's Prayer. It teaches us to pray that our morals and ethics will be like Christ's. In a word, Jesus teaches us how to pray for our spiritual lives.

WE ARE TO PRAY WITH PERSISTENCE (vv. 7, 8)

Jesus begins with some advice about our attitude.

> *"Ask and it will be given to you; seek and you will find; knock and the door will be opened to you. For every one who asks receives; he who seeks finds; and to him who knocks, the door will be opened."*

Jesus' language is unusually compelling because the three verbs "ask . . . seek . . . knock" command an ascending intensity. "Ask" implies asking for a conscious need. The word also suggests humility in asking, for it is commonly used of one asking a superior. The next step, "seek," involves asking but adds action. The idea is not merely to express one's need, but to get up and look around for help. It involves effort. "Knock" includes asking plus acting plus persevering — like someone who keeps pounding on a closed door! The stacking of these words is extremely forceful, but the fact that they are present imperatives gives them even more punch. In the Greek language there are two kinds of imperatives. The aorist imperative gives one definite command, such as "shut the door" or "pick up the newspaper." The present imperative, however, commands continuous action — "keep on shutting the door" or "keep on picking up the newspaper." So our text really reads: "Keep on asking and it will be given to you; keep on seeking and you will find; keep on knocking and the door will be opened to you."

These opening verses are remarkably intense, and there is no doubt that our Lord meant for them to be understood that way. Luke records the same words, word-for-word, in his Gospel (11:9, 10), but he precedes them with Jesus' mini-parable in verses 5-8:

> *Then he said to them, "Suppose one of you has a friend, and he goes to him at midnight and says, 'Friend, lend me three loaves, because a friend of mine on a journey has come to me, and I have nothing to set before him.' Then the one inside answers, 'Don't bother me. The door is already locked, and my children are with me in bed. I can't get up and give you anything.' I tell you, though he will not get up and give him the bread because he is his friend, yet because of the man's boldness he will get up and give him as much as he needs."*

Then comes Jesus' famous words, "So I say to you: Ask and it will be given to you; seek and you will find; knock and the door will be opened to you. For everyone who asks receives; he who seeks finds; and to him who knocks, the door will be opened" (Luke 11:9, 10).

Jesus is driving his point home, and the point is this: We are to passionately persist in prayer. We naturally persevere in our prayers when someone close to us is sick. If one of our children becomes ill, we pray without ceasing. Likewise, if we are in financial trouble or if we are hoping for a promotion or if we have a frightening or dangerous task ahead of us, we generally find it easy to pray.

But do we persist in our prayers for spiritual growth for ourselves and others? Do we "ask . . . seek . . . knock" for a pure mind? Do we keep on knocking for a forgiving spirit or for the removal of an angry or critical spirit? I think that Christians usually do not! Consider what would happen if God's people understood what Christ is saying here and put it to work. More about that a little later.

We give ourselves to passionate prayer for our spiritual development only when we sense our need for God's grace. God's kingdom requires righteousness — perfection. We are called to be holy as he is holy (Leviticus 19:2). Only "the pure in heart will see God" (Matthew 5:8). We know that though we do good things, we are evil — that all of us, Jews and Greeks, are under sin (Romans 3:9). The sight of God's perfect standard and our sin drives us to our knees and to his grace. We learn that there is no hope apart from his unearned favor. There is no hope for spiritual improvement apart from his continuing love and mercy. The one who sees this rejoices when he reads Jesus' invitation to "ask . . . seek . . . knock."

We are to ask and keep on asking for those things that will make us more like Jesus. We are to seek and keep on seeking. We are to knock and keep on knocking. Perseverance is the key to God's treasure, just as it often proves to be with earthly treasures. When Howard Carter, the British archaeologist, peered wide-eyed into an ancient Egyptian tomb in 1922, at first he saw nothing. For more than twenty centuries archaeologists, tourists, and tomb robbers had searched for the burial places of Egypt's pharaohs. It was believed that nothing remained undisturbed, especially in the Royal Valley where the ancient monarchs had been buried for over half a millennium. With only a few scraps of evidence Carter carried on his pursuit, privately financed because nobody felt there was anything left to be discovered. But he was convinced there was one remaining tomb.

Twice during his six-year search he came within two yards of the first stone step leading to the burial chamber, and finally he found it. "Can you see anything?" his assistants asked, as Carter's eyes adjusted. He was seeing, but he had difficulty speaking because he saw what no modern man had ever seen. Wooden animals, statues, chests, chariots, carved cobras, vases, daggers, jewels, a throne — and a hand-carved coffin of a teenage king. It was the priceless tomb and treasure of King Tutankhamen, the world's most exciting archaeological discovery. Howard Carter's great perseverance brought him King Tut's treasure.

How much greater our rewards when we persevere in praying for God's spiritual treasures! King Tut's treasures brought him no happiness; and if you were as rich as he, the effect would be the same. Besides, King Tut left it all behind.

The treasures Christ gives are eternally ours and eternally satisfying. But perseverance is the key. We may wonder why God wants us to persist intensely for things he surely wants to give us. The answer is, he wants to give us great spiritual treasures, but he will not give it to us until we are ready. Persistent prayer prepares us for those treasures.

WE ARE TO PRAY WITH CONFIDENCE (vv. 7-11)

Jesus' words teach us that we are not only to pray with persistence, but with confidence. The verses we have already studied shout assurance to us: "Ask and it will be given to you; seek and you will find; knock and the door will be opened to you." The only condition for our receiving spiritual treasure is persistence. If we persistently ask for increased spiritual growth and understanding and intimacy with God, we *will* receive! I am grateful this verse is not a blank check for just anything we want in life. God knows much better than we do what we need.

I have heard Howard Hendricks say that when he was a young man, certain mothers set their hopes on him in behalf of their daughters. One mother even said to him, "Howard, I just want you to know that I am praying you will be my son-in-law." Dr. Hendricks asked us very solemnly, "Have you ever thanked God for unanswered prayer?" I am grateful that God has not answered all my prayers too! And so are you. On the other hand, how wonderful it is that he has always answered your and my persistent prayers for spiritual growth.

Jesus assures us that this is true with illustrations taken from earthly fatherhood. "Which of you, if his son asks for bread, will give him a stone? Or if he asks for a fish, will give him a snake?" (vv. 9, 10).

The illustration is deliberately absurd. In the Galilean setting for the giving of the Sermon on the Mount, the people were familiar with the flat stones by the shore that looked exactly like their round, flat cakes of bread, and with fish (more likely eels) that looked very much like snakes. Can you imagine your son coming to tell you he is hungry and you give him a stone instead of bread? "Here son, enjoy!" you say mockingly as he cracks his teeth. "Oh, you didn't like that? Here, have a fish," and you give him a harmful snake or eel. No first-century father would be as ignorant or cruel. Today we cannot always be sure. Nevertheless, the illustration holds. God always gives us what is good.

Our Lord also crowns our assurance with the illustration of our heavenly Father: "If you, then, though you are evil, know how to give good gifts to your children, how much more will your Father in heaven give good gifts to those who ask him!" (v. 11).

Here is the familiar *a fortiori* argument that Jesus is so fond of. If it is true of the lesser, how much more of the greater. God is our Father, our *Abba*, our Dearest Father *par excellence*! Think of our earthly fathers at their very best and multiply that by infinity, and you have it. Isaiah says:

> *Can the mother forget the baby at her breast and have no compassion on the child she has borne? Though she may forget, I will not forget you! (49:15)*

The "how much more" of our text has an infinite ring.

An earthly father would never give his child a stone for bread, but sometimes he makes mistakes. At times earthly fathers think they are doing the right thing only to discover they were absolutely wrong! God never errs, though it is his policy to give greater quality and quantity than we imagine in our prayers. Luke's parallel quotation of this gives us a remarkable insight into the mechanics of God's giving greater "good gifts" to those who ask him.

> *"If you then, though you are evil, know how to give good gifts to your children, how much more will your Father in heaven give the Holy Spirit to those who ask him!" (11:13)*

Luke's substitution of "Holy Spirit" for "good gifts" is no contradiction because it is the Holy Spirit who bestows what is good. Moreover, the Holy Spirit knows what we need better than we do! Paul informs us in Romans 8:26, 27:

> *In the same way, the Spirit helps us in our weakness. We do not know what we ought to pray for, but the Spirit himself intercedes for us with groans that words cannot express. And he who searches our hearts knows the mind of the Spirit, because the Spirit intercedes for the saints in accordance with God's will.*

The result is, we get more "good gifts" than we ever imagined.

Our assurance is this: God will give us anything that is good for us spiritually (anything!) if we keep asking him for it! If you do not yet have eternal life through Jesus Christ, you may be sure he will give it to you if you ask with all your heart. If you are a believer but are short on Christian graces, you need to keep praying. If you often find yourself lying, if you begin to "ask" and "seek" and "knock," God will help you become a truth-teller. If you are not generous, make a habit of passionate prayer and he will give you a generous spirit. If you are not kind but persistently seek God for a kind spirit, he will give it to you.

Just think what would happen if we prayed for these things for ourselves and our brothers and sisters as intensely as we pray for our physical needs. The church would explode because a far greater proportion of its people would be living kingdom lives. Our pulpits would be filled with preachers of power. The mission fields would shrink as thousands more poured out to the harvest — with greater power.

Do we want the character of the kingdom in our lives through the fullness of the Holy Spirit? Then we have to do two things. First, ask persistently. Jesus says we are to ask and keep on asking, seek and keep on seeking, knock and keep on knocking. We are to beseech God constantly and passionately for spiritual blessing. Do we pray like that?

At the same time we are to ask confidently. Everyone who asks this way receives, and everyone who seeks like this finds, and everyone who knocks and keeps on knocking has the door opened to him. God will give us anything we ask for that is good for us spiritually. If we lack spiritually, it is our fault. As James says, "You do not have, because you do not ask God" (4:2). Over 200 years ago John Newton wrote the following hymn:

Come, my soul, thy case prepare;
Jesus loves to answer prayer;
He Himself has bid thee pray,
Therefore will not say thee nay.

Thou art coming to a King;
Large petitions with thee bring;
For His grace and power are such,
None can ever ask too much.

We can never ask too much spiritually. Let us ask and receive.

Someone once said, "Any discussion of the doctrine of prayer that does not issue in the practice of prayer is not only *not* helpful, but harmful." That is true. We would all do well to engage in the following actions:

1. Search out some spiritual qualities that you lack but would like to have. List them on your prayer list.
2. Pray passionately for them — keep asking, seeking, knocking.
3. Have confidence that God your Father will give them to you.

32

The Two Roads

MATTHEW 7:13, 14

Matthew 7:13, 14 records the beginning of the end of Jesus' Sermon on the Mount. After spelling out the character of the kingdom in the Beatitudes — the "Beautiful Attitudes" of those who are members of the kingdom of God (5:1-12) — and giving his disciples the two metaphors of salt and light (vv. 14-16) to illustrate how those who live out the Beatitudes affect the world, Jesus explained that he requires a righteousness that surpasses that of the scribes and Pharisees (vv. 17-20). He then presented relentless examples of what this surpassing righteousness is like (vv. 21-48). Then he gave specific instructions about giving, praying, fasting, materialism, worry, wrongly judging others, and prayer (6:1 — 7:11). He capped his comments on prayer with the Golden Rule (v. 12).

Our Lord then began a lengthy conclusion to his magnificent sermon. In effect, he was saying, "That's it, my friend. Now what are you going to do with it? There is no point in listening to the sermon if you are not going to do anything about it." The remainder of Matthew 7 is grand, motivational application. The Savior refuses to let his listeners bask in the grandeur of the sermon's thought. He knows that admiration without action is deadly, that conviction without commitment will dull one's spirituality.

He begins this section with a galvanizing opening statement: "Enter through the narrow gate." This is a command. The *King James Version* uses the word "straight" instead of "narrow." The two words mean the same thing.

Jesus adds, "Small is the gate and narrow the road that leads to life" (v. 14). In context, he is saying that all he has taught in the Sermon on the Mount taken together forms a "narrow gate." Such words have never been welcome, but they are particularly offensive to twenty-first-century ears. "Call me vain, call me proud, call me mean — but don't call me narrow!" People admire the urbane, the worldly-wise, the all-accepting. C. E. Jefferson writes:

> We often hear [narrow] used in a sinister and condemning sense, we sometimes use it so ourselves. We say, "Oh, yes, he is narrow," meaning that one side of his nature has been blighted, blasted. His mind is not full-orbed. His heart is not full grown. He is a dwarfed and stunted man, cramped by a defective education or squeezed out of shape by a narrowing environment.[1]

No one likes to be called narrow!

Now, in one sense it is good that Christians avoid this tag. We certainly do not want to be narrow and self-righteous like the list-carrying Pharisees. Nor do we want to be narrow and inflexibly dogmatic about matters in which the Scriptures are not clear, like the bishop who when he was visiting a small denominational college in 1870 took strong exception when the president happened to remark that in fifty years it might be possible for men to soar in the air like birds. The bishop was scandalized and replied, "Flight is strictly reserved for the angels and I beg you not to repeat your suggestion lest you be guilty of blasphemy!" Thirty-three years later Bishop Wright's sons, Orville and Wilbur, made the world's first flight at Kitty Hawk![2] We must avoid uninformed, pious narrowness at all costs.

On the other hand, we must embrace the narrowness that Christ recommends. Jesus says there are only two roads — one leading to destruction and one leading to life. And there is no middle way. Christ never said anything by accident, and what he said here was sublimely premeditated. He knew that nothing could be more calamitous than for a hearer (or reader) of the Sermon on the Mount to meditate on its precepts, perhaps even bow in admiration, but never experience its reality. This epilogue is perhaps the most important part of the entire Sermon on the Mount, for it is about getting on the right road and staying on it.

THE ROAD TO DESTRUCTION (v. 13)

> *"Wide is the gate and broad is the road that leads to destruction, and many enter through it."*

Jesus pictures here a large entrance to a city that opens onto a broad boulevard. The road has a wide entrance and is spacious, meaning it is easy to locate and to get onto. Because of its size, there are no limitations as to baggage. You can take anything along that you please. You do not have to leave anything behind. To stay on it, all you have to do is follow your inclinations. Absolutely no effort is required.

The implicit idea of this broad road is that it imposes no boundaries on what one thinks. Personal views do not make any difference. This was the early experience of C. S. Lewis as described in his autobiography:

> I was soon (in the famous words) altering "I believe" to "one does feel." And oh, the relief of it! . . . From the tyrannous noon of revelation I passed into the cool evening twilight of Higher Thought, where there was nothing to be obeyed, and nothing to be believed except what was either comforting or exciting.[3]

On the wide road if your thing is nature, that is okay. If it is meditation, that is okay. If it is morality or sensuality, that is okay too. The road has plenty of room for everybody as long as one's thinking does not turn to value judgments. It is okay to compare and contrast philosophies, but to say one is better than the other is anathema. The relative is absolutized, and the absolute is relativized.

Other than platitudes about the good of the majority or the consensus of the people, the wide road imposes few boundaries on conduct. It takes no effort to remain on its broad stretch. It inflicts a deceptive sense of freedom and independence. But the trip itself is all it has to offer, and it is unsatisfying throughout.

Though it is the wrong road, Jesus says that "many enter through it." The road is heavily traveled. In fact, most people prefer it! You are never alone on the broad road "that leads to destruction." Eventually the road comes to the edge of the abyss, and there it stops, but the traveler does not!

THE ROAD TO LIFE (v. 14)

"But small is the gate and narrow the road that leads to life, and only a few find it." Our Lord here pictures for us a tiny gate that is easily overlooked. You have to search for it to find it. Moreover, the road is narrow. It never broadens, no matter how far or how long one travels on it. The gate is evidently the kind through which you cannot bring any baggage, requiring us to leave everything behind.

The tiny gate is a perfect metaphor for the Beatitudes. Alexander Maclaren, the great preacher of a little more than 100 years ago, liked to poetically picture the first two Beatitudes as the sideposts of the small gate. One denoted the first Beatitude and the need for a consciousness of spiritual bankruptcy, and the other stood for the second Beatitude's demand for sorrow over sin. This is indeed a small gate, and few people are willing to shed what is necessary to get through it! No one naturally likes to be poor in spirit or to truly mourn their sins. We must come to God holding nothing in our hands except our inadequacy and our consciousness of sin.

Having entered the narrow gateway to life, the traveler finds that the road remains narrow. Christ is absolutely upfront about the fact that the road remains narrow and difficult. There is no attempt to lure us onto the road with assurances that though it will be difficult at first, the road's contour will eventually widen. The truth is, those who follow the road have to take up their cross (Mark 8:34) and suffer for and with Jesus Christ. But as our Lord said, "Blessed are those who are persecuted because of righteousness, for theirs is the kingdom of heaven" (Matthew 5:10).

This narrow road is not only difficult — it imposes boundaries on what we think and believe. But this does not mean the narrow road is repressive. Far from it! Certainly there have been those like Bishop Wright who mistakenly have become too restrictive, but the fact is, Jesus' narrow way enhances logic and aesthetics and science. As Dr. Charles Malik said in a 1984 Wheaton College commencement address, Christ is the one "who once made the university itself possible." Jesus said, "I am the way and the truth and the life," and he remains so!

On the narrow road our thoughts about God and truth are both enlarged and confined. Truth is not left up to the tyranny of democratic consensus. Those who follow Christ will not and may not believe what most people believe. And those on the narrow way will not be popular for their beliefs. For example, our thoughts about God are narrowed. Certain conceptions of God are true, and others are false. Certain views of him are degrading, and others are exalting. But in believing the truth, our vision of God goes far beyond any vision ever dreamed by anyone on the broad road. The Biblical vision of God is electrifying! Who would ever have dreamed of a God who was not confined by nature but was above nature, who holds things together by the word of his power, who is our Father but who also became a man in order to redeem us. So the narrow way brings an incredibly spectacular, immense conception of God.

Our thoughts regarding salvation are similarly narrowed. Jesus said, "I am the way and the truth and the life. No one comes to the Father except through me" (John 14:6). And those who have preached salvation through Christ have exhibited the same narrowness. Consider Peter before the Sanhedrin: "Salvation is found in no one else, for there is no other name under heaven given to men by which we must be saved" (Acts 4:12).

Our affections are also narrowed, for we are to love the Lord our God with all our heart and with all our soul and with all our might (Deuteronomy 6:5), to put no one else above or equal with him. The same goes for our conduct. There are things we cannot do. Everything is not okay. But in our boundaries we find liberation socially, sexually, ethically. The only free man or woman in these areas is the one who walks the straight and narrow way! Helmut Thielicke, the German theologian, says:

> But in talking about all this, have we not made an amazing discovery? As we have heard that this is a hard and narrow way that leads through dying and dark places, have we not suddenly seen in the narrowness the breadth,

> in the dying the living, and in him, who seems to make living so hard, the great liberator?[4]

The narrow way is completely fulfilling. It provides freedom and joy. And ultimately it leads to eternal life that Jesus defines as knowing him and the Father. "Now this is eternal life: that they may know you, the only true God, and Jesus Christ, whom you have sent" (John 17:3). There is no abyss at the end of the narrow road, but there is unspeakable glory!

It is no accident that Jesus placed this text at the beginning of the end of the Sermon on the Mount. He knew that at the end of the Sermon some would stand at the foot of the magisterial immensity of what he taught and praise it and laud it — and yet never enter the kingdom. That is why the opening line of the conclusion is a command: "Enter through the narrow gate." Jesus' parallel saying in Luke is, "Strive to enter through the narrow door" (13:24). It is not enough to listen to preaching about the gate. You must enter through it.

There can be no neutrality. You are either on the broad road leading to destruction or on the narrow road leading to life. You will never go through the narrow gate by accident or unawares. You must enter it thoughtfully and purposely. Have you done so? You must decide. No one else can do it for you. Moses told the people of Israel:

> *"This day I call heaven and earth as witnesses against you that I have set before you life and death, blessings and curses. Now choose life, so that you and your children may live." (Deuteronomy 30:19)*

Similarly, Joshua exhorted the people:

> *". . . choose for yourselves this day whom you will serve, whether the gods your forefathers served beyond the River, or the gods of the Amorites, in whose land you are living. But as for me and my household, we will serve the LORD." (Joshua 24:15)*

At the earliest preaching of the gospel, Peter declared:

> *"Repent and be baptized, every one of you, in the name of Jesus Christ for the forgiveness of your sins. And you will receive the gift of the Holy Spirit." (Acts 2:38)*

Which road are you on? Jesus said, "Enter through the narrow gate," and elsewhere "I am the gate" (John 10:9), but you must enter in. Have you? Will you?

33

Discerning False Preachers

MATTHEW 7:15-20

Chuck Swindoll tells the story about an unforgettable evening when a friend of his ate dog food. Contrary to what we might expect, he was not starving, nor was he being initiated into a fraternity. Rather, it happened at an elegant physician's home near Miami. The dog food was served on delicate little crackers with a wedge of imported cheese, bacon chips, and an olive, topped with a sliver of pimento. Hors d'oeuvres a la Alpo! The deed was not perpetrated by an enemy but by a friend. (With friends like that, who needs enemies!) She had just graduated from a gourmet cooking course and decided she would put her skills to the ultimate test — and did she ever. After doctoring up those miserable morsels, she placed them on a silver tray. With a sly grin she watched them disappear. Swindoll's friend could not get enough. He kept coming back for more. Evidently the woman's friends were a pretty laid-back group because everyone had a good laugh when she told them what they had been eating. To each their own.

That is a perfect illustration of what goes on in another realm — namely, religious deception. Every day professional Christians, phony preachers, are marketing their wares on shiny platters decorated in such a way that people do not know what they are really getting. Their dishes are topped with the language of orthodoxy — pious religious clichés and buzzwords — and are being eagerly consumed by the tragically grateful. They even pay for it, by the millions. That should never happen, and certainly the Lord does not want it to happen. That is why as he proceeds with the conclusion of the Sermon on the Mount, he gives advice to those who do not want to be led astray. The lengthy, driving conclusion began in verses 13 and 14 with the Lord's urging us to enter the narrow gate and to take the narrow road that the Sermon has prescribed. Now in verse 15 it is as if we can see our Lord

Jesus Christ standing by the fork that separates the narrow and broad way and saying, as our text records, "Watch out for false prophets. They come to you in sheep's clothing, but inwardly they are ferocious wolves."

THE CHARACTER OF FALSE TEACHERS (v. 15)

This opening line invites careful scrutiny because it tells us more than we might expect about those who would lead us astray. The most obvious thing it says is that false preachers or prophets will come. Jesus does not give false warnings. He does not put up a "wet paint" sign if there is no wet paint. His warning is based on historical reality. Israel had been subjected to a steady stream of false preachers throughout her history, and more would come in the future. Jesus, looking forward to the end of the age, said on another occasion that "many false prophets will appear and deceive many people" (Matthew 24:11). And the New Testament church was constantly assaulted by false preachers (as Paul's farewell address to the Ephesian elders in Acts 20:29-31 dramatically attests).

Jesus was crystal-clear — false preachers have and will come. Our churches *will* be assaulted by false preachers, and even if they withstand them, they will be assaulted again and again. We need to be prepared. We need to pray for our churches, for their leadership, that we will not come under the spell of false leaders.

Along with the statement that false preachers will come is a more positive one — that false preachers can be distinguished from genuine ones. Without contradicting his injunctions not to be judgmental and censorious (Matthew 7:1-5), Jesus encourages us to make clear distinctions regarding our preachers. In fact, he commands us to do so!

These are significant matters, but perhaps the most important thing he tells us in verse 15 is that the false prophets are those who "come to you in sheep's clothing." In other words, they look just like sheep. These false prophets, false preachers, are not your standard heretics. The most blatant obvious false preachers, whether tele-evangelists promising pie-in-the-sky *now* or whatever, are not what Jesus has in mind here. Jesus' language demands that we understand that these false teachers and their teaching are extremely subtle, as deceptive and subtle as the hostess and her Alpo hors d'oeuvres.

Dr. Martyn Lloyd-Jones says:

> The picture we need to have in our minds, therefore, should rather be this. The false prophet is a man who comes to us, and who at first has the appearance of being everything that could be desired. He is nice and pleasing and pleasant; he appears to be thoroughly Christian, and seems to say the right things. His teaching in general is quite all right and he uses many terms that should be used and employed by a true Christian teacher. He

> talks about God, he seems to be saying everything that a Christian should say. He is obviously in sheep's clothing, and his way of living seems to correspond. So, you do not suspect that there is anything wrong at all; there is nothing that at once attracts your attention or arouses your suspicions, nothing glaringly wrong.[1]

Dietrich Bonhoeffer adds:

> There is someone standing by my side, who looks just like a member of the Church. He is a prophet and a preacher. He looks like a Christian, he talks and acts like one. But dark powers are mysteriously at work; it was those who sent him into our midst. . . . He may even be unconscious himself of what he is doing. The devil can give him every encouragement and at the same time keeps him in the dark about his own motives.[2]

Though there is nothing *apparently* wrong with this messenger, there are things that are subtly wrong — terribly wrong. In terms suggested by the immediate preceding context of the Sermon on the Mount, there is no narrow gate in his message. This man's preaching is all right in that he says nothing that is untrue. The problem stems from what he does *not* say. He says many right things, but he also leaves out some indispensable points of belief. And that makes him exceedingly dangerous. He is truly a wolf "in sheep's clothing." His preaching also has another telltale characteristic — he says nothing that is offensive to the natural man. His message comforts and soothes and never warns of judgment. He wants everyone to speak well of him. He is like the false prophets in Jeremiah's time of whom the prophet said, "They dress the wound of my people as though it were not serious. 'Peace, peace,' they say, when there is no peace" (Jeremiah 6:14; cf. 8:11). They speak, according to Isaiah, "smooth things" and "prophesy illusions" (Isaiah 30:10, RSV). There is nothing to make anyone uneasy, but rather only things that make people feel good, content, and falsely assured. They characterize anyone who preaches otherwise as negative.

The result of such preachers' work is disastrous. Jesus says they are "ferocious wolves" — a horrific title! They are a shepherd's — and *the* Shepherd's — nightmare. They would destroy every sheep in the flock if undetected.

If false preachers came into most evangelical churches as blatant heretics, they would be banged over the head with Bibles and sent packing. But when they come with all the right language, credentials, and culture, they deceive the unwary elect.

> *For such men are false apostles, deceitful workmen, masquerading as apostles of Christ. And no wonder, for Satan himself masquerades as an*

> *angel of light. It is not surprising, then, if his servants masquerade as servants of righteousness. (2 Corinthians 11:13-15)*

Jesus commands us to be on our guard. "Watch out for false prophets. They come to you in sheep's clothing, but inwardly are ferocious wolves."

TESTING THE MESSENGERS (vv. 16-20)

Having given us his warnings, Jesus now tells us what tests to apply. He uses the classic Semitic way of phrasing an important principle, giving it both a negative and positive expression:

> *"By their fruit you will recognize them. Do people pick grapes from thornbushes, or figs from thistles? Likewise every good tree bears good fruit, but a bad tree bears bad fruit. A good tree cannot bear bad fruit, and a bad tree cannot bear good fruit. Every tree that does not bear good fruit is cut down and thrown into the fire. Thus, by their fruit you will recognize them." (vv. 16-20)*

Notice that he opens and closes his explanation with the same phrase: "By their fruit you will recognize them." The essence of a tree (what it really is) is revealed in its fruit. The word for "recognize" (other translations, "know," *epignosis*) means an exact or full knowledge of. One's fruits provide an exact, unerring knowledge of what one really is. The preacher's fruit is evident in two categories — what he says (his doctrine) and how he lives (his moral life).

I would like to suggest four doctrinal tests. First, *the false prophet avoids preaching on such things as the holiness, righteousness, justice, and wrath of God.* He never says he does not believe these truths. He just does not mention them, except in passing or to give his prayers a more ecclesiastical ring. Any exposition of these truths would be disconcerting, especially to the nonbelievers in his congregation. So he avoids them, and his people are ignorant of these essential doctrines. The main emphasis of his preaching is God's love, which he fails to keep in balance with God's justice or wrath.

Second, *he avoids preaching on the doctrine of the final judgment.* In this regard, two of America's most flourishing cults — the Mormons and the Jehovah's Witnesses — reject the Biblical doctrine of Hell in favor of a less stringent and less offensive approach.

Third, *false prophets fail to emphasize the fallenness and depravity of mankind.* The truths that man is sinful to the very core of his being and that he cannot save himself are consciously avoided. I once heard a prominent clergyman say he never preached on sin because people already know they are sinners (a very questionable premise!). What they need, he said, is to be built up, to be made to see their potential. He said he never used the word *sin* in his preaching. Prophets like this do not actually believe the Biblical assessment of man's predicament. We preach what we believe. If we do not preach it, it is because we do not believe it.

Fourth, *false prophets de-emphasize the substitutionary death and atonement of Christ*. They may talk about Christ's death on the cross, but they do not have the vicarious, substitutionary atonement in view. They may sentimentalize about it, they even sing about it, but they do not believe it. A prime example of this is Sir John Bowring, author of the magnificent hymn, "In the Cross of Christ I Glory." He was an English Unitarian and Utilitarian. He was hardly a believer in the Atonement.

False prophets talk about God. They wax eloquent on Jesus and even talk about his death on the cross. Many do not see them as heretics. They are likable — truly nice people — pleasant to be around. Sometimes churches grow under their ministries, but the following years are tragic, bringing a sea of unbelieving children and empty pews.

So much for the test of what they teach. There is also the test of how they live — the moral test. Here we really get to the heart of the matter.

The controlling realization here is that being a true Christian means there has been a radical change in the depth of the person through the grace of God. There is an awesomely deep connection between what comes out of us and what we are. The essence of the trees determines the fruit they produce. False prophets encourage us to try to make ourselves Christians by adding something to our lives instead of becoming something new, and their work never quite rings true. A wolf can wear sheep's clothing, but it cannot grow a sheep's coat. It is possible to put grapes on thorns, and figs on thistles, but they cannot grow there. It is possible to subscribe to the qualities of the Beatitudes, and yet never truly own them from within. But appearances can only be kept up for so long. Time will reveal the true nature of the fruit. Sooner or later we will know where a man stands. Believers are not to involve themselves in inquisitions or censorious judgment, but they must recognize the verdict of God when it comes, and they must be discerning, obeying Jesus' command to "watch out for false prophets."

True believers have been radically altered, and though they are far from perfection and often stumble and backslide, they do manifest the character of God's kingdom. There is a true ring to their poverty of spirit, their thirst after righteousness, their mercy, and their being peacemakers. They also show the fruit of the Spirit — "love, joy, peace, patience, kindness, goodness, faithfulness, gentleness and self-control" (Galatians 5:22, 23). Believers slip and stumble, but their fruit is real, flowing from their inner beings "as milk from the mother."[3]

Today whole groups of people are being served things they would never consciously eat, for the silver trays and attractive garnishes have them completely fooled. Here at the end of his great sermon, Jesus is warning his followers not to be superficial in evaluating prophets and preachers. Does what these prophets and preachers say measure up? What are they leaving out? Does how they live measure up? These are important tests, because false preachers are coming and are already here.

Our Lord's words warn us not to be superficial regarding our own lives. Sheep, is the fleece you are wearing really yours? Did you really grow it, or is it just a uniform? Trees, what kind of fruit are you bearing? Is the fruit really yours? Does it really come from the life within, or is it just so many ornaments?

34

Entering the Kingdom

MATTHEW 7:21-29

Sadly, it is really quite easy to be accorded the status of an evangelical Christian without being born-again. The process is essentially cultural. That is, if you will work at displaying certain cultural traits, you will be accepted. Here is how you do it. First, work on your vocabulary. Biblical history records that when the Gileadites and the Ephraimites were warring, the Gileadites developed a password to detect Ephraimites who when captured pretended to be Gileadites — the word *shibboleth*, which the Ephraimites (who had trouble with the *sh* sound) could only pronounce *Sibboleth*. It worked perfectly on the unsuspecting enemy, much to their dismay and demise (see Judges 12:4-7). We evangelicals have our *shibboleths*, but they are unfortunately rather easy to pick up. They are words like *fellowship*, *brother*, and *born-again*. Use these words with the right inflection and you are in.

Second, emulate certain social conventions. It is most effective to share similar attitudes about alcohol and tobacco, modesty and style of clothing, and so on. If you show the same likes and dislikes (especially dislikes), you will probably pass as a Christian. The ease with which one can assume the social conventions of the faithful has been facilitated by evangelical Christianity's gradual alignment with secular culture's materialism, pleasure-seeking, entertainment, economics, and fads.

Third, have the right heritage. If your parents are respectable Christians or, even better, Christian workers, you will probably be assumed to be a believer. And if you affect some civilities that apparently reflect a godly heritage, such as attending evening service and prayer meeting or tithing, you will be accepted as a Christian. Sometimes the desire of overly anxious parents to see their children become born-again has contributed to the heritage = salvation delusion. Some well-meaning parents have manipulated their children into a bogus confession of faith, baptism, and church membership. For these and similar reasons multitudes of unregenerate evangelicals are comfortably ensconced in their churches. And no one questions the authenticity of their faith!

By *evangelical* I mean a person who believes the Bible is divinely inspired and infallible and subscribes to doctrinal formulations that teach the total depravity of man, the inerrancy of the Scriptures, the substitutionary death and atonement of Christ, salvation by unmerited grace through personal faith in Christ (not through good works), the necessity of a transformed life, the existence of a literal Heaven and Hell, and the visible personal return of Jesus Christ to set up his kingdom of righteousness. Moreover, they believe in the proclamation of the gospel and the mission of winning the world for Christ.[1]

The question is, why would anyone willfully take up the so-called "narrow way" apart from being born-again? For many it is the path of least resistance. To do otherwise would impair comfortable family and social relationships. Besides, evangelical Christianity's preachers dominate the religious media. Its recording artists sell hundreds of thousands of CDs. A billion dollars is spent annually on its publications. Being born-again can be profitable. Jesus saves, but he also sells.

We also must remember that the Biblical lifestyle is a good way to live. Families that subscribe to Biblical models tend to be happier and healthier and stay together longer. It is not at all surprising that Christianity, being so wholesome, attracts those who would practice its style without knowing its inner reality. The human race has an incredible capacity for self-delusion, and nowhere is that more perfectly demonstrated than in the lives of thousands of evangelicals who are not born-again. What wise Solomon said in his day describes some people in our day too: "those who are pure in their own eyes, and yet are not cleansed of their filth" (Proverbs 30:12). I think that what John Newton, the eighteenth-century father of Evangelicalism, said is perfectly true:

> If I ever reach Heaven I expect to find three wonders there: first, to meet some I had not thought to see there; second, to miss some I had thought to meet there; and third, the greatest wonder of all, to find myself there.[2]

As we have come to expect, our Lord anticipated the problem of false profession by those in the church and deals with it here at the end of the Sermon on the Mount. The conclusion of that sermon is a driving warning against being sidetracked from the true faith. In verses 13-20 he warned us against the dangers that come from the outside. Now in verses 21-27 he warns us of dangers that come from ourselves. Specifically, they are: 1) the danger of basing your salvation on lip service, and 2) the danger of basing your salvation on lifestyle.

RELIGIOUS LIP SERVICE NOT ENOUGH (vv. 21-23)

> *"Not everyone who says to me, 'Lord, Lord,' will enter the kingdom of heaven, but only he who does the will of my Father who is in heaven. Many will say to me on that day, 'Lord, Lord, did we not prophesy in your name, and in your name drive out demons and perform many miracles?' Then I will tell them plainly, 'I never knew you. Away from me, you evildoers!'"*

The Master holds up the example of people who give a spectacular profession of belief as they stand before Christ, but they will be rejected on the day of judgment. John Stott has noted that this confession is remarkable on four points.[3] First, it is polite. They address Christ as "Lord." Even today that is a courteous, tolerant way to refer to Christ. Second, the confession is orthodox. The word "Lord" (*kurios*) can mean "Sir," but it is also a divine title. The context with its allusions to God as Christ's Father and Christ as Judge demands that we see it as the latter — God. Third, the confession is fervent. "Lord, Lord" is an appellation of enthusiasm and zeal. Fourth, the confession is public. These professing believers did not make some private confession of allegiance to Christ but did it in front of everyone. Moreover, they even did public works in the name of Christ. This is a model confession, a beautiful one. So what is wrong with it? Nothing! It would be wonderful if we all would make confessions like this.

But there *is* a problem. Correct orthodox belief will not give us eternal life. This is not to say that correct belief is not necessary for salvation — it is. Paul makes that clear in Romans 10:9, 10:

> *If you confess with your mouth, "Jesus is Lord," and believe in your heart that God raised him from the dead, you will be saved. For it is with your heart that you believe and are justified, and it is with your mouth that you confess and are saved.*

A man who refuses to say "Lord, Lord" will never enter the kingdom of heaven. All true Christians say, "Lord, Lord." But not all who say "Lord, Lord" are true Christians! Intellectual orthodoxy does not indicate saving faith. You can be absolutely correct in your belief about Christ's nature and person, his substitutionary atonement, his resurrection, and his return, you can have even fought against heretics, and yet not be truly saved.

Furthermore, zeal and fervency do not bring eternal life. Saying orthodox things with emotion is not enough. When I was a youth pastor in the 1960s, a young man right out of the youth culture of the day made a profession of faith in Christ. A few weeks later he stood in front of the church and passionately and articulately talked about Christ, exhorting the people to follow the Savior. About two weeks later the same young man rejected Christ in a most dramatic manner and gave evidence and testimony from his own lips that he had never believed any of it.

Finally, remarkable works do not bring eternal life. These professing believers say, "Lord, Lord, did we not prophesy in your name . . . ?" Prophesying, preaching, does not prove anything. Balaam gave an accurate message but was a hireling and a sinner (Numbers 22 — 25). Saul was used by God when he was under the spirit of prophecy, but he himself was lost. Fervent proclamation of truth does not prove spiritual reality. A preacher can be fervent simply because he likes his outline and likes to move people, but it does not prove anything about the man himself. These are sobering thoughts. The Lord does not want anyone to miss the point of all the great teaching that he had given in the Sermon on the Mount.

These professing believers also say, "Lord, Lord, did we not . . . in your name cast out demons?" Is it possible for a person to do that and yet be outside the kingdom? Yes, for the New Testament clearly says Judas had such power (Luke 10:17). Our Lord may allow power to course through a man though the man himself is lost.

Finally these professing believers say, "Lord, Lord, did we not . . . in your name . . . perform many miracles?" How can it be that these are lost? Jesus explains in Matthew 24:24, "For false Christs and false prophets will appear and perform great signs and miracles to deceive even the elect — if that were possible." Paul notes a similar phenomenon in 2 Thessalonians 2:8, 9:

> *And then the lawless one will be revealed, whom the Lord will overthrow with the breath of his mouth and destroy by the splendor of his coming. The coming of the lawless one will be in accordance with the work of Satan displayed in all kinds of counterfeit miracles, signs and wonders.*

In other words, a man may be able to do great things and get great results, but that says absolutely nothing about his salvation. We need to hear this well in a day when there are thousands who are claiming that in Christ they have supernatural powers. People say to me they have heard of some bizarre thing going on and will comment that it is okay because the individual uses Jesus' name every time he does it. Using his name does not prove anything.

Satan is still "the ruler of the kingdom of the air, the spirit who is now at work in those who are disobedient" (Ephesians 2:2), and he will do anything to keep people under his bondage, even if it means getting them to say "Lord, Lord" and endowing them with evil supernatural power.

Jesus says that orthodoxy, zeal, and spectacular displays of spiritual power do not prove a thing. Notice also his word "many" at the beginning of verse 22. There will not be a few, but *many* who do these things to whom he will say, "I never knew you. Away from me, you evildoers!" (NASB: "you who practice lawlessness") (v. 23). Sadly, multitudes of evangelical Christians are not born again — they are lost.

How can this be? Part of the answer is that they "practice lawlessness." Jesus gives the parallel, more positive reason at the end of verse 21, where he says that "he who does the will of my Father who is in heaven" will enter the kingdom of heaven. Multitudes of religious people, evangelicals included, are lost because they do not do God's will. What is Christ referring to? Is this salvation by works? No. In the context of the Sermon on the Mount, Jesus is referring to the Beatitudes and the deep ethical, spiritual obedience found in God's kingdom. "The will of my Father" refers to God's will as Jesus has revealed it in the Sermon on the Mount. Jesus is referring to a profound heart obedience that is not only on the surface but permeates our inner being. "The will of my Father" indicates the character and the conduct of the kingdom of God.

The way to test yourself is to look below the surface. Do not look at the apparent results or at the miracles or at your creedal orthodoxy, but rather look to see if your life conforms to the character of the kingdom — the Beautiful Attitudes of the kingdom of God. Are you poor in spirit? Are you meek? Do you have that positive quality of strength in saying, "Yes, I am a sinner. No matter what others do to me, I will stand up for truth and for God and for others"? Do you have a merciful spirit? Are you compassionate to those who are hurting and lost and in physical need? Do you forgive, or do you hold on to your grudges as your dearest possession? That is what Jesus is saying.

How do you respond to Jesus' exposition of the Law when he says, "For I say to you that unless your righteousness surpasses that of the scribes and Pharisees, you will not enter the kingdom of heaven" (Matthew 5:20)? How beautiful this is, and it is exactly the medicine our souls need.

RELIGIOUS LIFESTYLE NOT ENOUGH (vv. 24-27)

We all know the story about the house that was built on the rock and the house that was built on the sand. We also know that the houses are metaphors for two men's religious lives. The houses, the lives, looked *exactly* the same. In our terms, they both have chimneys, both have several bedrooms, the windows are shuttered, they are freshly painted in attractive colors, and the yards are well-kept. So it is with the edifices of their lives — they look the same. The two men attend the same church, sing the same songs, send their children to the same schools.

But one has been wise, and the other has been a fool (the Greek word used here is *moro*, from which we get *moron*). The wise man excavated down to the bedrock and grounded his house upon it. The foolish man built the seemingly identical building upon sand. The foundation of one man's life is solid, and that of the other is nonexistent. Donald Carson explains:

> The man who builds his house upon the shifting foundation is likened to the person who hears Jesus' words but who does not put them to practice. The man who builds his house upon the rock is likened to the person who not only hears Jesus' words but also puts them into practice. The difference between the two houses is therefore likened to the difference between obedience and disobedience.[4]

If we heed Jesus' soul-penetrating words, if we measure ourselves by his standards, if we evaluate our ethics by his ethics, if we strain after the Sermon's great teaching in prayer and piety, we are building upon the rock. The foolish man is shallow in his thinking and lays a shallow foundation on the sand. He cannot be troubled with thinking things through. He is concerned with having a house (life) that simply looks nice. It looks like his church friend's life, but it is all outward, it is all style! Oh, that Jesus' words would penetrate our evangelical hearts! It is not our cultural distinctions that save us. It is not our evangelical civilities. It is not our evangelical experience. It is not our heritage. It is a personal relationship with Jesus Christ that is so profound and growing that it produces his character, the character of his kingdom, in our lives. It is not just on the surface, though it can and ought to be seen. This is radical! It is the difference between life and death.

Jesus says that the storms will reveal whether we have the true foundation or not. His primary reference here is to the final judgment because in the Old Testament and elsewhere in Jewish writings the storm serves as a symbol for God's judgment (see, for example, Ezekiel 13:11b). The storm can also refer to life's difficulties. Sometimes a gracious, dark, hurling storm hits the house on the sand, and its owner finds out that he is lacking. How tragic to find this out only in the final judgment. Many will cry, "Lord, Lord" from beneath the rubble of their life's house, and he will say, "I never knew you." How tragic!

As believers, we are in a privileged and dangerous position. As members of his church we call him, "Lord, Lord," and we see his power at work among us. But we must make sure that we truly know him.

It is easy to fool the pastor, our friends, and even ourselves. All we have to do is learn the vocabulary and adapt some cultural conventions. But Jesus does not want any of us to fall to such delusion. It is apparent as he concludes the Sermon on the Mount that he is instilling some healthy fear into our lives. In verse 13 he warns of "destruction." In verses 15-20 he speaks of branches being burned. And in verses 21-29 he refers to the possibility of his publicly rejecting us and of the edifice of our lives suffering total destruction. Can you blame our Lord? After all, the issue is Heaven or Hell.

> The pages of the Bible strain metaphor and exhaust the resources of language in describing the holy delights of the new heaven and the new earth, still to come; but they scarcely do less in outlining the horrors and terrors of hell. The latter is variously described as the place of outer darkness, the place where the worm will not die, the place of exclusion and rejection, the place of burning and torment, the place where there will be weeping and grinding of teeth. I am not trying to give you hell's coordinates, nor place it on a map. Just as I find myself unable to describe the new heaven and earth except in the metaphors of Scripture, so I cannot describe hell except in the metaphors of Scripture. But those metaphors are staggering.[5]

Jesus believed in Heaven and Hell (in fact, he said twice as much about Hell as about Heaven), and he came to deliver us from Hell. He wants us to take note of our lives and where they are going!

Do you know Christ, or do you just know the vocabulary? Do you have a relationship with Jesus Christ, or are you riding on your heritage? Is the fruit of the Spirit evident in your life? Can the character of the kingdom be seen there? Is Jesus alive in your life? Do you love him? These are important questions, and they have nothing to do with lip service and style.

I hope all of us will examine our hearts by the standards Jesus set down and not by our culture or anything else in this world. May we, like the hearers of old, respond to Jesus' words:

> *When Jesus had finished these words, the crowds were amazed at his teaching; for he was teaching them as one having authority, and not as their scribes. (Matthew 7:28, 29,* NASB*)*

35

The Sermon on the Move

MATTHEW 8:1-3

Matthew 8:1-3, which records what immediately happened when Jesus descended the mount after giving his sermon, is intimately involved with the Beatitudes. Jesus delivered the Beatitudes at the beginning of the Sermon on the Mount, the Beautiful Attitudes of the true children of God describing the inner character of those who are members of the kingdom. Then in the remainder of the Sermon, Jesus described how those who have the character of the kingdom live their lives in this world. Jesus did not want this marvelous teaching to be wasted. So as he descended the mount he gave one last illustration of what the character of the kingdom is like, a living illustration of the healing of a leprous man.

An understanding of the man's predicament reveals the fullness of Christ's teaching. Dr. Luke (in the parallel account in Luke 5:12) describes him as "covered with leprosy." The disease had run its full course. Leprosy, today called Hansen's disease (after the man who diagnosed its cause), is not a rotting infection as is commonly thought, nor are horrible outward physical deformities directly imposed by the disease. The research of doctor and missionary Paul Brand and others has proven that the disfigurement associated with Hansen's disease comes solely because the warning system of pain is gone. The disease brings numbness to the extremities as well as to the ears, eyes, and nose. The devastation that follows comes from such incidents as reaching one's hand into a charcoal fire to retrieve a dropped potato or washing one's face with water so hot that it burns or gripping a hoe too tightly while working in the fields, so that great trauma is done to the hands causing them to ultimately become stumps.[1] Dr. Brand calls the disease a "painless hell," and it truly is. The poor man Jesus met as he came down the mountain had not been able to feel for years. His body was mutilated from head to foot and was foul and rotting.

The lot of a leper in Israel in those days is summed up in Leviticus 13:45, 46:

> *The person with such an infectious disease must wear torn clothes, let his hair be unkempt, cover the lower part of his face and cry out, "Unclean! Unclean!" As long as he has the infection he remains unclean. He must live alone; he must live outside the camp.*

We can hardly imagine the humiliation and isolation of a leper's life. He was ostracized from society and had to assume a disheveled appearance. And then there was the ultimate degradation, having to cry "Unclean! Unclean!" whenever he came in range of the normal population. Lepers were typically beggars. There was little else they could do. By Jesus' time, rabbinical teaching had made matters even worse with absurd restrictions. If a leper even stuck his head inside a house, it was pronounced unclean. It was illegal to greet a leper. Lepers had to remain at least 100 cubits away if they were upwind, and four cubits if downwind. Josephus, the famous Jewish historian, summed it up, saying that lepers were treated "as if they were, in effect, dead men."[2]

In addition to this, it was thought that those who had leprosy had contracted it because of some great personal sin. People jumped to this erroneous conclusion because in past history such people as Miriam (Numbers 12:6-10), Uzziah (2 Chronicles 26:19), and Gehazi (2 Kings 5:25-27) had been judged with leprosy.

The lot of a leper in Christ's time was just as horrible. A leper was sick and rotting, with no hope of healing. Because of his contamination, he was barred from society and made to cry, "Unclean! Unclean!" And though there was some reason for this (leprosy was at that time considered to be terribly contagious, though it is not), this did nothing to palliate lepers' misery. The unreasonable strictures of the rabbis and the assumption that lepers were great sinners made the situation unbearable. However, the plight of the leper illustrated the effects of sin, though the leper was actually not any more sinful than anyone else. R. C. Trench, the great Greek scholar and the inspiration for and first editor of the monumental *Oxford English Dictionary* (*OED*), recognized this, saying that though the leper was not worse or guiltier than his fellow Jews, nevertheless he was a parable of sin — an "outward and visible sign of innermost spiritual corruption." The leper is a physical illustration of the heart of every human being! If for a moment we could see a visible incarnation of ourselves apart from the cleansing work of Christ, we would see ourselves as the walking dead — forms dead in their trespasses and sins — forms trying to cover themselves with filthy rags.

Christ meeting the leper as he descended the mount was no chance encounter! It was divinely choreographed. We see in Matthew 8 not the Sermon on the Mount but the Sermon on the Move as Jesus authenticates and illustrates his message. And from the perspective of the leper (and ours as well), we see what is involved in obtaining and experiencing the healing touch of Christ. These few verses tell us how to obtain and experience that touch.

REQUESTING THE HEALING TOUCH OF CHRIST (vv. 1, 2)

"When he came down from the mountainside, large crowds followed him." A vast throng had attended his teaching, and now they descended the slope together, having heard the greatest sermon ever preached. What a magnificent scene! But then something startling happened, for Matthew adds, "A man with leprosy came and knelt before him." No doubt the din of the descending multitude was considerable, but above it, persistent and clear, was heard "Unclean! Unclean!" The leper steadily made his way to Jesus as the people fell back on either side, fearing contamination. Perhaps some cursed him, but he kept coming until he was almost to Jesus, crying the refrain of his pitiful life — "Unclean! Unclean!" Then the Master was face to face with a foul, decaying leper, "covered with leprosy" from head to toe.

Here we see the first and fundamental qualification for obtaining the healing touch of Jesus — an awareness of one's condition. The poor man not only *said* he was unclean — he *knew* he was. All he had to do was hold what was left of his hand before his eyes, and if he was prone to any illusions, they vanished in an ugly moment. Moreover, he saw himself as perfectly hopeless. There was nothing he could do to help himself. Everyone else had probably given up on him too. His many years of illness probably meant that even some in his family had discontinued their prayers for him. He was painfully aware of his condition, and in this he exemplified the blessed spiritual awareness found in the very first words of Christ's great sermon: "Blessed are the poor in spirit, for theirs is the kingdom of heaven. Blessed are those who mourn, for they will be comforted" (Matthew 5:3, 4).

The man had spent years mourning his condition. The piteous refrain, "Unclean! Unclean!" had shaped his whole psyche. I suspect that the theological truth had permeated his heart as well. He acknowledged there was nothing within him that would commend him to God. He was in the perfect posture to receive grace. God does not come to the self-sufficient, those who think they have no need or imagine they can make it on their own. He comes to the bankrupt in spirit, those who mourn their condition. It is entirely possible (and probable) that the leper had been sitting beyond the range of the crowd and was galvanized by Jesus' opening words and the masterful argument that followed. The Holy Spirit caused the truth to pierce his heart and brought him to Jesus as his only hope.

This is the only way we can come to Christ too — saying, "Unclean!

Unclean!" If we come saying, "only partly unclean" or "25 percent clean," he will not receive us. Have you come to Christ totally unclean? Only then does he give the healing touch we need.

We see the second qualification in the first sentence of verse 2: "A man with leprosy came and knelt before him." We see here worshipful submission. The word translated "knelt" (NASB, "bowed") takes us into the leper's heart. The basic meaning of the word in early Greek literature was "to kiss," as in kissing the earth as one lay prostrate before the gods. In the Greek translation of the Old Testament this word was used for the Hebrew word for bowing down.[3] Luke tells us "he fell on his face" (5:12), which enhances the picture. The humble leper put his whole soul into obeisance and adoration as he lay prostrate before Christ. He worshiped Christ as the only possible source of his healing. The lesson is clear. Christ's healing touch does not come with casual, irreverent acknowledgment. It comes as we bow before him in realization that he is our *only* hope.

The third factor in obtaining the healing touch of Christ is faith. The leper demonstrated remarkable faith. "A man with leprosy came and knelt before him and said, 'Lord, if you are willing, you can make me clean.'"

In the original, Mark indicates that he repeated this several times (1:40). How poignant this picture is with the prostrate leper repeating in the hoarse voice typical of those with advanced leprosy, "Lord, if you are willing, you can make me clean. Lord, if you are willing, you can make me clean. Lord, if you are willing, you can make me clean." No doubt he had heard of Jesus' miraculous power and had been listening to him that day and had come to the conclusion that Christ was omnipotent. But even more significant the man said, "You can make *me* clean." He believed Jesus could save even him. Before I came to Christ, I never doubted Jesus' power to save others. But I thought I was the one case his power did not cover. Often when a person is under the conviction of sin, he secretly thinks he is beyond God's grace.

If we are going to ask for the healing touch of Jesus Christ we will recognize our condition, bowing before him in reverence as the only source of healing and forgiveness.

EXPERIENCING THE HEALING TOUCH OF CHRIST (v. 3)

As the leper lay at Jesus' feet before the multitude, Jesus looked at the leper as that man had never been looked at before. Mark 1:41 says Jesus was "moved with compassion" (NASB). Jesus felt the man's pain. Then came the sublime apex of the encounter: "Jesus reached out his hand and touched the man." Perhaps it had been twenty or even thirty years since the leper had been touched by a non-leprous hand. Perhaps he was a father and had once known the embrace of his children and his wife, but that was years ago. In fact, according to Jewish law, no one could come closer than six feet to him. But now Christ touched him, and as Bishop Westcott says, the word "expresses more than superficial contact."[4] The Greek word used here is often translated "to take hold of." Jesus, at the very least, placed his hand firmly on the leper. How beautiful Christ is! He did not have to do that. He could have spoken a word or simply willed the healing. But he chose to lay his hand on the poor man right there in front of the multitude. The onlookers were appalled. The disciples were shocked. Jesus was now ceremonially unclean — and besides he might catch the disease, they thought. Why did he do this?

There are some very human reasons. Reaching out was the instinct of his loving heart. He also wanted to clear away any fears the man had. He wanted the leper to feel his willingness and sympathy. There was also the matter of identification. Jesus' touch said, "I am with you. I understand." But besides those human reasons, there was an overshadowing theological reason. The touch of Jesus' pure hand on the rotting leper was a parable of the Incarnation. In the Incarnation Jesus took on our flesh, then became sin for us, though he himself never sinned. In the Incarnation, he took our sins upon himself and gave us his cleanliness.

Jesus took on our flesh, our sins, our filth. "God made him who had no sin to be sin for us, so that in him we might become the righteousness of God" (2 Corinthians 5:21). Jesus lay hold of our flesh and touched us and healed us.

That leper's healing was dramatic. "Jesus reached out his hand and touched the man. 'I am willing,' he said. 'Be clean.' Immediately he was cured of his leprosy." The cleansing was instantaneous. Moreover, it was not some unverifiable case of a mysterious backache going away or hearing restored. Everyone saw it — the face, the brows, the eyelashes, the nose, the ears, the hair were all instantly restored! The claw-like hands and the stubs the man called feet were completely whole. No doubt a rolling roar rose from the multitude as the realization of what had happened set in! We can only guess at how the leper reacted. I would guess he no longer said, "Unclean! Unclean!" but "I'm clean! I'm clean! I'm clean!" That is how it was for us when Jesus touched us and took away our sins.

That is what God can do for anyone in a split second of belief. If you come to him, fully aware of the leprosy of your sin, and if your attitude is one of worshipful reverence, realizing he is the only possible source of your healing, if you come believing that he can heal you, you will be saved — healed from your soul's sin.

May we experience his individual touch in each of our lives today and always!

Soli Deo Gloria!

Notes

Chapter One: The Riches of Poverty

1. Charles Colson, *Who Speaks for God?* (Wheaton, Ill.: Crossway Books, 1985), p. 153.
2. John R. W. Stott, *The Message of the Sermon on the Mount* (Downers Grove, Ill.: InterVarsity Press, 1979), p. 33.
3. D. A. Carson, *The Sermon on the Mount* (Grand Rapids, Mich.: Baker, 1978), p. 16.
4. D. Martyn Lloyd-Jones, *Studies in the Sermon on the Mount*, Vol. 1 (Grand Rapids, Mich.: Eerdmans, 1959), p. 47.
5. Carson, *The Sermon on the Mount*, p. 17.
6. Edward H. Sugden, ed., *John Wesley's Fifty-three Sermons* (Nashville: Abingdon, 1983), pp. 231-232.
7. David F. Wells, *No Place for Truth or Whatever Happened to Evangelical Theology?* (Grand Rapids, Mich.: Eerdmans, 1993), p. 183.
8. R. Kent Hughes, *Romans: Righteousness from Heaven* (Wheaton, Ill.: Crossway Books, 1991), pp. 89-96, where the author expands Paul's logic that salvation is by *faith alone* in respect to Abraham (vv. 1-5), David (vv. 6-8), the Gentiles (vv. 9-12), the Law (vv. 13-15) — *sola fide* (v. 16).
9. George L. Lawlor, *The Beatitudes Are for Today* (Grand Rapids, Mich.: Baker, 1974), pp. 40, 41.

Chapter Two: The Comfort of Mourning

1. Charles Colson, *Who Speaks for God?* (Wheaton, Ill.: Crossway Books, 1985), pp. 136-137.
2. *Ibid.*, p. 137.
3. C. H. Spurgeon, *Lectures to My Students* (Grand Rapids, Mich.: Zondervan, 1969), p. 166.
4. Oswald Sanders, *Spiritual Leadership* (Chicago: Moody Press, 1967), p. 60.
5. Edward H. Sugden, ed., *John Wesley's Fifty-three Sermons* (Nashville: Abingdon, 1983), p. 239.
6. Thomas F. Roeser, "There Is One Thing Worse Than Sin," *Chicago Sun-Times*, August 22, 1983.
7. George L. Lawlor, *The Beatitudes Are for Today* (Grand Rapids, Mich.: Baker, 1974), pp. 40, 41.
8. Colson, *Who Speaks for God?,* p. 138.

Chapter Three: The Strength of Gentleness

1. William Henley, "Invictus," in *The Home Book of Verse*, selected and arranged by Burton E. Stevenson, 9th edition (New York: Henry Holt & Co., n.d.), pp. 3500, 3501.
2. Colin Brown, *The New International Dictionary of New Testament Theology*, Vol. 2 (Grand Rapids, Mich.: Zondervan, 1979), pp. 256, 257.
3. William Barclay, *A New Testament Wordbook* (New York: Harper & Brothers, n.d.), p. 103.
4. M. R. Vincent, *Word Studies in the New Testament* (Gainesville, Fla.: Associated Publishers and Authors, 1972), p. 30.
5. Barclay, *A New Testament Wordbook*, p. 104.
6. Hugh Martin, *The Beatitudes* (New York: Harper & Brothers, 1953), pp. 44, 45.
7. D. Martyn Lloyd-Jones, *Studies in the Sermon on the Mount*, Vol. 1 (Grand Rapids, Mich.: Eerdmans, 1959), p. 69.

Chapter Five: The Dividend of Mercy

1. John R. Claypool, *The Preaching Event* (Waco, Tex.: Word, 1980), p. 39.
2. *Ibid.*, pp. 37-40.

3. Robert Guelich, *The Sermon on the Mount* (Waco, Tex.: Word, 1982), pp. 88, 89.
4. Haddon Robinson, *Biblical Preaching* (Grand Rapids, Mich.: Baker, 1980), p. 150.
5. Corrie ten Boom, *The Hiding Place* (Grand Rapids, Mich.: Chosen Books, 1971), p. 215.

CHAPTER SIX: THE REWARD OF PURITY

1. Reprinted in *Chicago Sun-Times*, February 17, 1982.
2. William Barclay, *A New Testament Wordbook* (New York: Harper, n.d.), p. 69.
3. D. Martyn Lloyd-Jones, *Studies in the Sermon on the Mount*, Vol. 2 (Grand Rapids, Mich.: Eerdmans, 1959), p. 111.

CHAPTER SEVEN: THE PATERNITY OF PEACE

1. Will and Ariel Durant, *The Lessons of History* (New York: Simon & Schuster, 1968), p. 81.
2. *Ibid.*, p. 86.

CHAPTER EIGHT: THE JOY OF PERSECUTION

1. William Blake, "The Auguries of Innocence" (lines 59-62), *The Complete Poetry and Prose of William Blake*, revised edition, ed. David V. Erdman (Berkeley, Calif.: University of California Press, 1982), p. 491.
2. Hugh Martin, *The Beatitudes* (New York: Harper & Brothers, 1953), p. 75.
3. Joseph Bayly, *The Gospel Blimp* (Richardson, Tex.: Windward Press, 1969), p. 32.
4. Dietrich Bonhoeffer, *The Cost of Discipleship* (New York: Macmillan, 1969), pp. 100, 101.

CHAPTER NINE: "THE SALT OF THE EARTH"

1. W. Phillip Keller, *Salt for Society* (Waco, TX: Word, n.d.), p. 100.
2. William Barclay, *The Gospel of Matthew*, Vol. 1 (Philadelphia: Westminster, n.d.), p. 116
3. Malcolm Muggeridge, *Christ in the Media* (Grand Rapids, MI: Eerdmans, 1977), p. 46.
4. F. W. Boreham, *A Bunch of Everlasting* (Nashville: Abingdon, n.d.), p. 186.

CHAPTER TEN: "THE LIGHT OF THE WORLD"

1. Mishna, Sukkah 5:2, 3, *The Mishna*, Herbert Danby, trans. (Oxford: Oxford, 1974).
2. James M. Boice, *The Sermon on the Mount* (Grand Rapids, MI: Zondervan, 1972), p. 80
3. Martyn Lloyd-Jones, *The Sermon on the Mount*, Vol. 1 (Grand Rapids, MI: Eerdmans, n.d.), p. 174.
4. John R. W. Stott, *Christian Counter-Culture* (Downers Grove, IL: InterVarsity Press, 1978), p. 62.
5. *Speaker's Bible*, Vol. 8 (Grand Rapids, MI: Baker, n.d.), p. 108.
6. C. S. Lewis, *The Weight of Glory and Other Addresses* (Grand Rapids, MI: Eerdmans, 1973), p. 13.

CHAPTER ELEVEN: JESUS ON RIGHTEOUSNESS

1. John R. W. Stott, *Christian Counter-Culture* (Downers Grove, IL: InterVarsity Press, 1978), p. 72.
2. Harvey McArthur, *Understanding the Sermon on the Mount* (New York: Harper & Bros., n.d.), p. 26.
3. *Ibid.*, p. 39.
4. *Ibid.*
5. James M. Boice, *The Sermon on the Mount* (Grand Rapids, MI: Zondervan, 1972), pp. 93, 94.
6. Quoted by Stott, *Christian Counter-Culture*, p. 38.
7. Albert Bengel, *Bengel's New Testament Commentary*, Vol. 1 (Grand Rapids, MI: Kregel, n.d.), p. 108.
8. E. C. Reisinger, *Today's Evangelism: Its Message and Methods* (Philippsburg, NJ: P & R, 1982), p. 17.

9. Edwin Newman, *Strictly Speaking* (New York: Macmillan, 1974), pp. 111-113.

CHAPTER TWELVE: A RIGHTEOUS PERSON'S RELATIONSHIPS

1. See Alan F. Johnson's excellent article, "Jesus and Moses: Rabbinic Backgrounds and Exegetical Concerns in Matthew 5," in *The Living and Active Word of God: Studies in Honor of Samuel J. Schultz* Morris Inch and Ronald Youngblood, (Winona Lake, IN: Eisenbrauns, 1983), pp. 85-107, esp. p. 87.
2. Alexander Balmain Bruce, "Matthew," in *The Expositor's Greek Testament*, Vol. 1, ed. W. Robertson Nicoll (Grand Rapids, MI: Eerdmans, n.d.), p. 107.
3. Martyn Lloyd-Jones, *The Sermon on the Mount*, Vol. 1 (Grand Rapids, MI: Eerdmans, n.d.), p. 228.

CHAPTER THIRTEEN: RADICAL PURITY

1. *Time*, August 21, 1972.
2. Alexander Balmain Bruce, *The Expositor's Greek Testament*, Vol. 1 (Grand Rapids, MI; Erdmans, n.d.), p. 108.
3. Robert Guelich, *The Sermon on the Mount* (Waco, TX: Word, 1991), p. 194.
4. Albert Bengel, *Bengel's New Testament Commentary*, Vol. 1 (Grand Rapids, MI: Kregel, 1981), p. 114.
5. Oswald Chambers, *My Utmost for His Highest* (New York: Dodd, Mead and Company, 1935), p. 181.
6. John R. W. Stott, *Christian Counter-Culture* (Downers Grove, IL: InterVarsity Press, 1978), p. 89.

CHAPTER FOURTEEN: JESUS' TEACHING ON DIVORCE

1. Quoted from J. Allan Peterson, *The Myth of Greener Grass* (Wheaton, IL: Tyndale, 1983), p. 17.
2. James B. Hurley, *Man and Woman in Biblical Perspective* (Grand Rapids, MI: Zondervan, 1981), pp. 99-102.
3. See *ibid.*, pp. 102, 103.
4. John R. W. Stott, *Christian Counter-Culture* (Downers Grove, IL: InterVarsity Press, 1978), pp. 96, 97.
5. John Murray, *Divorce* (Phillipsburg, NJ: The Presbyterian and Reformed Publishing Company, 1972), p. 63.
6. *Ibid.*, pp. 74, 75. Murray's classic work establishes beyond doubt that "is not bound" means "is not bound in marriage."
7. *The Wittenberg Door*, No. 65, February/March 1982, p. 24, quoting an ad from *TV Guide*.
8. Martyn Lloyd-Jones, *The Sermon on the Mount*, Vol. 1 (Grand Rapids, MI: Eerdmans, n.d.), p. 261.

CHAPTER FIFTEEN: RADICAL TRUTHFULNESS

1. Mortimer Adler, *How to Read a Book* (New York: Simon and Schuster, 1972), p. 165.
2. Edward Hastings, ed., *The Speakers' Bible*, Vol. 6 (Grand Rapids, MI: Baker, 1971), p. 130, quoting from Greville Macdonald's *Reminiscences of a Specialist*.
3. See *The Mishna*, Herbert Danby, trans. (Oxford: Oxford, 1974), pp. 408-421.
4. D. A. Carson, *The Sermon on the Mount* (Grand Rapids, MI: Baker, 1978), p. 47.
5. Helmut Thielicke, *Life Can Begin Again* (Minneapolis: Fortress, 1980), p. 55.
6. Hastings, ed., *The Speakers' Bible*, Vol. 6, p. 128.
7. Macdonald, *Reminiscences of a Specialist*.
8. Thielicke, *Life Can Begin Again*, p. 59.
9. William Barclay, *Ephesians* (Philadelphia: Westminister, 1976), p. 183.

CHAPTER SIXTEEN: WRONGS AND RIGHTS

1. *The Mishna*, trans. Herbert Danby (Oxford: Oxford, 1974), pp. 332-346.
2. John R. W. Stott, *Christian Counter-Culture* (Downers Grove, IL: InterVarsity Press, 1978), pp. 108, 109.
3. Joachim Jeremias, *The Sermon on the Mount* (Minneapolis: Fortress, 1963), p. 28:

   Jesus — and this is very important for an understanding of this matter — is not speaking of a simple insult; it is much more the case of a quite specific insulting blow: the blow given to the disciples of Jesus as heretics. It is true that this is not specifically stated, but it follows from the observation that in every instance where Jesus speaks of insult, persecution, anathema, dishonor to the disciples, he is concerned with outrages that arise because of the discipleship itself. If you are dishonored as a heretic, says Jesus, then you should not go to law about it; rather you should show yourselves to be truly my disciples by the way in which you bear the hatred and the insult, overcome the evil, forgive the injustice.
4. *Ibid.*
5. Carson, *The Sermon on the Mount* (Grand Rapids, MI: Baker, 1978), p. 50.
6. Alexander Maclaren, *Expositions of Holy Scripture: Daniel and the Minor Prophets,* Vol. 6 (Grand Rapids, MI: Baker, 1974), p. 214.

CHAPTER SEVENTEEN: SUPERSEDING LOVE

1. *Christian Century*, Vol. LXXV, October 1, 1958, pp. 1104-1107.
2. C. S. Lewis, *God in the Dock*, Walter Hooper, ed. (Grand Rapids, MI: Eerdmans, 1970), pp. 181, 182.
3. Warren Wiersbe, *Walking with the Giants* (Grand Rapids, MI: Baker, 1976), p. 93.
4. Alfred Plummer, *S. Matthew* (London: Paternoster, 1910), p. 89.
5. William Barclay, *Matthew*, Vol. 1 (Philadelphia: Westminster, n.d.), pp. 174, 175.
6. Martyn Lloyd-Jones, *The Sermon on the Mount*, Vol. 1 (Grand Rapids, MI: Eerdmans, n.d.), p. 313.
7. C. S. Lewis, *Mere Christianity* (London: Fontana, revised edition 1964), p. 114.

CHAPTER EIGHTEEN: CHRISTIANITY WITHOUT HYPOCRISY

1. Walter Bauer, William Arndt, and Wilbur Gingrich, *A Greek-English Lexicon of the New Testament* (Chicago: University of Chicago Press, 1957), p. 84,
2. C. S. Lewis, *The Weight of Glory and Other Addresses* (Grand Rapids, MI: Eerdmans, 1973), p. 2.
3. James Montgomery Boice, *The Sermon on the Mount* (Grand Rapids, MI: Zondervan, 1972), p. 185.
4. Note: These questions are suggested by D. A. Carson, *The Sermon on the Mount* (Grand Rapids, MI: Baker, 1978), pp. 60, 61.
5. Martyn Lloyd-Jones, *Studies in the Sermon on the Mount*, Vol. 2 (Grand Rapids, MI: Eerdmans, n.d.), p. 15.

CHAPTER NINETEEN: THE LORD'S PRAYER: THE FATHER

1. James M. Boice, *The Sermon on the Mount* (Grand Rapids, MI: Zondervan, 1972), p. 192 is the source of this brief listing of the Lord's Prayer.
2. Dietrich Bonhoeffer, *The Cost of Discipleship* (New York: Macmillan, n.d.), p. 184.
3. Joachim Jeremias, *The Lord's Prayer* (Minneapolis: Fortress Press, 1980), pp. 19, 20.
4. *Ibid.*, p. 20.
5. J. I. Packer, *Knowing God* (Downers Grove, IL: InterVarsity Press, 1973), p. 182.
6. Everett Fullam, *Living the Lord's Prayer* (Grand Rapids, MI: Chosen Books, 1980), pp. 27, 28.

CHAPTER TWENTY: THE LORD'S PRAYER: THE NAME

1. Nels Ferré, *Strengthening the Spiritual Life* (London: Collins, 1956), p. 1.
2. William Barclay, *The Beatitudes and Lord's Prayer for Everyman* (New York: Harper & Row, 1964), p. 179.

3. Ernst Lohmeyer, *Our Father* (New York: Harper & Row, 1965), p. 81.
4. Barclay, *Beatitudes and Lord's Prayer,* pp. 187, 188.

CHAPTER TWENTY-ONE: "YOUR KINGDOM COME"

1. John R. W. Stott, *Christian Counter-Culture* (Downers Grove, IL: InterVarsity Press, 1978), p. 147.
2. Ernst Lohmeyer, *Our Father* (New York: Harper & Row, 1965), p. 104.
3. *Oxford English Dictionary, in loc.*
4. Quoted by James Boice, *The Sermon on the Mount* (Grand Rapids, MI: Zondervan, 1972), p. 208.
5. Helmut Thielicke, *Our Heavenly Father* (Grand Rapids, MI: Baker, 1980), p. 60.
6. *Ibid.*, p. 62.
7. *Ibid.*, p. 57.
8. Charles Colson, *Who Speaks for God?* (Wheaton, IL: Crossway Books, 1985), pp. 28, 29.

CHAPTER TWENTY-TWO: "YOUR WILL BE DONE"

1. Helmut Thielicke, *Our Heavenly Father* (Grand Rapids, MI: Baker, 1980), pp. 70, 71.
2. William Barclay, *The Beatitudes and Lord's Prayer for Everyman* (New York: Harper & Row, 1975), p. 208.
3. Martin E. Marty, *The Hidden Discipline* (St. Louis: Concordia, 1912), p. 73.
4. *World Vision*, April 1977, p. 12.
5. *Ibid.*, p. 13.

CHAPTER TWENTY-THREE: THE LORD'S PRAYER: THE BREAD

1. Helmut Thielicke, *Our Heavenly Father* (Grand Rapids, MI: Baker, 1980), pp. 77, 78.
2. William Barclay, *The Beatitudes and Lord's Prayer for Everyman* (New York: Harper & Row, 1975), pp. 219, 220. See also Joachim Jeremias, *The Lord's Prayer* (Minneapolis: Fortress Press, 1980), pp. 23, 24.
3. Thielicke, *Our Heavenly Father*, p. 79.
4. *Ibid.*, p. 81.
5. See Ernst Lohmeyer, *Our Father* (New York: Harper & Row, 1965), p. 148:

   And this thought is further underlined by the fact that while in the Old Testament there are many vivid pictures which paint the glory of the final kingdom, in the words of Jesus there is only one, which is drawn many times, the picture of the marriage feast or the king's feast, of eating and drinking or reclining at table with the patriarchs, in Abraham's bosom, and the pictures of harvest or sowing only serve to show the great context in which "our bread" is situated. One might almost say that from this point of view to pray for the coming of the kingdom and to pray "Give us our bread today" amounted to the same thing.

CHAPTER TWENTY-FOUR: THE LORD'S PRAYER: FORGIVENESS

1. F. C. Cook, ed., *Speaker's Commentary* (New York: C. Scribner's, 1878-1896), p. 30.
2. Bruce Metzger, ed., *Oxford Annotated Apocrypha* (Oxford, England: Oxford University Press, 1977), p. 164.
3. I. Thomas, *Puritan Quotations* (Chicago: Moody Press, 1975), p. 111.
4. Charles Haddon Spurgeon, *Metropolitan Tabernacle Pulpit*, Vol. 24 (Pasadena, TX: Pilgrim Publications, 1969), p. 694.
5. C. S. Lewis, *Fern-seed and Elephants,* Walter Hooper, ed. (Glasgow: Fontana/ Collins, 1975), pp. 39, 40.
6. *Ibid.*, p. 42.

CHAPTER TWENTY-FIVE: THE LORD'S PRAYER: TEMPTATION

1. Joachin Jeremias, *The Lord's Prayer* (Minneapolis: Fortress, 1980), p. 29.

2. *Ibid.*, p. 30, quoting b, Berakoth 60b. in *The Babylonian Talmud*, p. 378.
3. William Barclay, *The Beatitudes and the Lord's Prayer for Everyman* (New York: Harper & Row, 1975), p. 247.
4. Charles Haddon Spurgeon, *Metropolitan Tabernacle Pulpit*, Vol. 24 (Pasadena, TX: Pilgrim Publications, 1969), p. 143.
5. Helmut Thielicke, *Our Heavenly Father* (Grand Rapids, MI: Baker, 1980), p. 133.

Chapter Twenty-six: The Lord's Prayer: Glory

1. *The Apostolic Fathers*, I, The Loeb Classical Library, ed. E. H. Warmington (Cambridge, MA: Harvard University Press, 1970).
2. Ernst Lohmeyer, *Our Father* (New York: Harper & Row), pp. 230, 231.
3. *Ibid.*, p. 241.
4. A. W. Tozer, *The Knowledge of the Holy* (New York: Harper & Row), p. 62.
5. F. W. Farrar, *The Lord's Prayer* (New York: Thomas Whittaker, 1893), p. 221.
6. Helmut Thielicke, *Our Heavenly Father* (Grand Rapids, MI: Baker, 1974), p. 152.
7. Farrar, *The Lord's Prayer*, p. 217.
8. Alan Redpath, *Victorious Praying* (Old Tappan, NJ: Revell, 1957), p. 127.

Chapter Twenty-seven: Lasting Treasure

1. William Barclay, *Matthew*, Vol. 1 (Philadelphia: Westminster, n.d.), p. 244.
2. Edward Hastings, ed., *The Speaker's Bible*, Vol. 6 (Grand Rapids, MI: Baker, 1971), p. 173.
3. George Macdonald, *Christ in Creation* (Carol Stream, IL: Harold Shaw, 1978), p. 204.
4. Martyn Lloyd-Jones, *The Sermon on the Mount*, Vol. 2 (Grand Rapids, MI: Eerdmans, 1960), p. 85.

Chapter Twenty-eight: Unclouded Vision

1. Os Guinness, *The Gravedigger Files* (Downers Grove, IL: InterVarsity Press, n.d.), p. 84.
2. *Ibid.*, p. 132.
3. *Speaker's Bible,* Vol. 6 (Grand Rapids, MI: Baker, 1971), p. 118.
4. Martyn Lloyd-Jones, *Studies in the Sermon on the Mount* (Grand Rapids, MI: Eerdmans, 1960), pp. 95, 96.

Chapter Twenty-nine: "Do Not Worry . . . But Seek First"

1. James M. Boice, *The Sermon on the Mount* (Grand Rapids, MI: Zondervan, 1972), p. 252, quoting *Time* Magazine, March 31, 1961, pp. 44, 46.
2. *Sermons of Martin Luther*, Vol. 5, ed. John N. Lenker (Grand Rapids, MI: Baker, 1983), p. 112.
3. John R. W. Stott, *Christian Counter-Culture* (Downers Grove, IL: InterVarsity Press, 1978), p. 161.
4. *Ibid.*, p. 164.
5. *Ibid.*
6. *Sermons of Martin Luther*, Vol. 5, p. 115.
7. George Macdonald, *Better Than Gold* (publishing information unknown), p. 45.

Chapter Thirty-two: The Two Roads

1. C. E. Jefferson, *The Character of Jesus* (New York: Thomas Y. Crowell, 1908), p. 107.
2. *Daily Bread*, H. G. B., September 21, 1984.
3. C. S. Lewis, *Surprised by Joy* (New York: Harcourt, Brace & World, Inc., 1955), p. 63.
4. Helmut Thielicke, *Life Can Begin Again* (Minneapolis: Fortress, 1980), p. 182.

CHAPTER THIRTY-THREE: DISCERNING FALSE PREACHERS

1. Martyn Lloyd-Jones, *The Sermon on the Mount*, Vol. 2 (Grand Rapids, MI: Eerdmans, 1960), p. 243.
2. Dietrich Bonhoeffer, *The Cost of Discipleship* (New York: Macmillan, 1969), pp. 212, 213.
3. Albert Bengel, *Bengel's New Testament Commentary,* Vol. 1, Charlton T. Lewis and Marvin R. Vincent, trans. (Grand Rapids, MI: Kregel, 1981), p. 134.

CHAPTER THIRTY-FOUR: ENTERING THE KINGDOM

1. R. V. Pierard, "Evangelicalism," in *Evangelical Dictionary of Theology*, Walter A. Elwell, ed. (Grand Rapids, MI: Baker, 1984), p. 379.
2. *The New Dictionary of Thoughts,* Tyron Edwards, ed. (New York: Standard Book Pub., 1936), p. 251.
3. John R. W. Stott, *Christian Counter-Culture* (Downers Grove, IL: InterVarsity Press, 1978), pp. 206, 207.
4. Donald Carson, *The Sermon on the Mount* (Grand Rapids, MI: Baker, 1978), p. 132.
5. *Ibid.*, p. 134.

CHAPTER THIRTY-FIVE: THE SERMON ON THE MOVE

1. Philip Yancey, *Where Is God When It Hurts?* (Grand Rapids, MI: Zondervan, 1997), p. 32.
2. William Barclay, *Matthew*, Vol. 2 (Philadelphia: Westminster Press, n.d.), p. 301.
3. *The New International Dictionary of New Testament Theology,* Colin Brown, gen. ed. (Grand Rapids, MI: Zondervan, 1976), pp. 875-877.
4. Brooke Foss Westcott, *Christian Aspects of Life* (New York: Macmillan, n.d.), p. 354.

Scripture Index

General Index

Index of Sermon Illustrations

Cambridge student gives to every panhandler who comes along — and goes bankrupt, 135
Alexander Maclaren on how resisting our persecutors is sometimes the loving response, for their sake, 136
C. S. Lewis in *Mere Christianity*: act in love toward your neighbors, and soon you will really love them, 144
The reforms brought about through Christians such as William Wilberforce, Elizabeth Fry, and Florence Nightingale, 172
Bismarck, seeing a wounded soldier's longing eyes, gives him his last cigar, 216

Compromise
Roman Emperor Julian in Henrik Ibsen play on Christians who have no joy in life and just want to die, 79
Pastors who fall morally, 105
Chuck Swindoll says he will get sick if he hears of one more fallen pastor, 105
Origen of Alexandria had himself physically emasculated to overcome sensual desires, 108
James Montgomery Boice: most prayers in our churches on Sunday mornings, even those offered by preachers, are not made to God but to men, 150
Minister tells pastors that whatever they desire is God's will for them, but is later convicted for fraud, 182
Author's friend, along with several others, goes into the ministry but later leaves it and also his family, 193-194
Two men about to be martyred; one says he will never deny Christ but does, and the other fears he will but does not, 196
Os Guinness, in *The Gravedigger Files*, on our preferring aerobics to apologetics, fitness to faithfulness, shapeliness to godliness, 211
Christians' defense of child labor in the mines and of slavery on economic grounds, 215
Teen saved out of youth counterculture, testifies passionately about his faith before the whole church, two weeks later dramatically rejects Christ, 255-256

Confession
Thief confesses, twin brothers reconcile, 45

Conversion
English judge's conversion a greater miracle of grace than a thief's, 23
Colson describes the night he turned to God, 31
Mark McCann — violent, angry, hateful — is converted and weeps the first time he sees Jesus' name in the Bible, 136
Missionary Everett Fullam describes baptism of three Nigerians, who rejoiced to know there is one God, not many warring gods, 157
Author was drawn to God because a loving pastor modeled God as a loving Father, 165

Conversion Without Repentance
Mickey Cohen "converted," a Christian gangster, 15
Teen saved out of youth counterculture, testifies passionately about his faith before the whole church, two weeks later dramatically rejects Christ, 255-256

Conviction
Martin Luther on the Law humbling us so we will turn to Christ, 94-95
Martyn Lloyd-Jones on how we avoid facing the conviction of the Holy Spirit, 103

Courage
Despite disease and opposition, William Wilberforce almost single-handedly defeats slavery in the British Empire, 80
Martyrs Hugh Latimer and Nicholas Ridley know they are lighting a candle that will never be put out, 85
The reforms brought about through Christians such as William Wilberforce, Elizabeth Fry, and Florence Nightingale, 172
Two men about to be martyred; one says he will never deny Christ but does, and the other fears he will but does not, 196

Criticism of Pastors
Richard DeHaan's tongue-in-cheek list of criticisms made against pastors, 227
Man whose mother criticizes every prospective wife he brings home; when he brings home someone just like her, his father can't stand her, 227
Neighbor watches a pastor nail up a trellis in his backyard, just to see what he will say when he hits his thumb, 229

Darkness
Lady Macbeth plotting murder under cover of darkness, 84
Poem on the certainty of darkness someday surrendering to Christ, 88

Denial of Sin
Comparison of moral fall of two Congressmen, one unrepentant, 29
Author's friend, along with several others, goes into the ministry but later leaves it and also his family, 193-194

The Devil
Helmut Thielicke on "*the* tempter . . . *the* liar," 197
Luther hymn about "the prince of darkness grim," 198

Discernment
Chuck Swindoll's friend eats dog food at a party without knowing it, 247

About the Book Jacket

The design of the book jacket brings together the talents of several Christian artists. The design centers around the beautiful banner created by artist Marge Gieser. It is photographed here on the jacket at about one-twentieth of its original size.

The banner was constructed specifically for the book cover.

The other artists contributing their talents to the creation of the jacket were: Bill Koechling, photography; Paul Higdon, design and typography; and Cindy Kiple, art direction.